STORM   MONET   PSYLOCKE   RACHEL GREY   JUBILEE   ...ND
REYES

MARC GUGGENHEIM
WRITER

HARVEY
TOLIBAO   &   ## DEXTER
SOY
PENCILERS

ED
TADEO   DEXTER
SOY   CRAIG
YEUNG   SCOTT
HANNA   NORMAN
LEE   HARVEY
TOLIBAO
INKERS

PAUL
MOUNTS   JOE
CARAMAGNA
COLORIST   ### LETTERER

COVER ART: TERRY DODSON & RACHEL DODSON
EDITORS: JEANINE SCHAEFER & TOM BRENNAN
X-MEN GROUP EDITOR: NICK LOWE

COLLECTION EDITOR: **JENNIFER GRÜNWALD**   ASSISTANT EDITOR: **SARAH BRUNSTAD**
ASSOCIATE MANAGING EDITOR: **ALEX STARBUCK**   EDITOR, SPECIAL PROJECTS: **MARK D. BEAZLEY**
SENIOR EDITOR, SPECIAL PROJECTS: **JEFF YOUNGQUIST**   SVP PRINT, SALES & MARKETING: **DAVID GABRIEL**

EDITOR IN CHIEF: **AXEL ALONSO**   CHIEF CREATIVE OFFICER: **JOE QUESADA**
PUBLISHER: **DAN BUCKLEY**   EXECUTIVE PRODUCER: **ALAN FINE**

X-MEN VOL. 4: EXOGENOUS. Contains material originally published in magazine form as X-MEN #18-22. First printing 2015. ISBN# 978-0-7851-9233-6. Published by MARVEL WORLDWIDE, INC., a subsidiary of MARVEL ENTERTAINMENT, LLC. OFFICE OF PUBLICATION: 135 West 50th Street, New York, NY 10020. Copyright © 2014 and 2015 Marvel Characters, Inc. All rights reserved. All characters featured in this issue and the distinctive names and likenesses thereof, and all related indicia are trademarks of Marvel Characters, Inc. No similarity between any of the names, characters, persons, and/or institutions in this magazine with those of any living or dead person or institution is intended, and any such similarity which may exist is purely coincidental. **Printed in Canada.** ALAN FINE, EVP - Office of the President, Marvel Worldwide, Inc. and EVP & CMO Marvel Characters B.V.: DAN BUCKLEY, Publisher & President - Print, Animation & Digital Divisions; JOE QUESADA, Chief Creative Officer; TOM BREVOORT, SVP of Publishing; DAVID BOGART, SVP of Operations & Procurement, Publishing; C.B. CEBULSKI, SVP of Creator & Content Development; DAVID GABRIEL, SVP Print, Sales & Marketing; JIM O'KEEFE, VP of Operations & Logistics; DAN CARR, Executive Director of Publishing Technology; SUSAN CRESPI, Editorial Operations Manager; ALEX MORALES, Publishing Operations Manager; STAN LEE, Chairman Emeritus. For information regarding advertising in Marvel Comics or on Marvel.com, please contact Niza Disla, Director of Marvel Partnerships, at ndisla@marvel.com. For Marvel subscription inquiries, please call 800-217-9158. **Manufactured between 12/26/2014 and 2/2/2015 by SOLISCO PRINTERS, SCOTT, QC, CANADA.**

10 9 8 7 6 5 4 3 2 1

They are the faculty and students of the Jean Grey School for Gifted Youngsters, a school meant to protect and train mutants, the next step in human evolution. They are the X-Men!

After finding an infant boy alone in the wreckage of a destroyed building, Jubilee — an orphan herself — decided to raise the child with the X-Men as part of their extended family and named him Shogo.

Not long after Shogo and Jubilee arrived at the Jean Grey School, trouble followed in the form of Arkea, a malevolent and infectious alien being capable of destroying the world. After briefly inhabiting Shogo, Arkea fought the X-Men and formed a new evil sisterhood that included the Enchantress, Typhoid Mary, Selene and Lady Deathstroke. Storm, Rachel Grey, Psylocke, Monet, Jubilee and Karima Shapandar took down the sisterhood with the help of Arkea's brother, John Sublime, destroying Arkea permanently in the process.

Unbeknownst to the team, Shogo's father — a criminal mastermind calling himself "The Future" — had recently broken out of a high-security prison with one thing on his mind: to take back his son. After launching a series of guerrilla attacks on the school, The Future abducted Jubilee to his safe house. With the help of Kymera, Storm's daughter from an alternate future, and a bit of Shogo's blood, the X-Men were able to shut down his weaponized forest and defeat The Future.

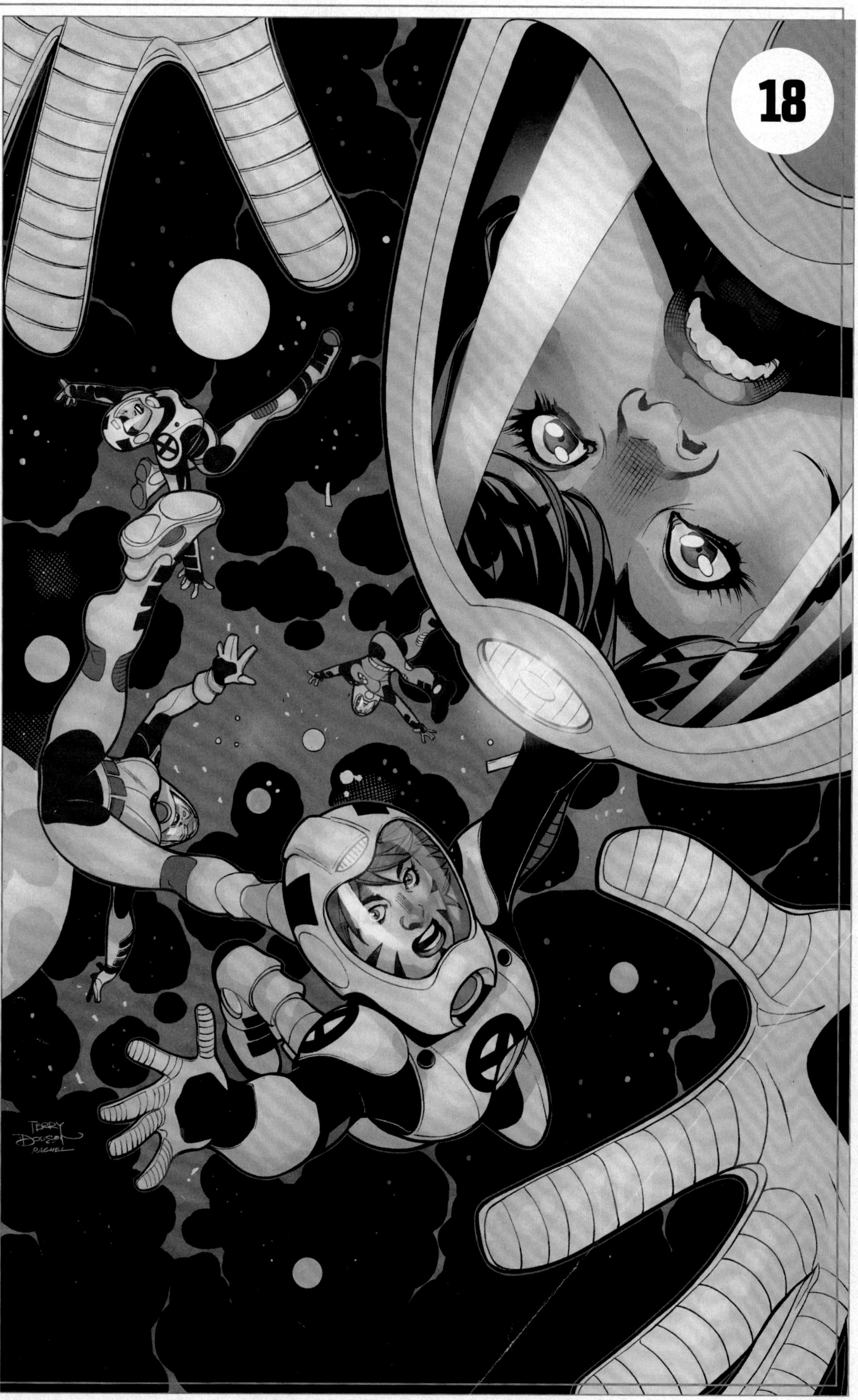
18
TERRY DODSON
RACHEL

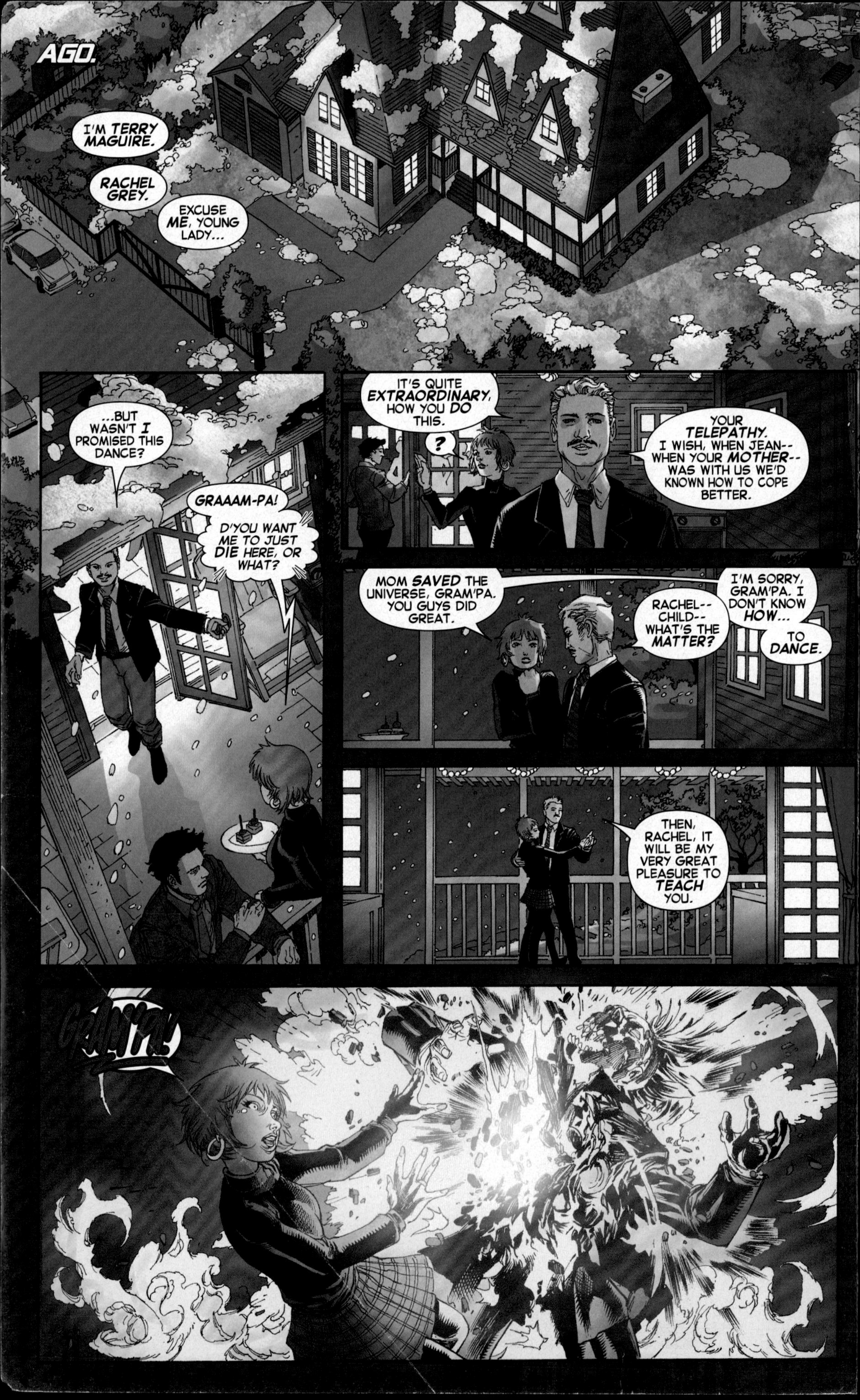
AGO.
I'M TERRY MAGUIRE.
RACHEL GREY.
EXCUSE ME, YOUNG LADY...
...BUT WASN'T I PROMISED THIS DANCE?
GRAAAM-PA!
D'YOU WANT ME TO JUST DIE HERE, OR WHAT?
IT'S QUITE EXTRAORDINARY, HOW YOU DO THIS.
?
YOUR TELEPATHY. I WISH, WHEN JEAN-- WHEN YOUR MOTHER-- WAS WITH US WE'D KNOWN HOW TO COPE BETTER.
MOM SAVED THE UNIVERSE, GRAM'PA. YOU GUYS DID GREAT.
RACHEL-- CHILD-- WHAT'S THE MATTER?
I'M SORRY, GRAM'PA. I DON'T KNOW HOW...
TO DANCE.
THEN, RACHEL, IT WILL BE MY VERY GREAT PLEASURE TO TEACH YOU.

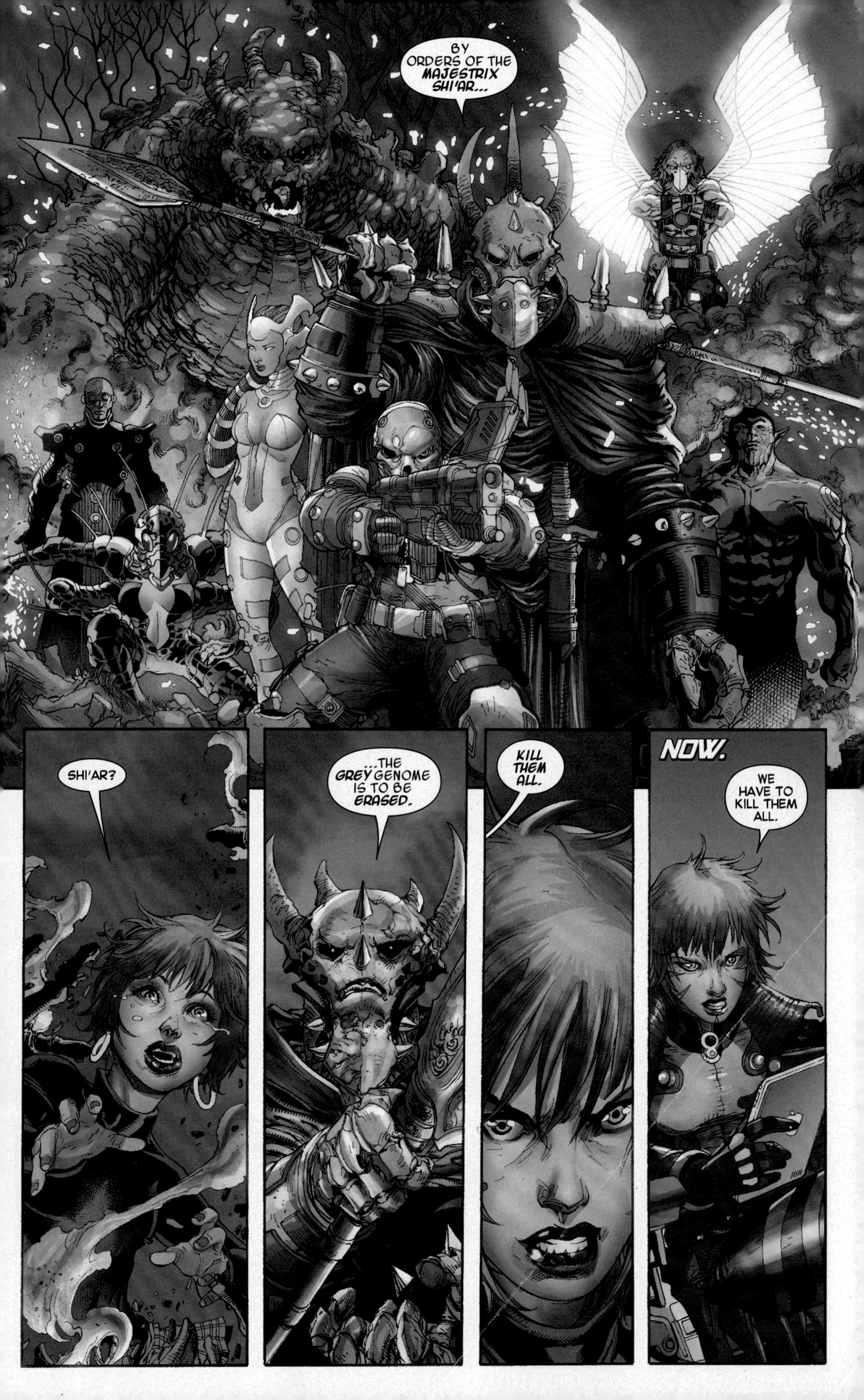

BY ORDERS OF THE MAJESTRIX SHI'AR...
SHI'AR?
...THE GREY GENOME IS TO BE ERASED.
KILL THEM ALL.
NOW.
WE HAVE TO KILL THEM ALL.

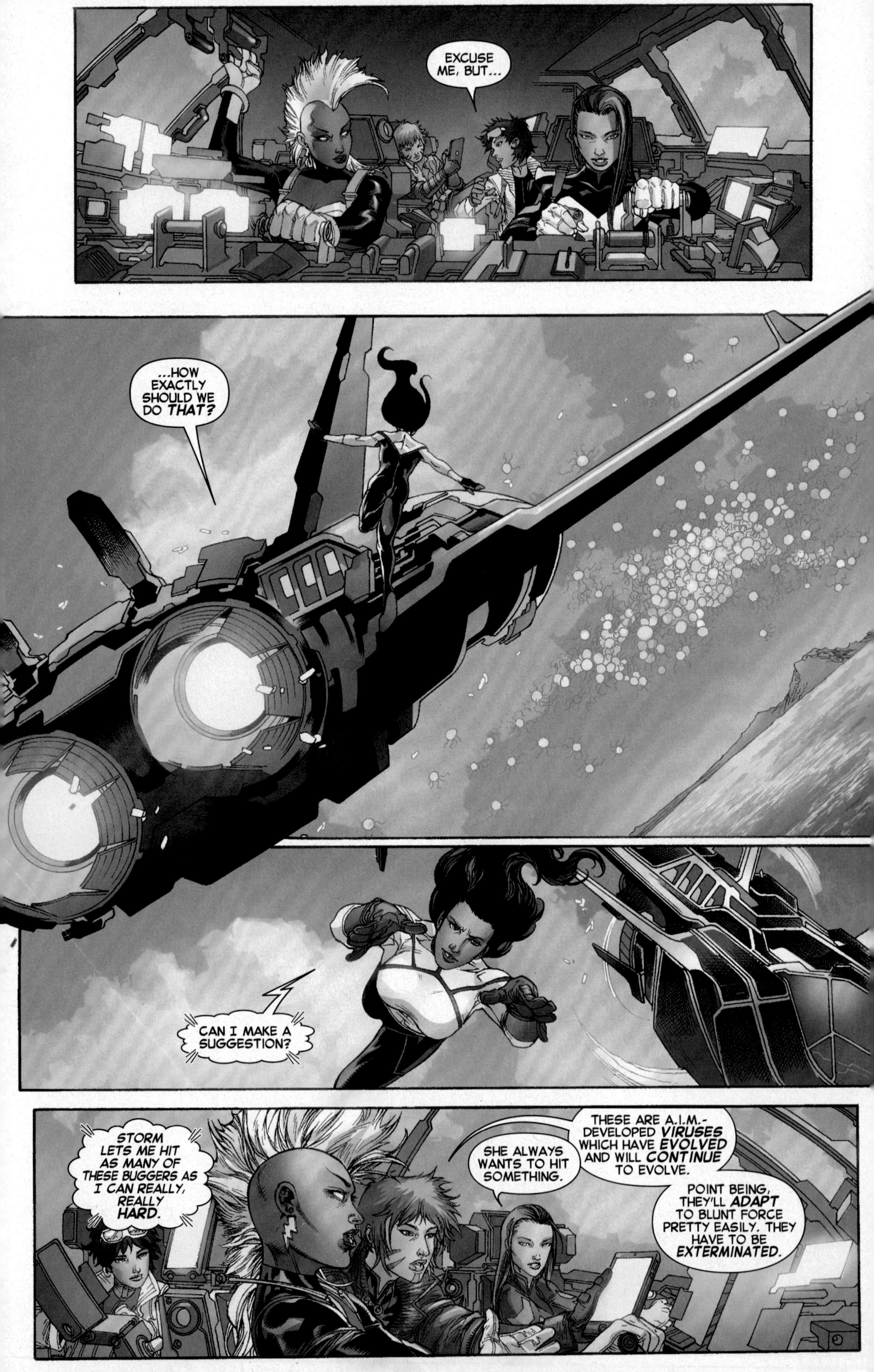
EXCUSE ME, BUT...
...HOW EXACTLY SHOULD WE DO THAT?
CAN I MAKE A SUGGESTION?
STORM LETS ME HIT AS MANY OF THESE BUGGERS AS I CAN REALLY, REALLY HARD.
SHE ALWAYS WANTS TO HIT SOMETHING.
THESE ARE A.I.M.-DEVELOPED VIRUSES WHICH HAVE EVOLVED AND WILL CONTINUE TO EVOLVE.
POINT BEING, THEY'LL ADAPT TO BLUNT FORCE PRETTY EASILY. THEY HAVE TO BE EXTERMINATED.

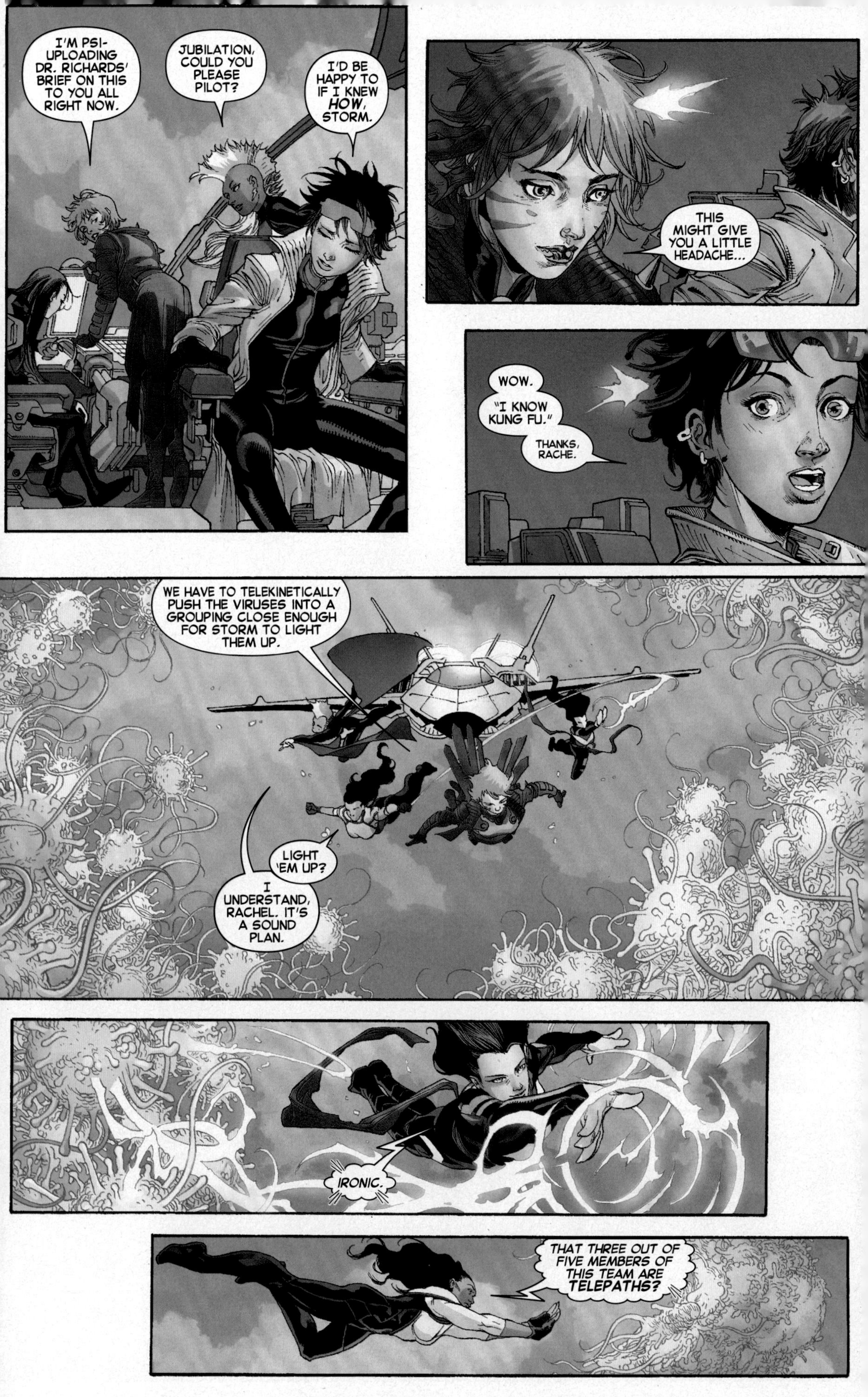
I'M PSI-UPLOADING DR. RICHARDS' BRIEF ON THIS TO YOU ALL RIGHT NOW.
JUBILATION, COULD YOU PLEASE PILOT?
I'D BE HAPPY TO IF I KNEW HOW, STORM.
THIS MIGHT GIVE YOU A LITTLE HEADACHE...
WOW.
"I KNOW KUNG FU."
THANKS, RACHE.
WE HAVE TO TELEKINETICALLY PUSH THE VIRUSES INTO A GROUPING CLOSE ENOUGH FOR STORM TO LIGHT THEM UP.
LIGHT 'EM UP?
I UNDERSTAND, RACHEL. IT'S A SOUND PLAN.
IRONIC.
THAT THREE OUT OF FIVE MEMBERS OF THIS TEAM ARE TELEPATHS?

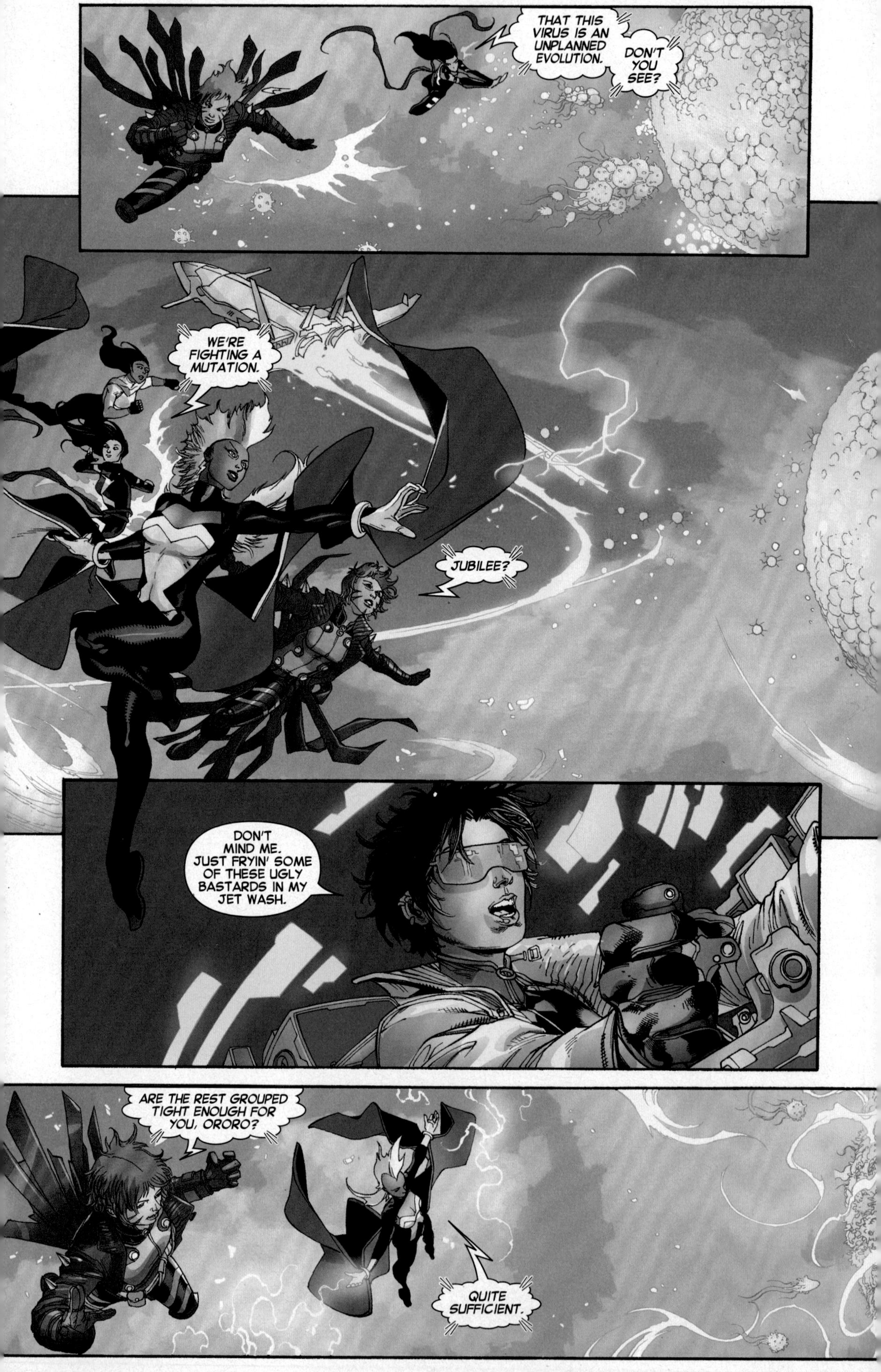
THAT THIS VIRUS IS AN UNPLANNED EVOLUTION.
DON'T YOU SEE?
WE'RE FIGHTING A MUTATION.
JUBILEE?
DON'T MIND ME. JUST FRYIN' SOME OF THESE UGLY BASTARDS IN MY JET WASH.
ARE THE REST GROUPED TIGHT ENOUGH FOR YOU, ORORO?
QUITE SUFFICIENT.

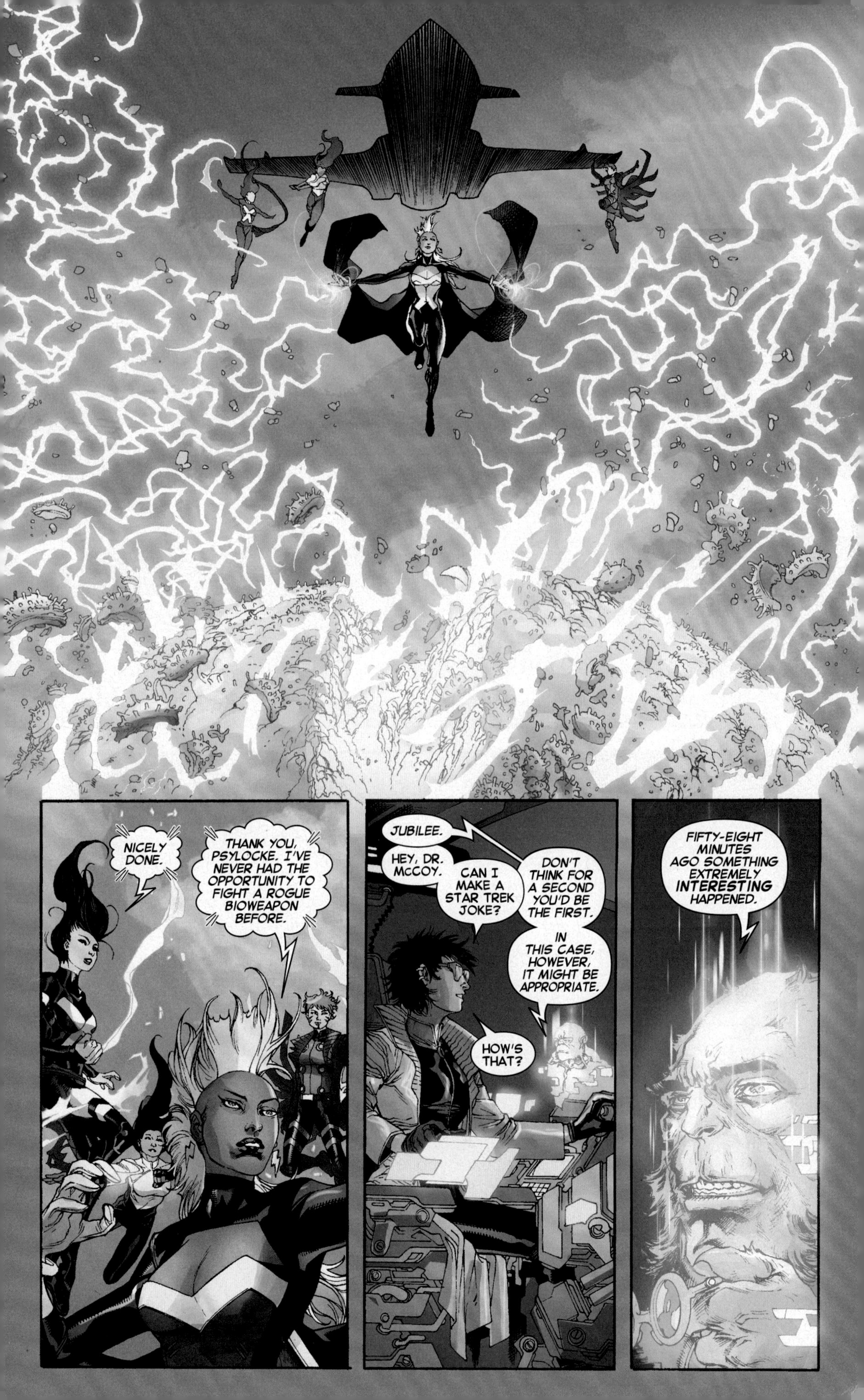
NICELY DONE.
THANK YOU, PSYLOCKE. I'VE NEVER HAD THE OPPORTUNITY TO FIGHT A ROGUE BIOWEAPON BEFORE.
JUBILEE.
HEY, DR. McCOY.
CAN I MAKE A STAR TREK JOKE?
DON'T THINK FOR A SECOND YOU'D BE THE FIRST.
IN THIS CASE, HOWEVER, IT MIGHT BE APPROPRIATE.
HOW'S THAT?
FIFTY-EIGHT MINUTES AGO SOMETHING EXTREMELY INTERESTING HAPPENED.

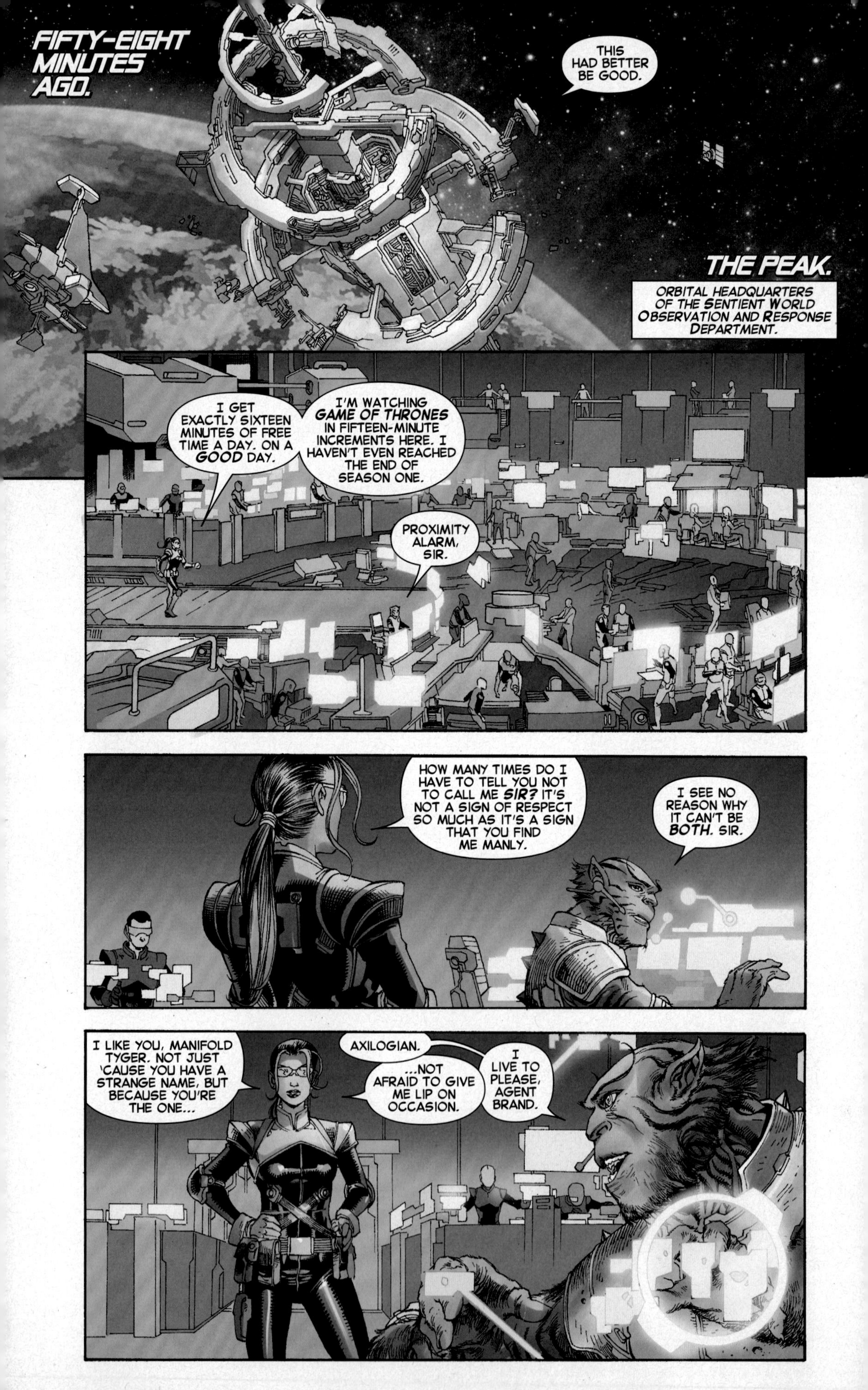
FIFTY-EIGHT MINUTES AGO.
THIS HAD BETTER BE GOOD.
THE PEAK.
ORBITAL HEADQUARTERS OF THE SENTIENT WORLD OBSERVATION AND RESPONSE DEPARTMENT.
I GET EXACTLY SIXTEEN MINUTES OF FREE TIME A DAY. ON A GOOD DAY.
I'M WATCHING GAME OF THRONES IN FIFTEEN-MINUTE INCREMENTS HERE. I HAVEN'T EVEN REACHED THE END OF SEASON ONE.
PROXIMITY ALARM, SIR.
HOW MANY TIMES DO I HAVE TO TELL YOU NOT TO CALL ME SIR? IT'S NOT A SIGN OF RESPECT SO MUCH AS IT'S A SIGN THAT YOU FIND ME MANLY.
I SEE NO REASON WHY IT CAN'T BE BOTH. SIR.
I LIKE YOU, MANIFOLD TYGER. NOT JUST 'CAUSE YOU HAVE A STRANGE NAME, BUT BECAUSE YOU'RE THE ONE...
AXILOGIAN.
...NOT AFRAID TO GIVE ME LIP ON OCCASION.
I LIVE TO PLEASE, AGENT BRAND.

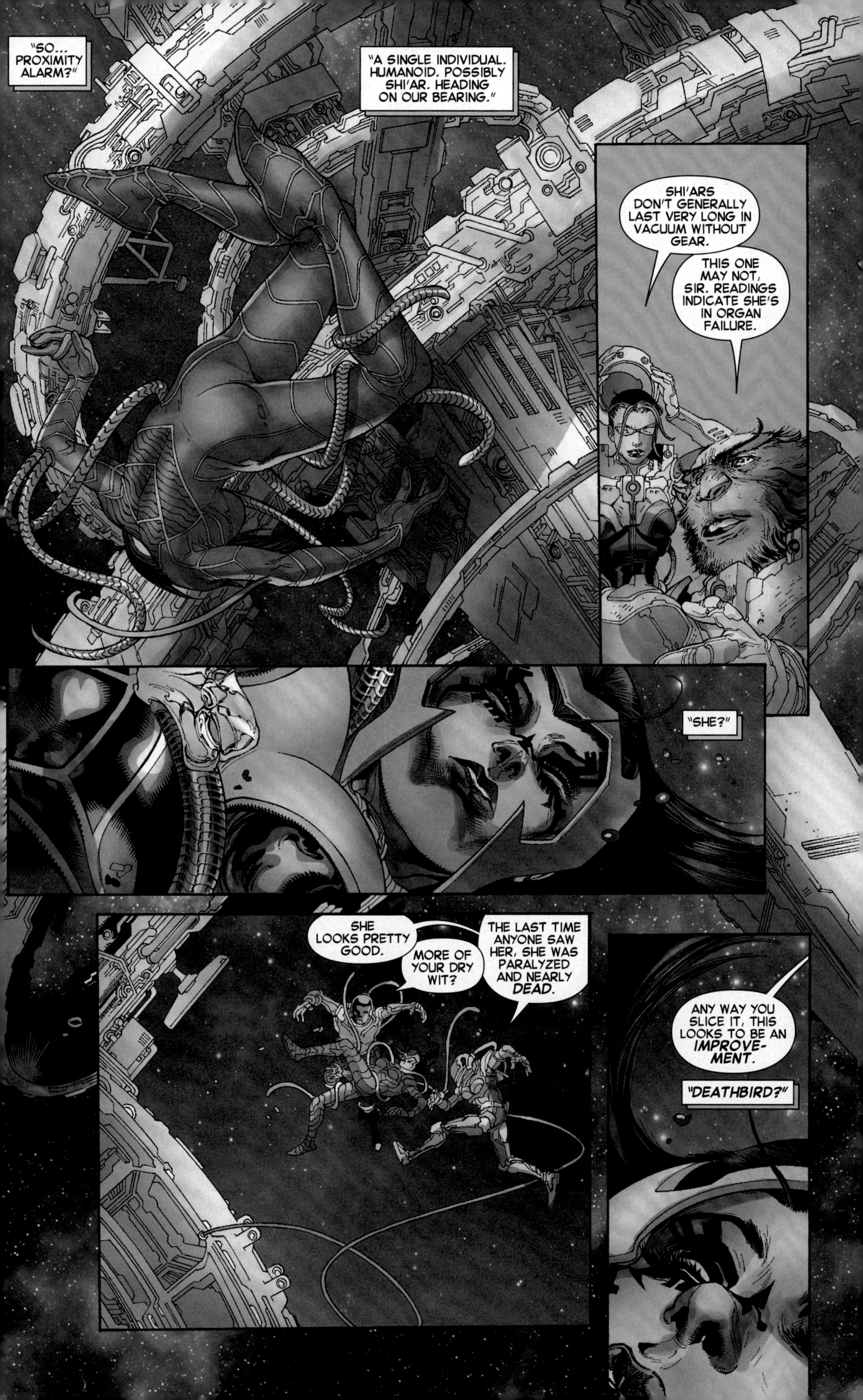
"SO... PROXIMITY ALARM?"
"A SINGLE INDIVIDUAL. HUMANOID. POSSIBLY SHI'AR. HEADING ON OUR BEARING."
SHI'ARS DON'T GENERALLY LAST VERY LONG IN VACUUM WITHOUT GEAR.
THIS ONE MAY NOT, SIR. READINGS INDICATE SHE'S IN ORGAN FAILURE.
"SHE?"
SHE LOOKS PRETTY GOOD.
MORE OF YOUR DRY WIT?
THE LAST TIME ANYONE SAW HER, SHE WAS PARALYZED AND NEARLY *DEAD*.
ANY WAY YOU SLICE IT, THIS LOOKS TO BE AN *IMPROVE-MENT*.
"DEATHBIRD?"

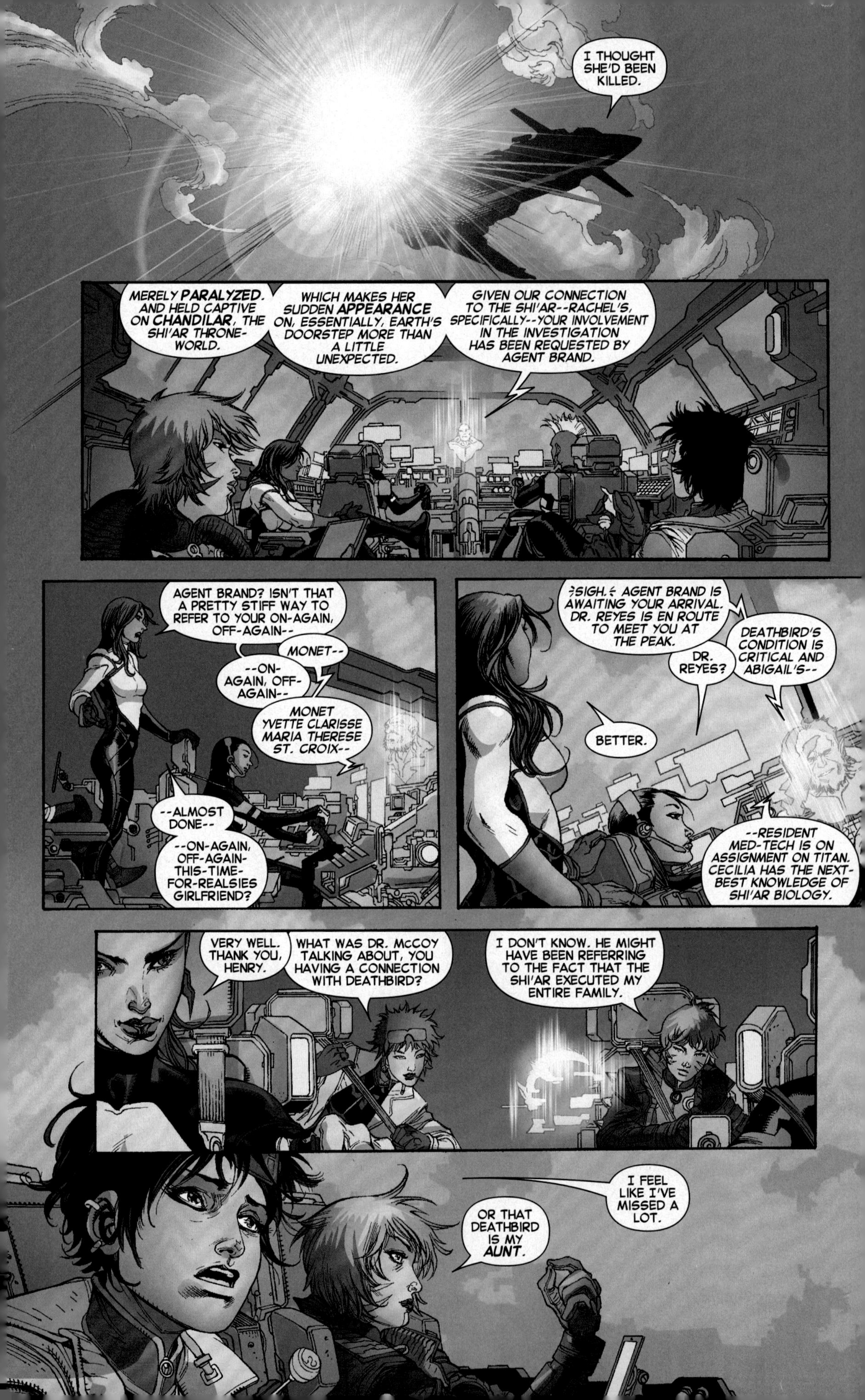

I THOUGHT SHE'D BEEN KILLED.
MERELY PARALYZED. AND HELD CAPTIVE ON CHANDILAR, THE SHI'AR THRONE-WORLD.
WHICH MAKES HER SUDDEN APPEARANCE ON, ESSENTIALLY, EARTH'S DOORSTEP MORE THAN A LITTLE UNEXPECTED.
GIVEN OUR CONNECTION TO THE SHI'AR--RACHEL'S, SPECIFICALLY--YOUR INVOLVEMENT IN THE INVESTIGATION HAS BEEN REQUESTED BY AGENT BRAND.
AGENT BRAND? ISN'T THAT A PRETTY STIFF WAY TO REFER TO YOUR ON-AGAIN, OFF-AGAIN--
MONET--
--ON-AGAIN, OFF-AGAIN--
MONET YVETTE CLARISSE MARIA THERESE ST. CROIX--
--ALMOST DONE--
--ON-AGAIN, OFF-AGAIN-THIS-TIME-FOR-REALSIES GIRLFRIEND?
SIGH. AGENT BRAND IS AWAITING YOUR ARRIVAL. DR. REYES IS EN ROUTE TO MEET YOU AT THE PEAK.
DR. REYES?
DEATHBIRD'S CONDITION IS CRITICAL AND ABIGAIL'S--
BETTER.
--RESIDENT MED-TECH IS ON ASSIGNMENT ON TITAN. CECILIA HAS THE NEXT-BEST KNOWLEDGE OF SHI'AR BIOLOGY.
VERY WELL. THANK YOU, HENRY.
WHAT WAS DR. McCOY TALKING ABOUT, YOU HAVING A CONNECTION WITH DEATHBIRD?
I DON'T KNOW. HE MIGHT HAVE BEEN REFERRING TO THE FACT THAT THE SHI'AR EXECUTED MY ENTIRE FAMILY.
OR THAT DEATHBIRD IS MY AUNT.
I FEEL LIKE I'VE MISSED A LOT.

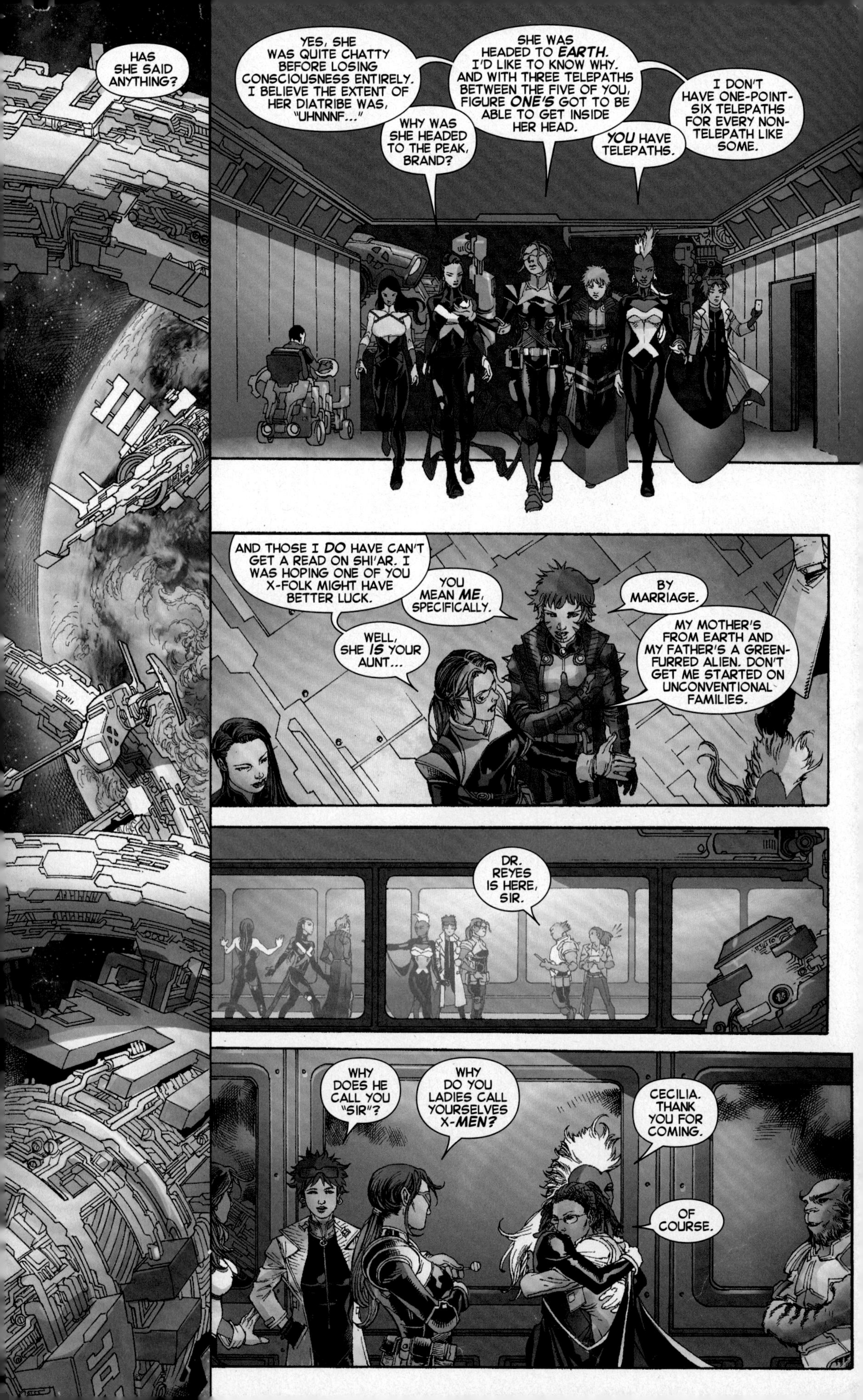
HAS SHE SAID ANYTHING?
YES, SHE WAS QUITE CHATTY BEFORE LOSING CONSCIOUSNESS ENTIRELY. I BELIEVE THE EXTENT OF HER DIATRIBE WAS, "UHNNNF..."
WHY WAS SHE HEADED TO THE PEAK, BRAND?
SHE WAS HEADED TO EARTH. I'D LIKE TO KNOW WHY. AND WITH THREE TELEPATHS BETWEEN THE FIVE OF YOU, FIGURE ONE'S GOT TO BE ABLE TO GET INSIDE HER HEAD.
YOU HAVE TELEPATHS.
I DON'T HAVE ONE-POINT-SIX TELEPATHS FOR EVERY NON-TELEPATH LIKE SOME.
AND THOSE I DO HAVE CAN'T GET A READ ON SHI'AR. I WAS HOPING ONE OF YOU X-FOLK MIGHT HAVE BETTER LUCK.
YOU MEAN ME, SPECIFICALLY.
WELL, SHE IS YOUR AUNT...
BY MARRIAGE.
MY MOTHER'S FROM EARTH AND MY FATHER'S A GREEN-FURRED ALIEN. DON'T GET ME STARTED ON UNCONVENTIONAL FAMILIES.
DR. REYES IS HERE, SIR.
WHY DOES HE CALL YOU "SIR"?
WHY DO YOU LADIES CALL YOURSELVES X-MEN?
CECILIA. THANK YOU FOR COMING.
OF COURSE.

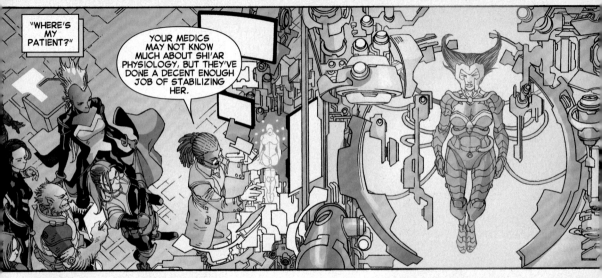

"WHERE'S MY PATIENT?"

YOUR MEDICS MAY NOT KNOW MUCH ABOUT SHI'AR PHYSIOLOGY, BUT THEY'VE DONE A DECENT ENOUGH JOB OF STABILIZING HER.

HOW DID SHE MAKE IT ALL THIS WAY? OUR INFORMATION IS THAT SHE WAS *PARALYZED*.

I SEE NO SIGN OF PARALYSIS.

ALL OF THESE INJURIES ARE *FRESH*. I'D ESTIMATE ONE DAY, TWO TOPS. AND--

WHAT'S UP?

I...NEED TO RUN SOME TESTS. DO YOU FOLKS HAVE A *LAB* I MIGHT BE ABLE TO USE?

WE HAVE *FIVE*.

MANIFOLD TYGER, GO WITH HER, PLEASE.

AM I THE ONLY ONE FREAKED OUT BY HOW FREAKED OUT SHE WAS JUST THEN?

PERHAPS NOW WOULD BE AN APPROPRIATE TIME TO PURSUE THE LINE OF INQUIRY AGENT BRAND SUGGESTS.

CAN YOU GIVE US THE ROOM?

KNOCK YOURSELVES OUT.

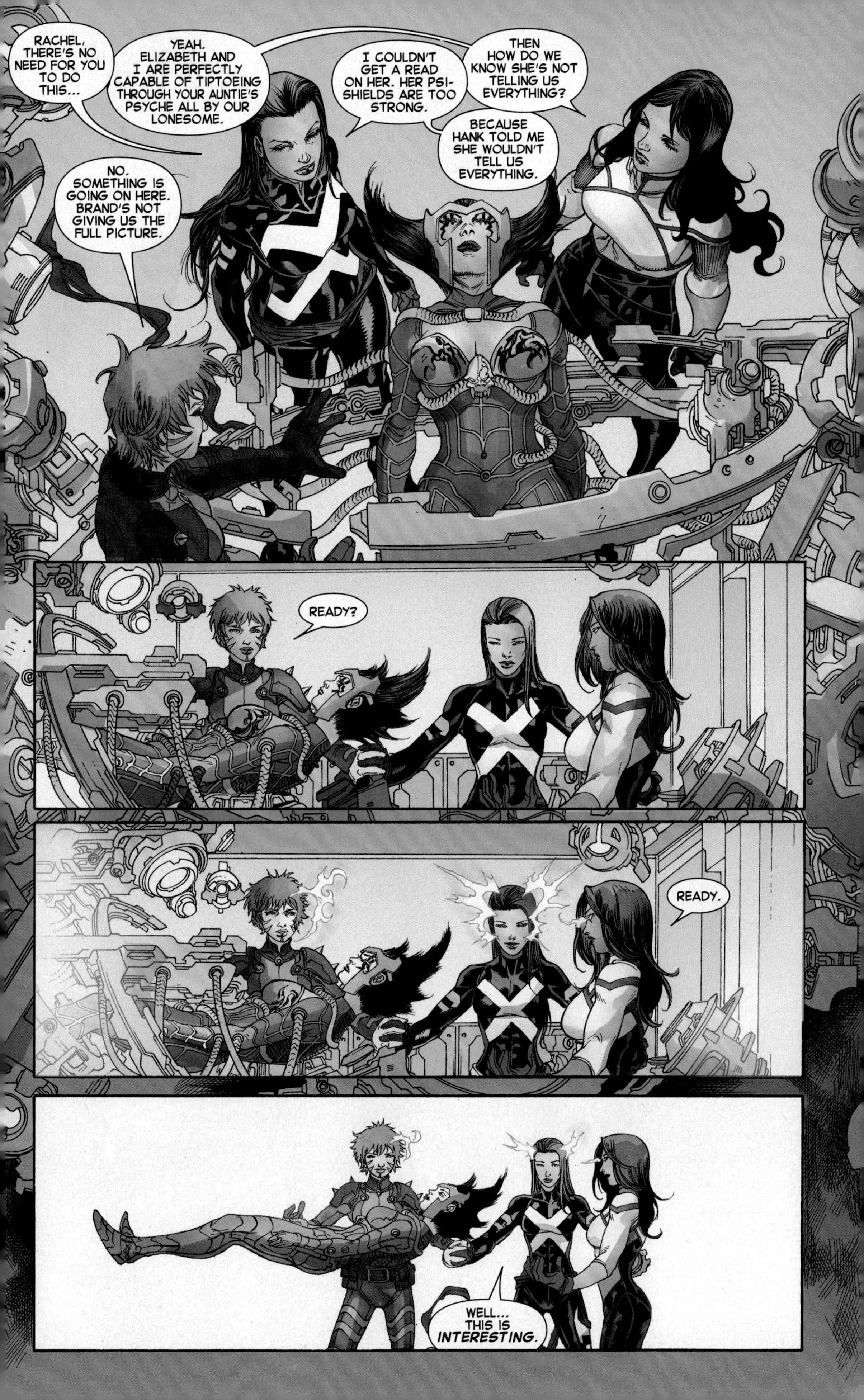
RACHEL, THERE'S NO NEED FOR YOU TO DO THIS...
YEAH. ELIZABETH AND I ARE PERFECTLY CAPABLE OF TIPTOEING THROUGH YOUR AUNTIE'S PSYCHE ALL BY OUR LONESOME.
NO. SOMETHING IS GOING ON HERE. BRAND'S NOT GIVING US THE FULL PICTURE.
I COULDN'T GET A READ ON HER. HER PSI-SHIELDS ARE TOO STRONG.
THEN HOW DO WE KNOW SHE'S NOT TELLING US EVERYTHING?
BECAUSE HANK TOLD ME SHE WOULDN'T TELL US EVERYTHING.
READY?
READY.
WELL... THIS IS INTERESTING.

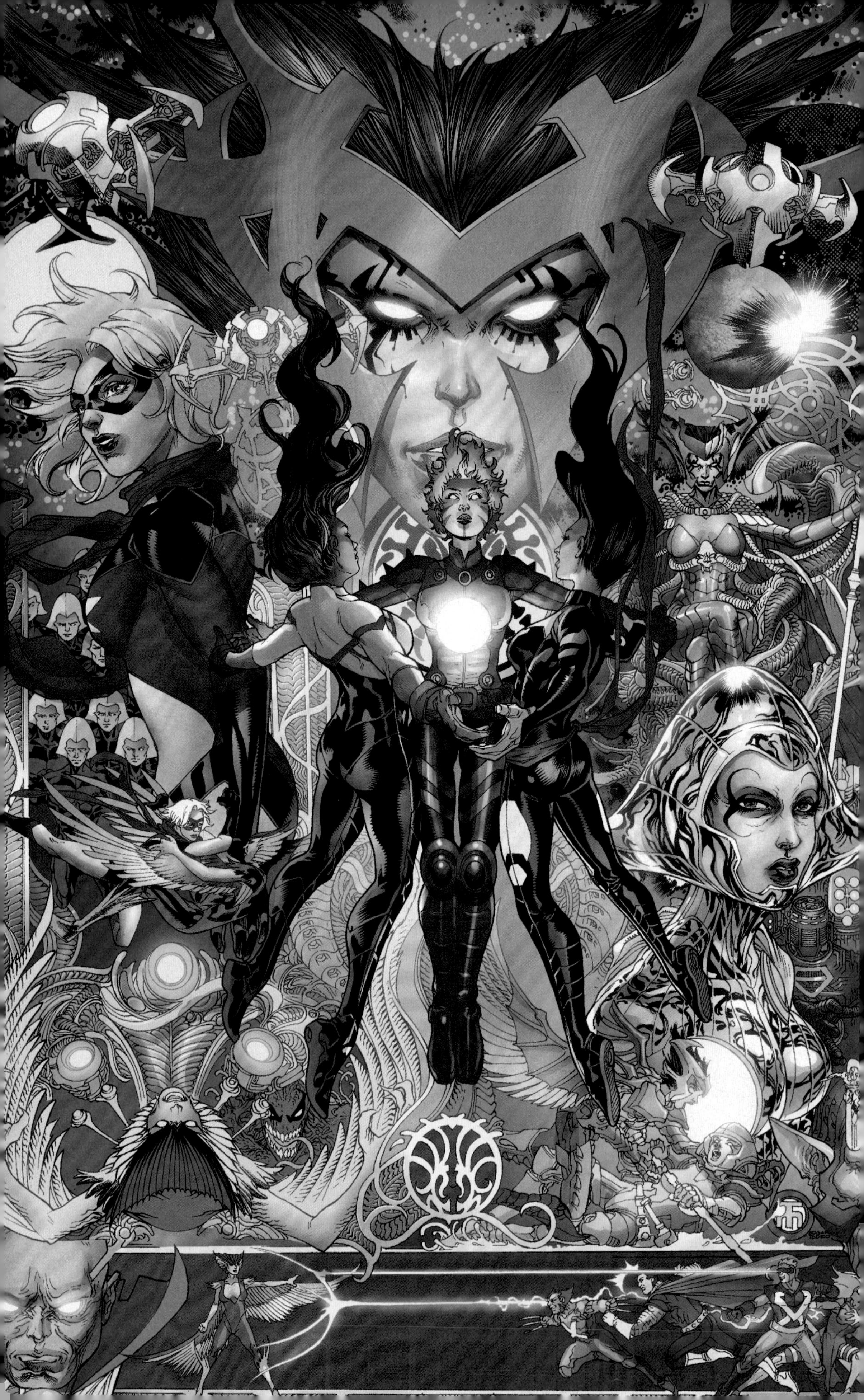

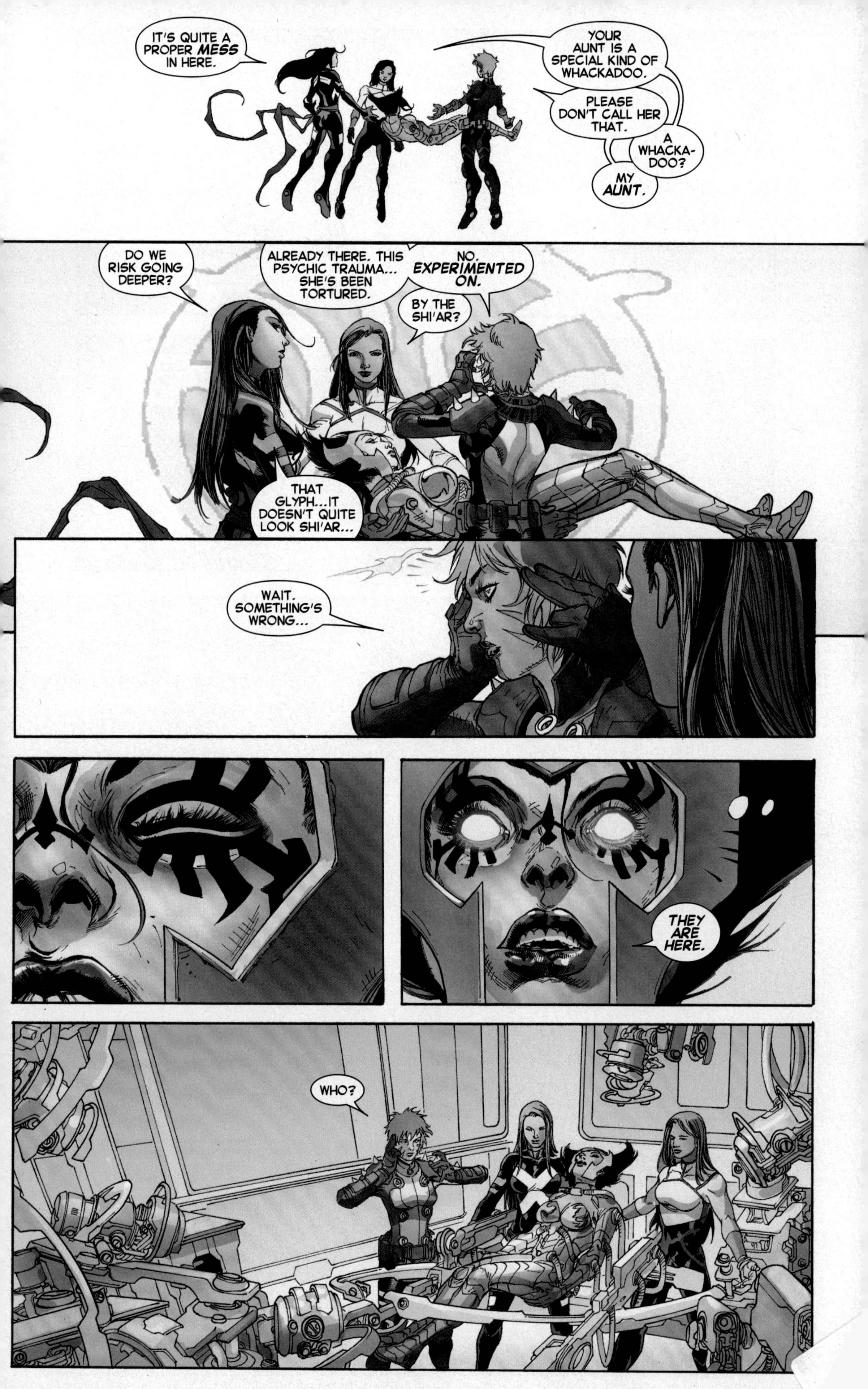
IT'S QUITE A PROPER MESS IN HERE.
YOUR AUNT IS A SPECIAL KIND OF WHACKADOO.
PLEASE DON'T CALL HER THAT.
A WHACKA-DOO?
MY AUNT.
DO WE RISK GOING DEEPER?
ALREADY THERE. THIS PSYCHIC TRAUMA... SHE'S BEEN TORTURED.
NO. EXPERIMENTED ON.
BY THE SHI'AR?
THAT GLYPH...IT DOESN'T QUITE LOOK SHI'AR...
WAIT. SOMETHING'S WRONG...
THEY ARE HERE.
WHO?

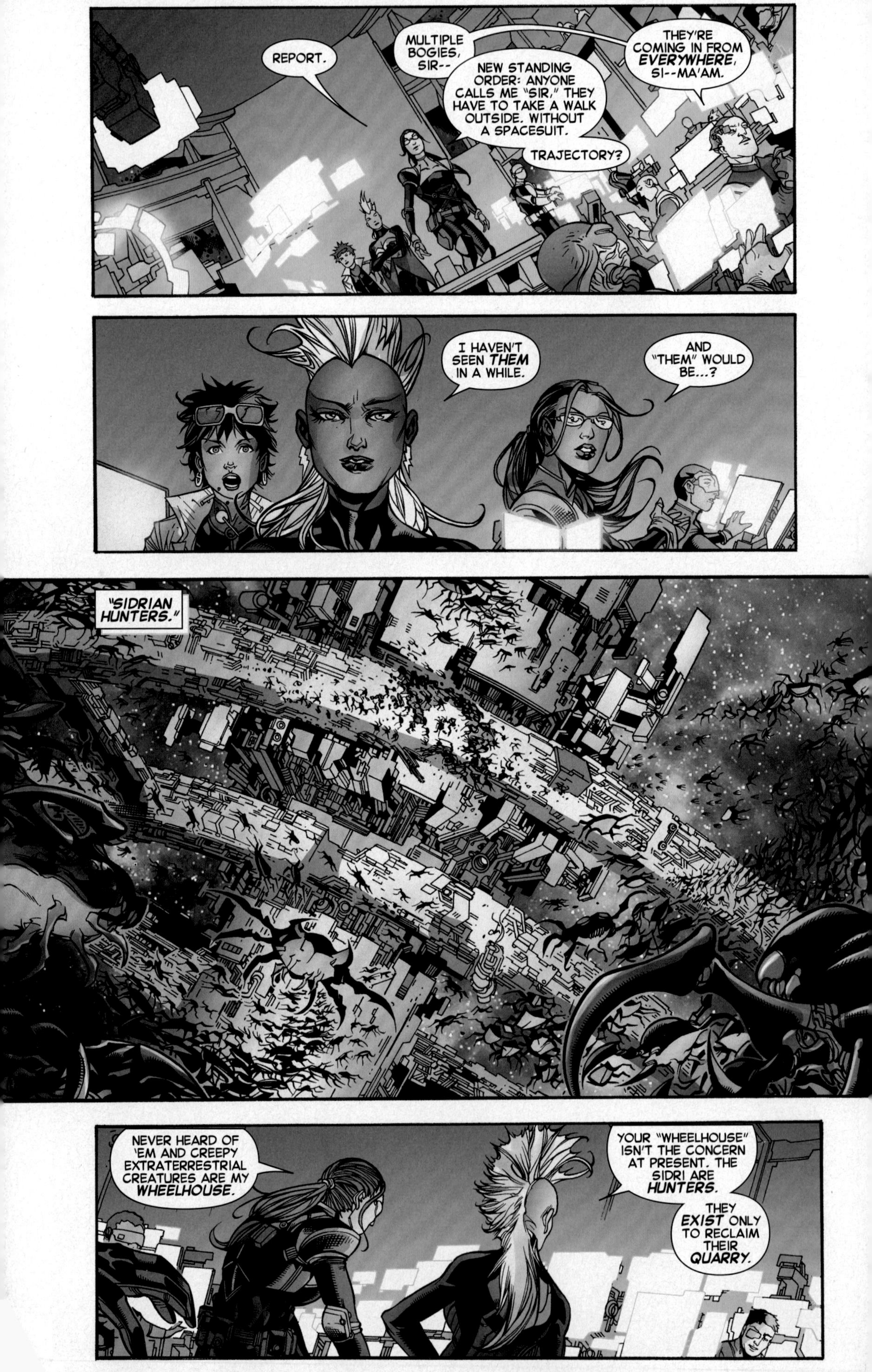
REPORT.
MULTIPLE BOGIES, SIR--
NEW STANDING ORDER: ANYONE CALLS ME "SIR," THEY HAVE TO TAKE A WALK OUTSIDE. WITHOUT A SPACESUIT.
TRAJECTORY?
THEY'RE COMING IN FROM EVERYWHERE, SI--MA'AM.
I HAVEN'T SEEN THEM IN A WHILE.
AND "THEM" WOULD BE...?
"SIDRIAN HUNTERS."
NEVER HEARD OF 'EM AND CREEPY EXTRATERRESTRIAL CREATURES ARE MY WHEELHOUSE.
YOUR "WHEELHOUSE" ISN'T THE CONCERN AT PRESENT. THE SIDRI ARE HUNTERS.
THEY EXIST ONLY TO RECLAIM THEIR QUARRY.

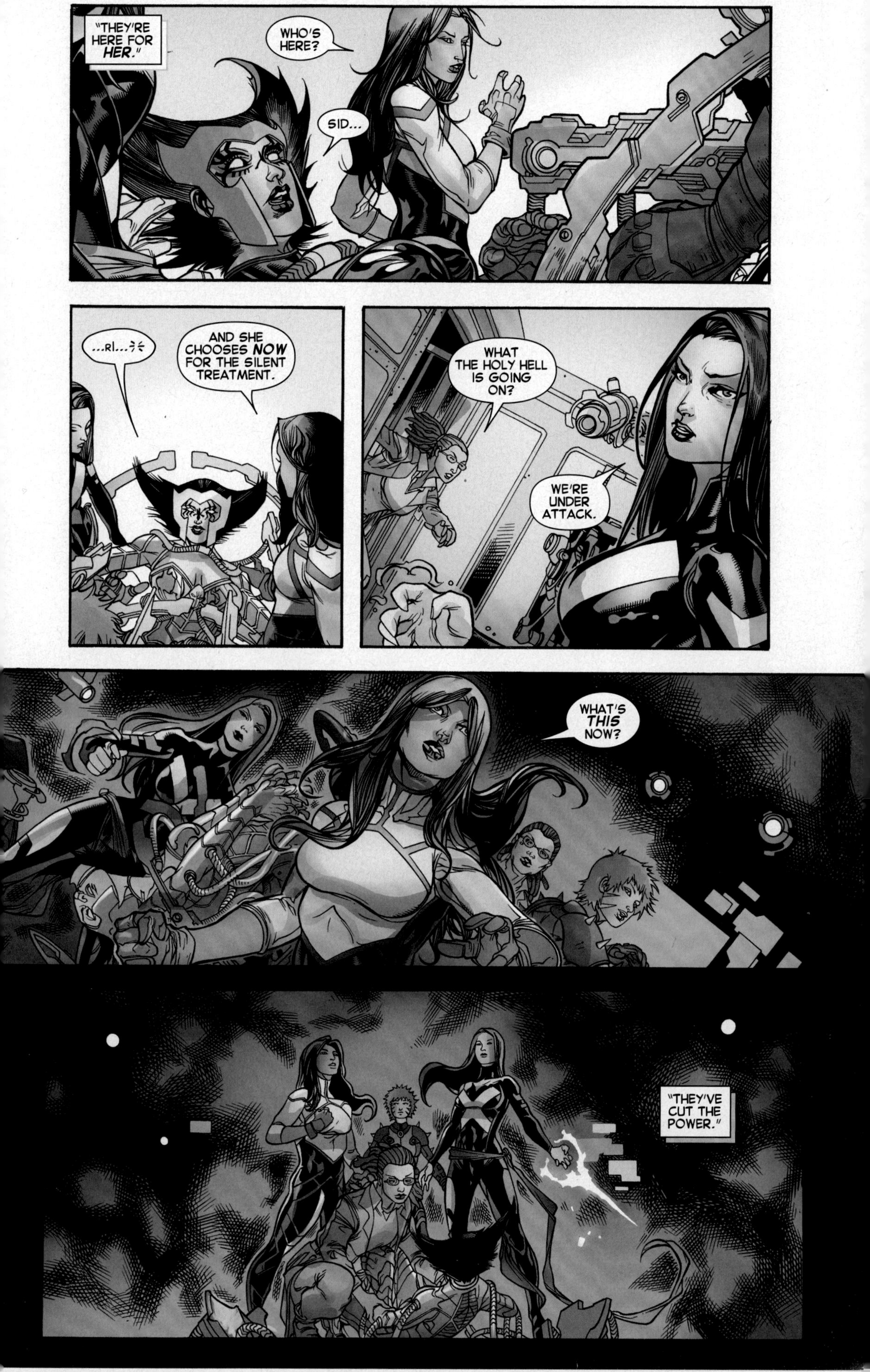
"THEY'RE HERE FOR HER."
WHO'S HERE?
SID...
...RI...
AND SHE CHOOSES NOW FOR THE SILENT TREATMENT.
WHAT THE HOLY HELL IS GOING ON?
WE'RE UNDER ATTACK.
WHAT'S THIS NOW?
"THEY'VE CUT THE POWER."

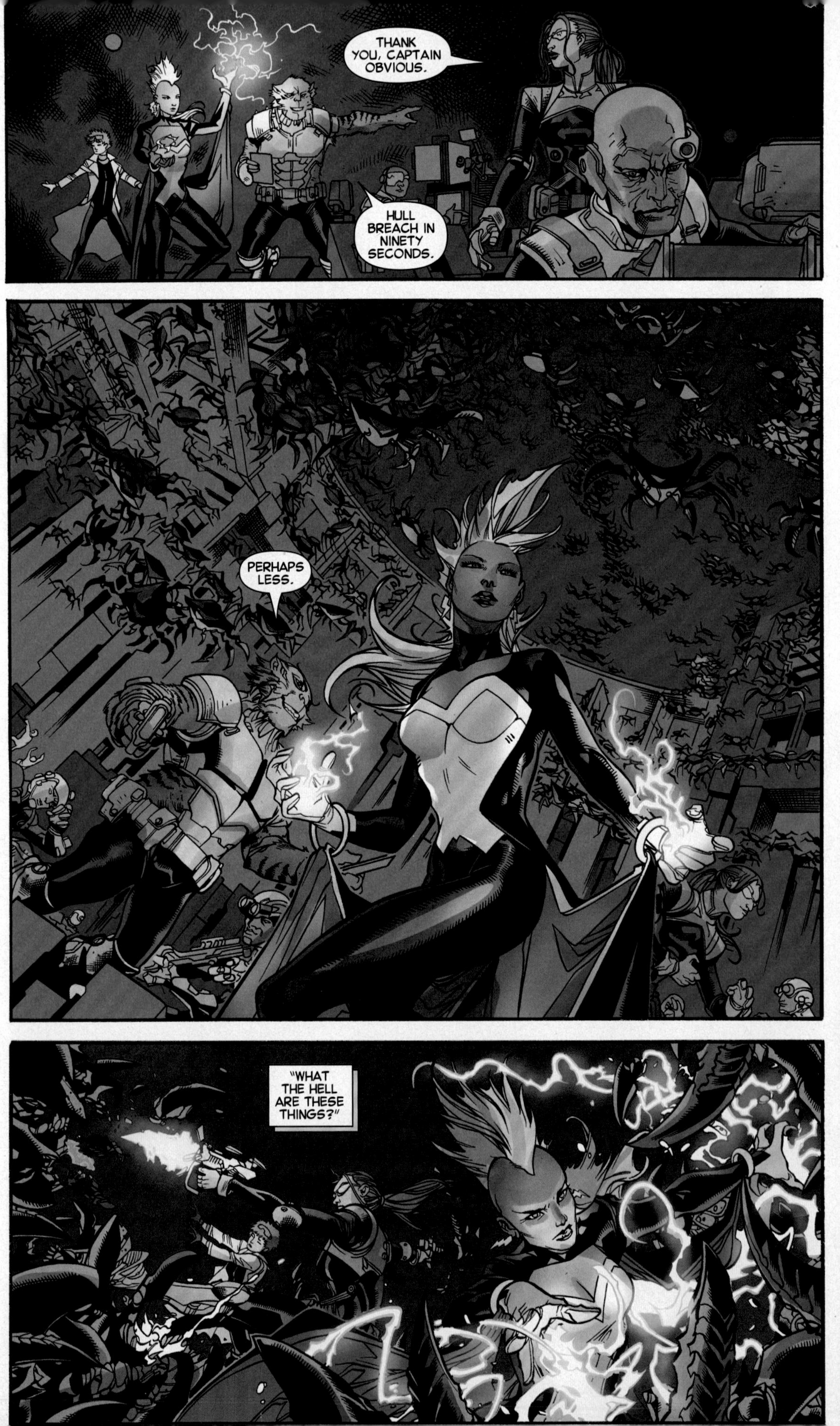
THANK YOU, CAPTAIN OBVIOUS.
HULL BREACH IN NINETY SECONDS.
PERHAPS LESS.
"WHAT THE HELL ARE THESE THINGS?"

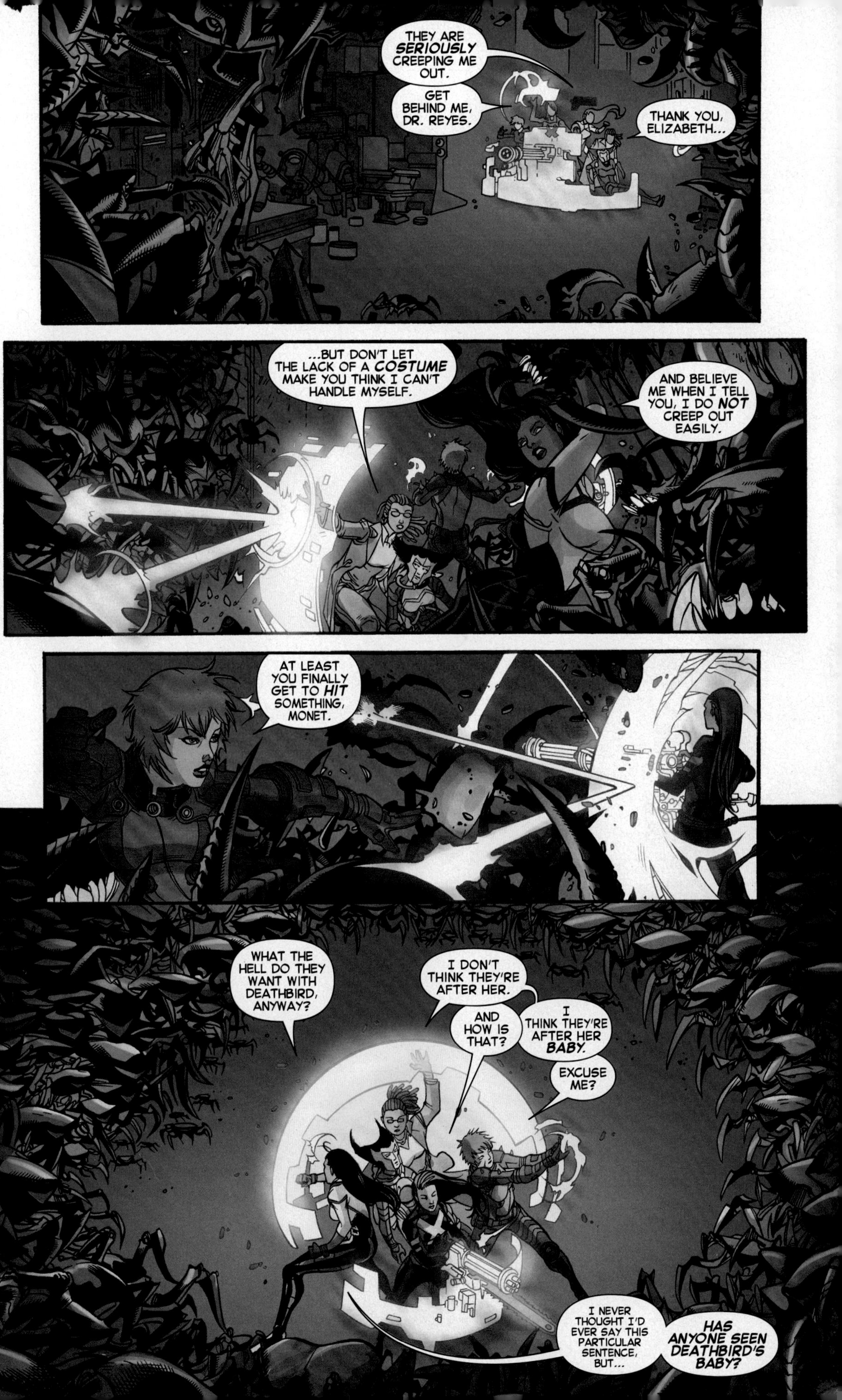
THEY ARE SERIOUSLY CREEPING ME OUT.
GET BEHIND ME, DR. REYES.
THANK YOU, ELIZABETH...
...BUT DON'T LET THE LACK OF A COSTUME MAKE YOU THINK I CAN'T HANDLE MYSELF.
AND BELIEVE ME WHEN I TELL YOU, I DO NOT CREEP OUT EASILY.
AT LEAST YOU FINALLY GET TO HIT SOMETHING, MONET.
WHAT THE HELL DO THEY WANT WITH DEATHBIRD, ANYWAY?
I DON'T THINK THEY'RE AFTER HER.
AND HOW IS THAT?
I THINK THEY'RE AFTER HER BABY.
EXCUSE ME?
I NEVER THOUGHT I'D EVER SAY THIS PARTICULAR SENTENCE, BUT...
HAS ANYONE SEEN DEATHBIRD'S BABY?

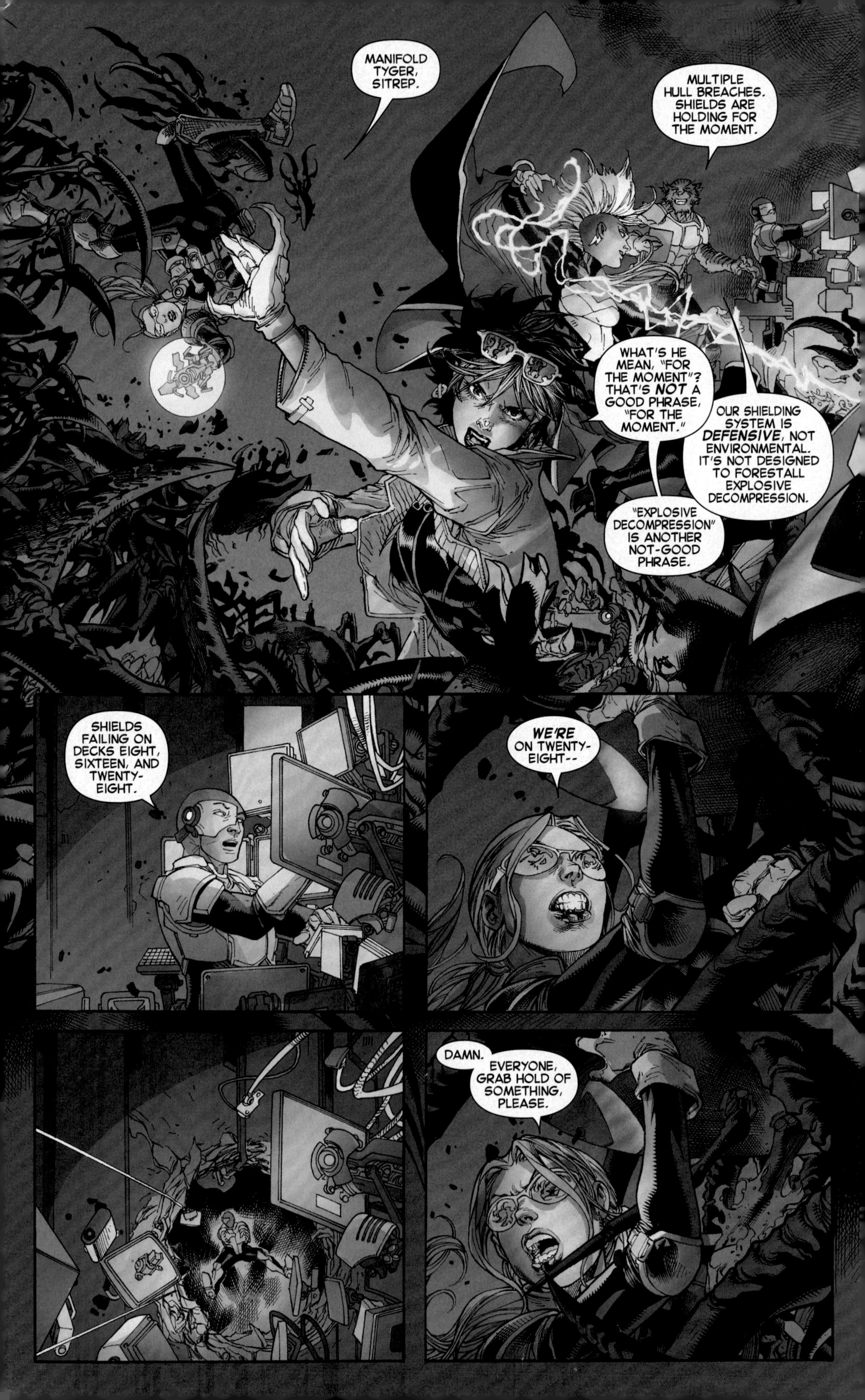

MANIFOLD TYGER, SITREP.
MULTIPLE HULL BREACHES. SHIELDS ARE HOLDING FOR THE MOMENT.
WHAT'S HE MEAN, "FOR THE MOMENT"? THAT'S NOT A GOOD PHRASE, "FOR THE MOMENT."
OUR SHIELDING SYSTEM IS DEFENSIVE, NOT ENVIRONMENTAL. IT'S NOT DESIGNED TO FORESTALL EXPLOSIVE DECOMPRESSION.
"EXPLOSIVE DECOMPRESSION" IS ANOTHER NOT-GOOD PHRASE.
SHIELDS FAILING ON DECKS EIGHT, SIXTEEN, AND TWENTY-EIGHT.
WE'RE ON TWENTY-EIGHT--
DAMN.
EVERYONE, GRAB HOLD OF SOMETHING, PLEASE.

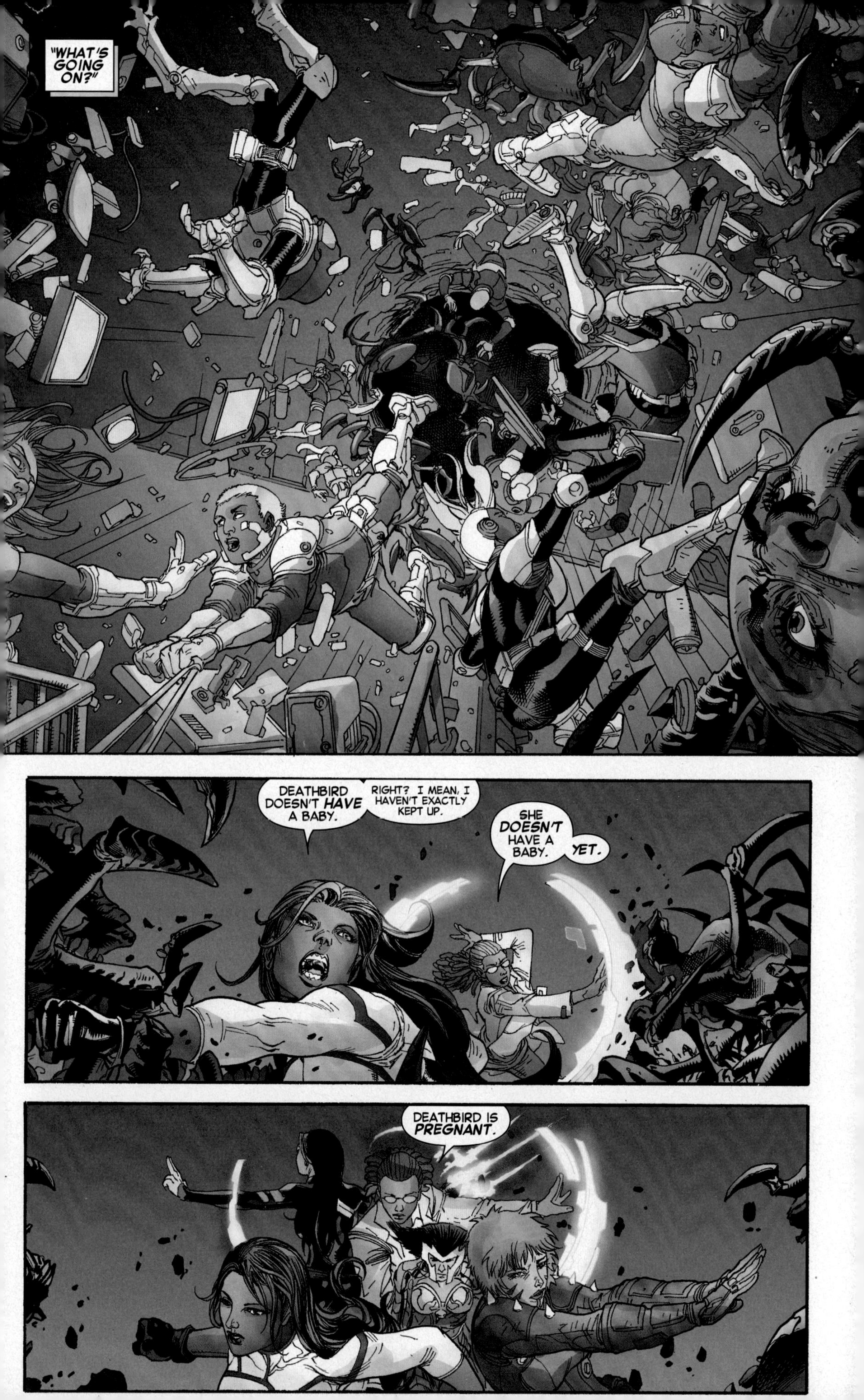
"WHAT'S GOING ON?"
DEATHBIRD DOESN'T HAVE A BABY.
RIGHT? I MEAN, I HAVEN'T EXACTLY KEPT UP.
SHE DOESN'T HAVE A BABY.
YET.
DEATHBIRD IS PREGNANT.

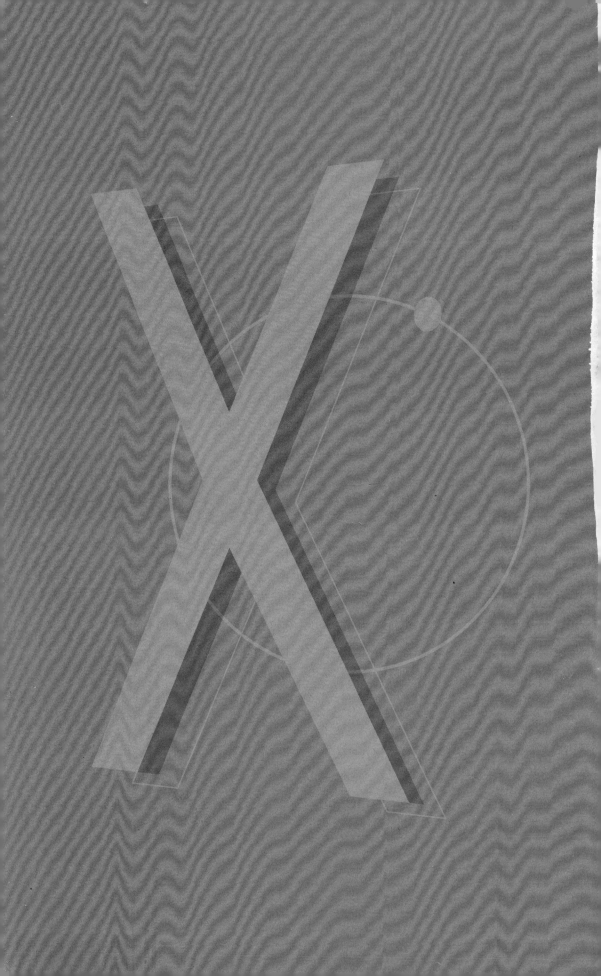

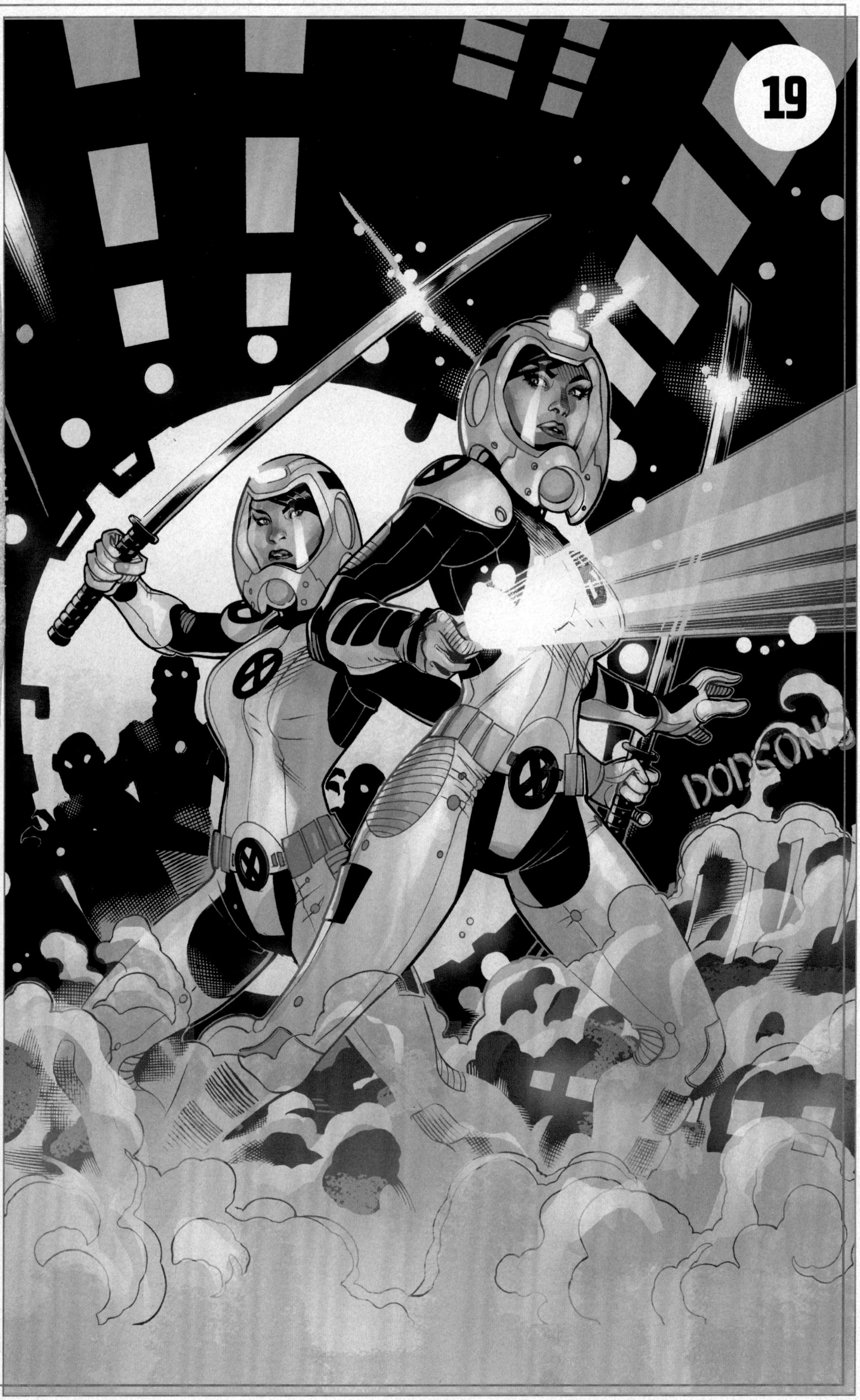
19
DODSON

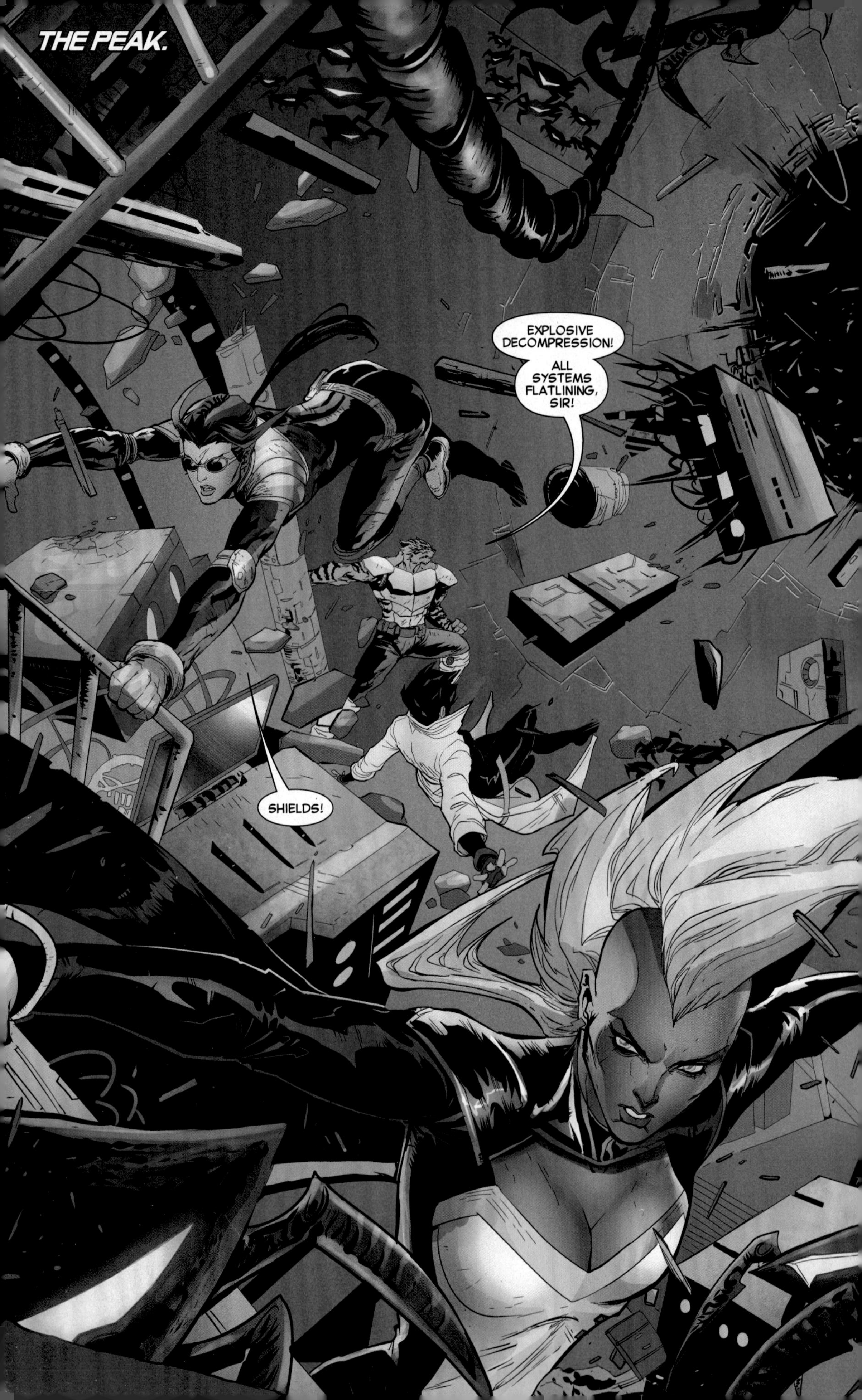
THE PEAK.
EXPLOSIVE DECOMPRESSION!
ALL SYSTEMS FLATLINING, SIR!
SHIELDS!

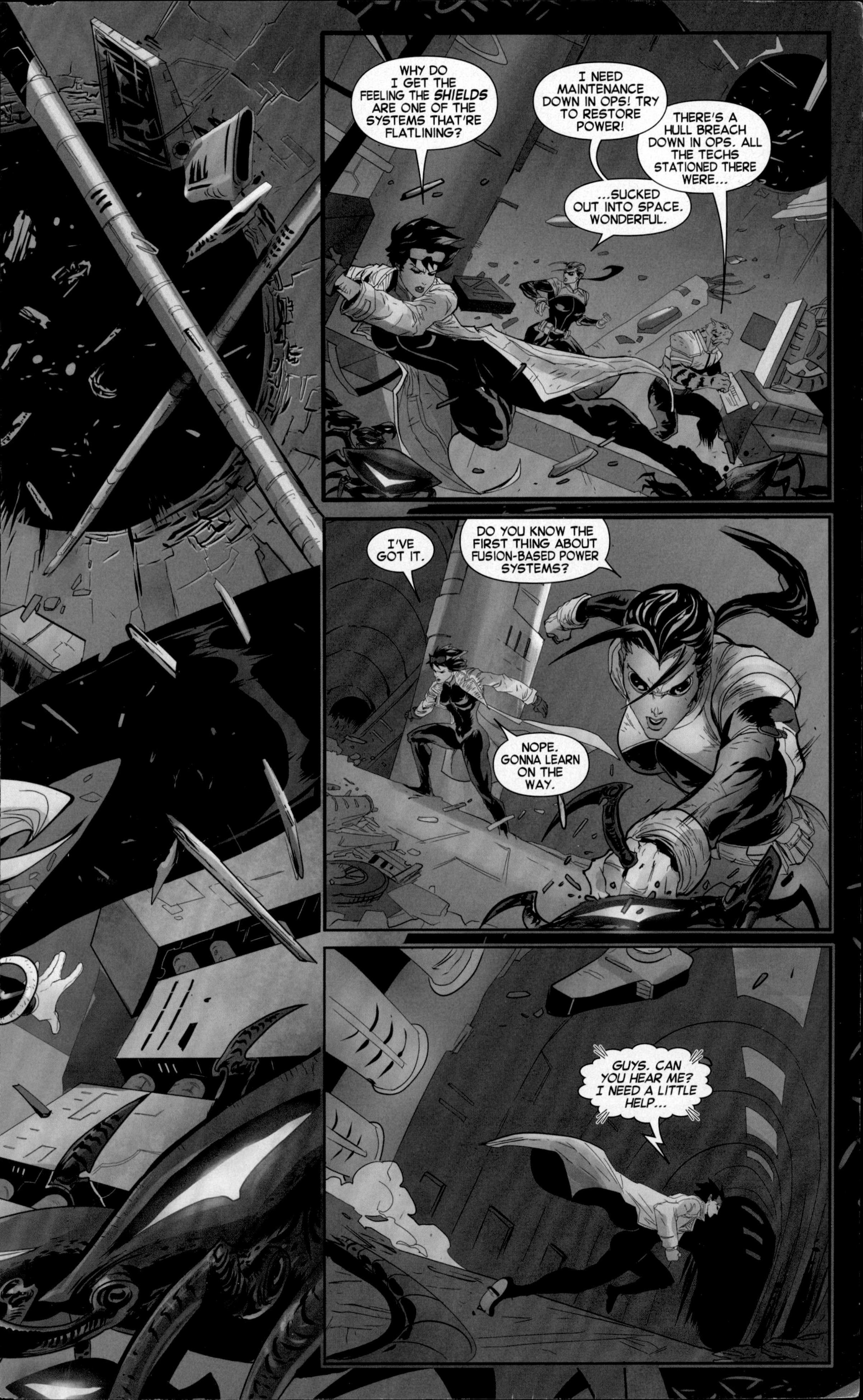
WHY DO I GET THE FEELING THE *SHIELDS* ARE ONE OF THE SYSTEMS THAT'RE FLATLINING?
I NEED MAINTENANCE DOWN IN OPS! TRY TO RESTORE POWER!
THERE'S A HULL BREACH DOWN IN OPS. ALL THE TECHS STATIONED THERE WERE...
...SUCKED OUT INTO SPACE. WONDERFUL.
I'VE GOT IT.
DO YOU KNOW THE FIRST THING ABOUT FUSION-BASED POWER SYSTEMS?
NOPE. GONNA LEARN ON THE WAY.
GUYS. CAN YOU HEAR ME? I NEED A LITTLE HELP...

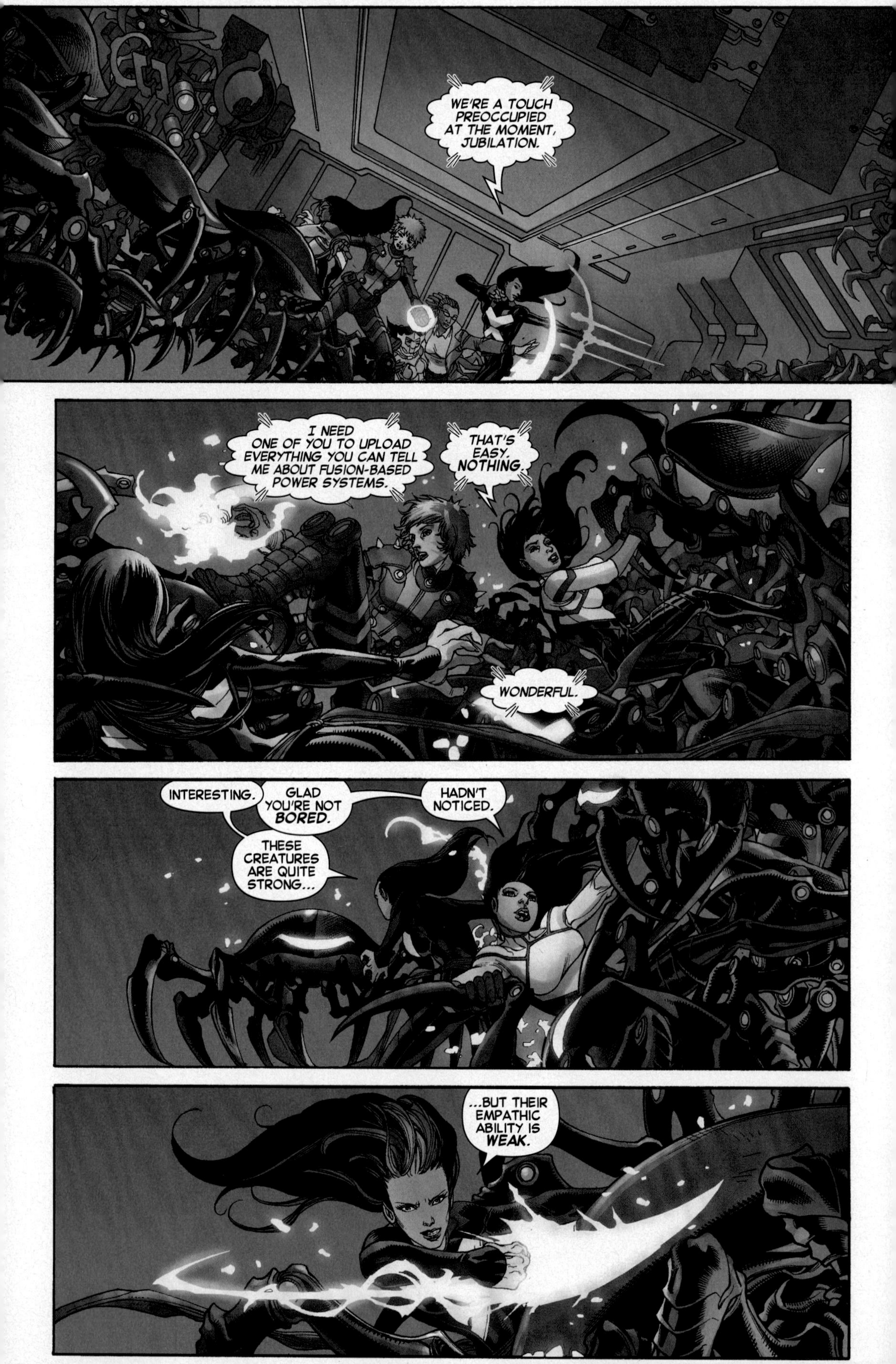
WE'RE A TOUCH PREOCCUPIED AT THE MOMENT, JUBILATION.
I NEED ONE OF YOU TO UPLOAD EVERYTHING YOU CAN TELL ME ABOUT FUSION-BASED POWER SYSTEMS.
THAT'S EASY. NOTHING.
WONDERFUL.
INTERESTING.
GLAD YOU'RE NOT BORED.
HADN'T NOTICED.
THESE CREATURES ARE QUITE STRONG...
...BUT THEIR EMPATHIC ABILITY IS WEAK.

I FEEL IT, TOO. THEY'RE VULNERABLE TO *PSYCHIC ATTACK.*

INDEED.

PSINIKT

"YO."

JEAN GREY SCHOOL FOR HIGHER LEARNING. YOUR ONE-STOP SHOP FOR MUTATION EDUCATION.

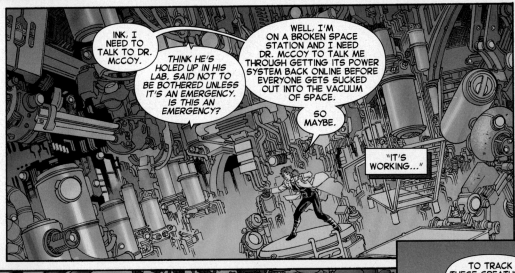

INK, I NEED TO TALK TO DR. MCCOY.

THINK HE'S HOLED UP IN HIS LAB. SAID NOT TO BE BOTHERED UNLESS IT'S AN EMERGENCY. IS THIS AN EMERGENCY?

WELL, I'M ON A BROKEN SPACE STATION AND I NEED DR. MCCOY TO TALK ME THROUGH GETTING ITS POWER SYSTEM BACK ONLINE BEFORE EVERYONE GETS SUCKED OUT INTO THE VACUUM OF SPACE.

SO MAYBE.

"IT'S WORKING..."

...THEY'RE IN RETREAT. CECILIA, GUARD DEATHBIRD. AND WE'RE GONNA NEED YOUR *SHUTTLE.*

FOR WHAT?

TO TRACK THESE CREATURES BACK TO THEIR *HOME.*

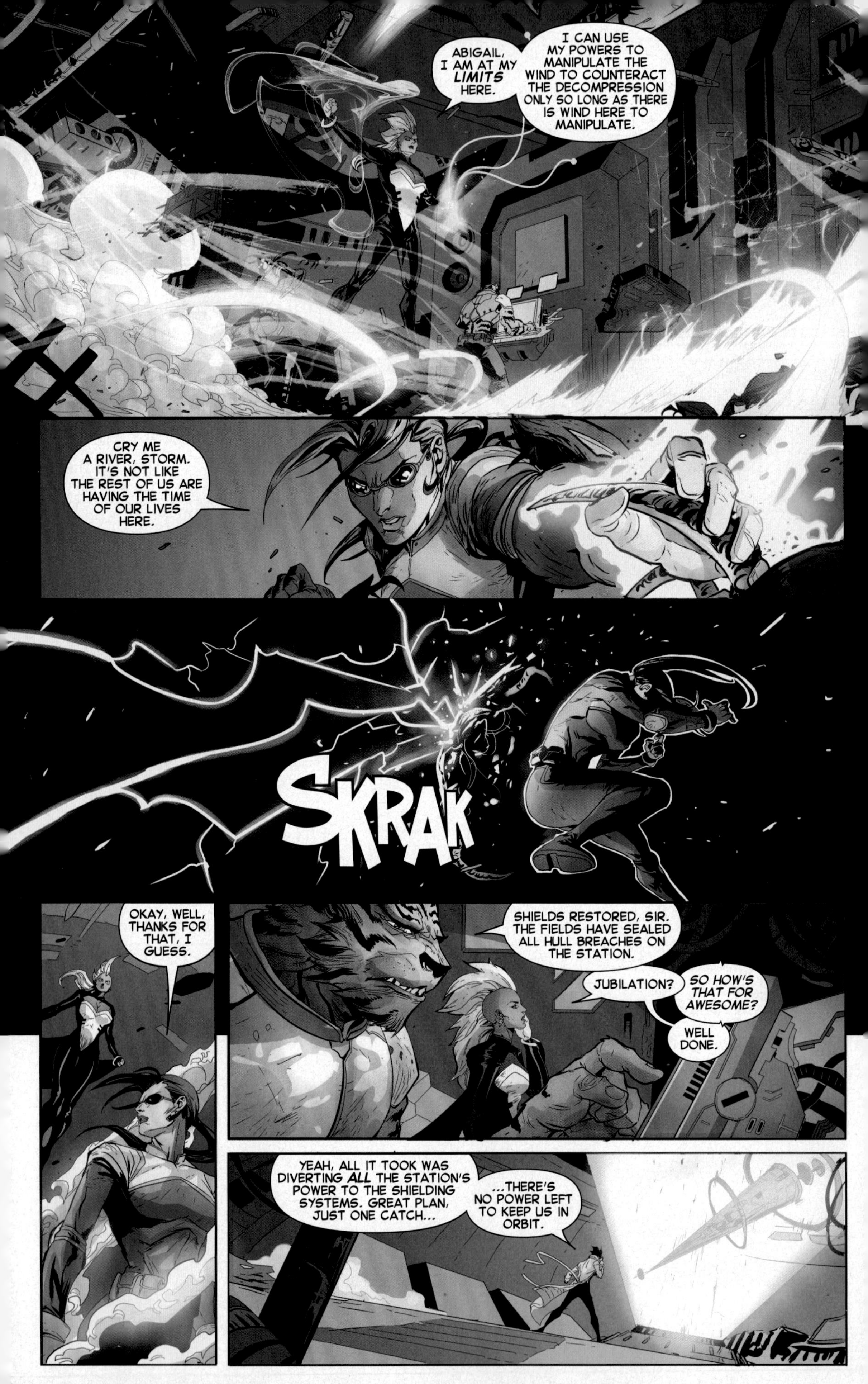
ABIGAIL, I AM AT MY LIMITS HERE.
I CAN USE MY POWERS TO MANIPULATE THE WIND TO COUNTERACT THE DECOMPRESSION ONLY SO LONG AS THERE IS WIND HERE TO MANIPULATE.
CRY ME A RIVER, STORM. IT'S NOT LIKE THE REST OF US ARE HAVING THE TIME OF OUR LIVES HERE.
SKRAK
OKAY, WELL, THANKS FOR THAT, I GUESS.
SHIELDS RESTORED, SIR. THE FIELDS HAVE SEALED ALL HULL BREACHES ON THE STATION.
JUBILATION?
SO HOW'S THAT FOR AWESOME?
WELL DONE.
YEAH, ALL IT TOOK WAS DIVERTING ALL THE STATION'S POWER TO THE SHIELDING SYSTEMS. GREAT PLAN, JUST ONE CATCH...
...THERE'S NO POWER LEFT TO KEEP US IN ORBIT.

YOU LOST THE BUGGERS, DIDN'T YOU?

I HAVEN'T LOST THEM, MONET.

WELL, I DON'T SEE THEM.

I'VE BEEN FOLLOWING THE TRAIL OF THEIR HEAT SIGNATURE.

AND?

...

AND *THAT* I'VE LOST.

WHAT DO YOU SAY, BOSS? HEAD BACK?

UNLESS CECILIA IS SUCCESSFUL IN REVIVING DEATHBIRD, WE WON'T GET ANY ANSWERS BACK AT THE PEAK.

TRUE. BUT WE COULD HELP STORM AND JUBILEE OUT. THE STATION WAS LOOKING PRETTY GNARLY FROM THE OUTSIDE.

WHY, MONET, THAT ALMOST SOUNDED *CONSIDERATE.*

TELL ANYONE AND I'LL BREAK YOUR SPINE.

THE SIDRI ARE *HUNTERS.* *SOMEONE* SENT THEM AFTER DEATHBIRD.

WHO?

I THINK...

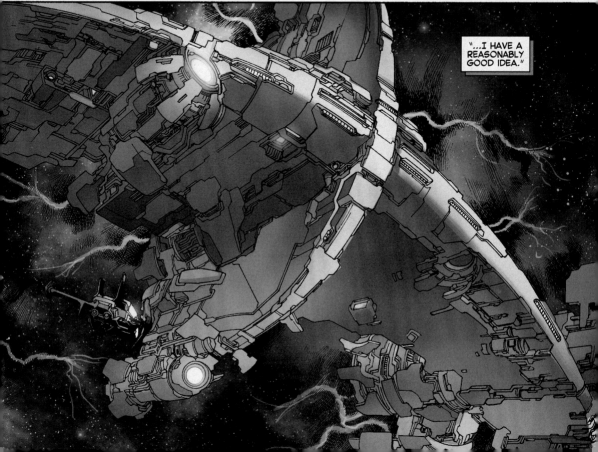

"...I HAVE A REASONABLY GOOD IDEA."

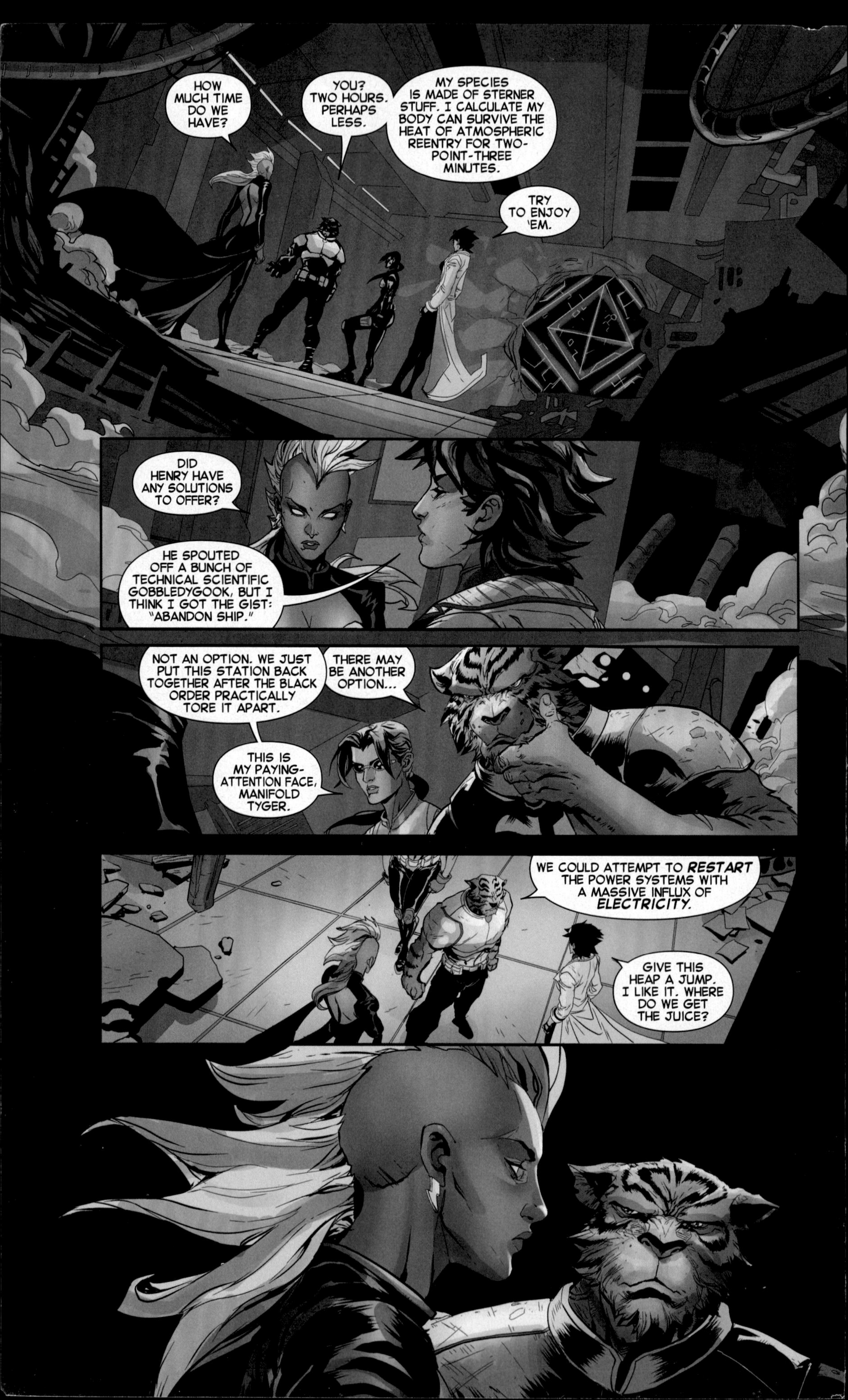
HOW MUCH TIME DO WE HAVE?
YOU? TWO HOURS. PERHAPS LESS.
MY SPECIES IS MADE OF STERNER STUFF. I CALCULATE MY BODY CAN SURVIVE THE HEAT OF ATMOSPHERIC REENTRY FOR TWO-POINT-THREE MINUTES.
TRY TO ENJOY 'EM.
DID HENRY HAVE ANY SOLUTIONS TO OFFER?
HE SPOUTED OFF A BUNCH OF TECHNICAL SCIENTIFIC GOBBLEDYGOOK, BUT I THINK I GOT THE GIST: "ABANDON SHIP."
NOT AN OPTION. WE JUST PUT THIS STATION BACK TOGETHER AFTER THE BLACK ORDER PRACTICALLY TORE IT APART.
THERE MAY BE ANOTHER OPTION...
THIS IS MY PAYING-ATTENTION FACE, MANIFOLD TYGER.
WE COULD ATTEMPT TO **RESTART** THE POWER SYSTEMS WITH A MASSIVE INFLUX OF ***ELECTRICITY.***
GIVE THIS HEAP A JUMP. I LIKE IT. WHERE DO WE GET THE JUICE?

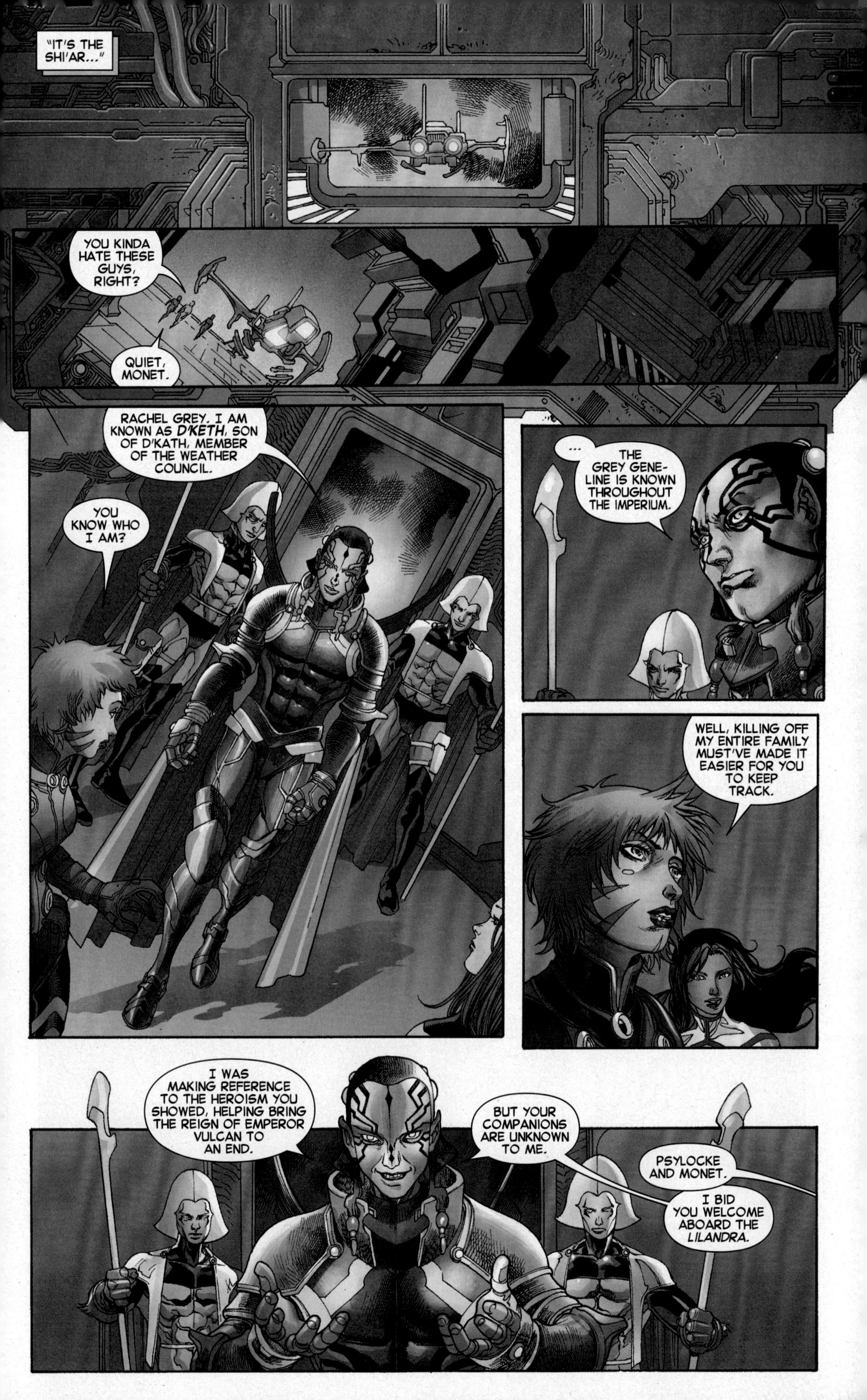
"IT'S THE SHI'AR..."
YOU KINDA HATE THESE GUYS, RIGHT?
QUIET, MONET.
RACHEL GREY. I AM KNOWN AS D'KETH, SON OF D'KATH, MEMBER OF THE WEATHER COUNCIL.
YOU KNOW WHO I AM?
... THE GREY GENE-LINE IS KNOWN THROUGHOUT THE IMPERIUM.
WELL, KILLING OFF MY ENTIRE FAMILY MUST'VE MADE IT EASIER FOR YOU TO KEEP TRACK.
I WAS MAKING REFERENCE TO THE HEROISM YOU SHOWED, HELPING BRING THE REIGN OF EMPEROR VULCAN TO AN END.
BUT YOUR COMPANIONS ARE UNKNOWN TO ME.
PSYLOCKE AND MONET.
I BID YOU WELCOME ABOARD THE LILANDRA.

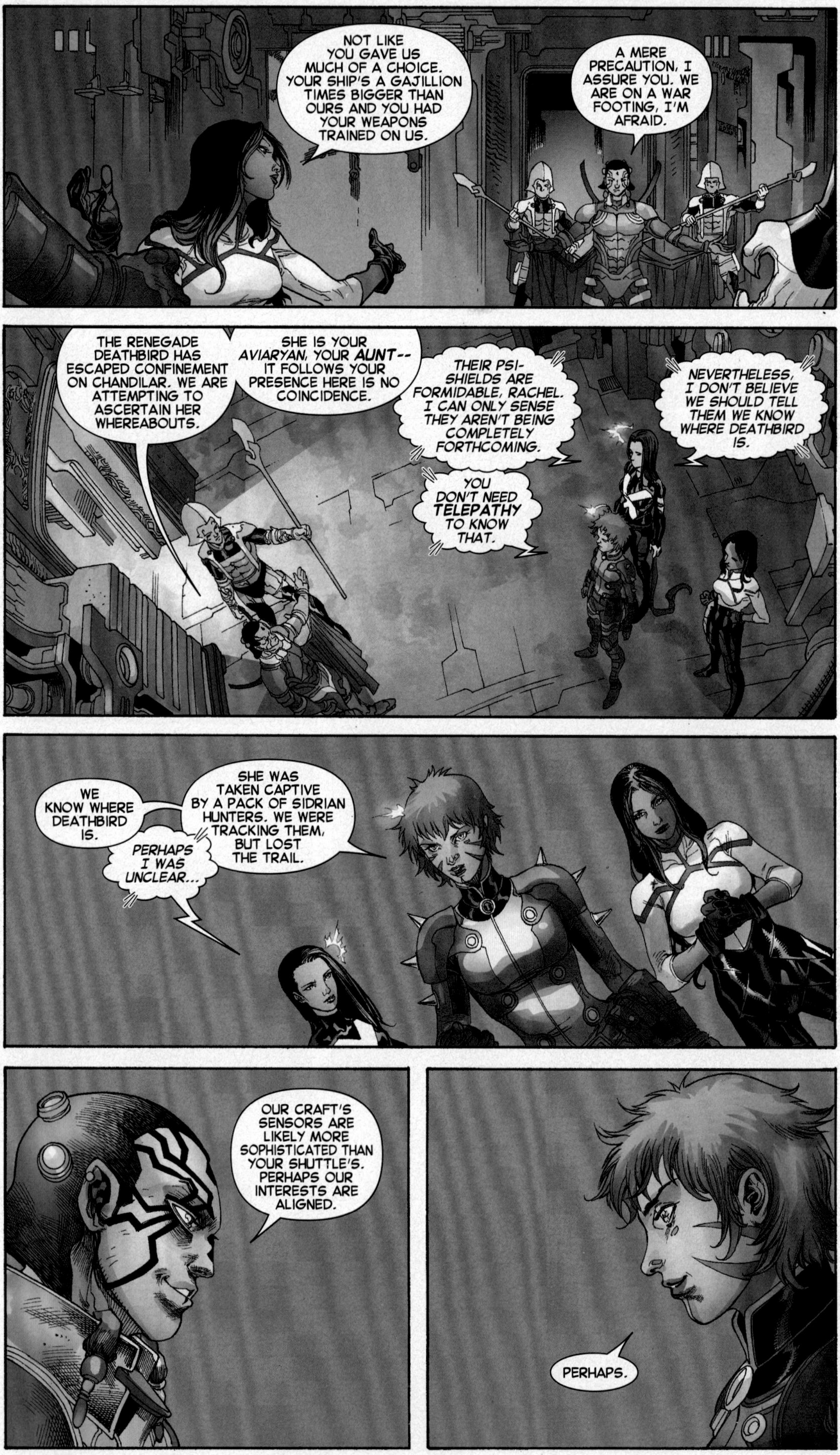
NOT LIKE YOU GAVE US MUCH OF A CHOICE. YOUR SHIP'S A GAJILLION TIMES BIGGER THAN OURS AND YOU HAD YOUR WEAPONS TRAINED ON US.
A MERE PRECAUTION, I ASSURE YOU. WE ARE ON A WAR FOOTING, I'M AFRAID.
THE RENEGADE DEATHBIRD HAS ESCAPED CONFINEMENT ON CHANDILAR. WE ARE ATTEMPTING TO ASCERTAIN HER WHEREABOUTS.
SHE IS YOUR AVIARYAN, YOUR AUNT-- IT FOLLOWS YOUR PRESENCE HERE IS NO COINCIDENCE.
THEIR PSI-SHIELDS ARE FORMIDABLE, RACHEL. I CAN ONLY SENSE THEY AREN'T BEING COMPLETELY FORTHCOMING.
YOU DON'T NEED TELEPATHY TO KNOW THAT.
NEVERTHELESS, I DON'T BELIEVE WE SHOULD TELL THEM WE KNOW WHERE DEATHBIRD IS.
WE KNOW WHERE DEATHBIRD IS.
PERHAPS I WAS UNCLEAR...
SHE WAS TAKEN CAPTIVE BY A PACK OF SIDRIAN HUNTERS. WE WERE TRACKING THEM, BUT LOST THE TRAIL.
OUR CRAFT'S SENSORS ARE LIKELY MORE SOPHISTICATED THAN YOUR SHUTTLE'S. PERHAPS OUR INTERESTS ARE ALIGNED.
PERHAPS.

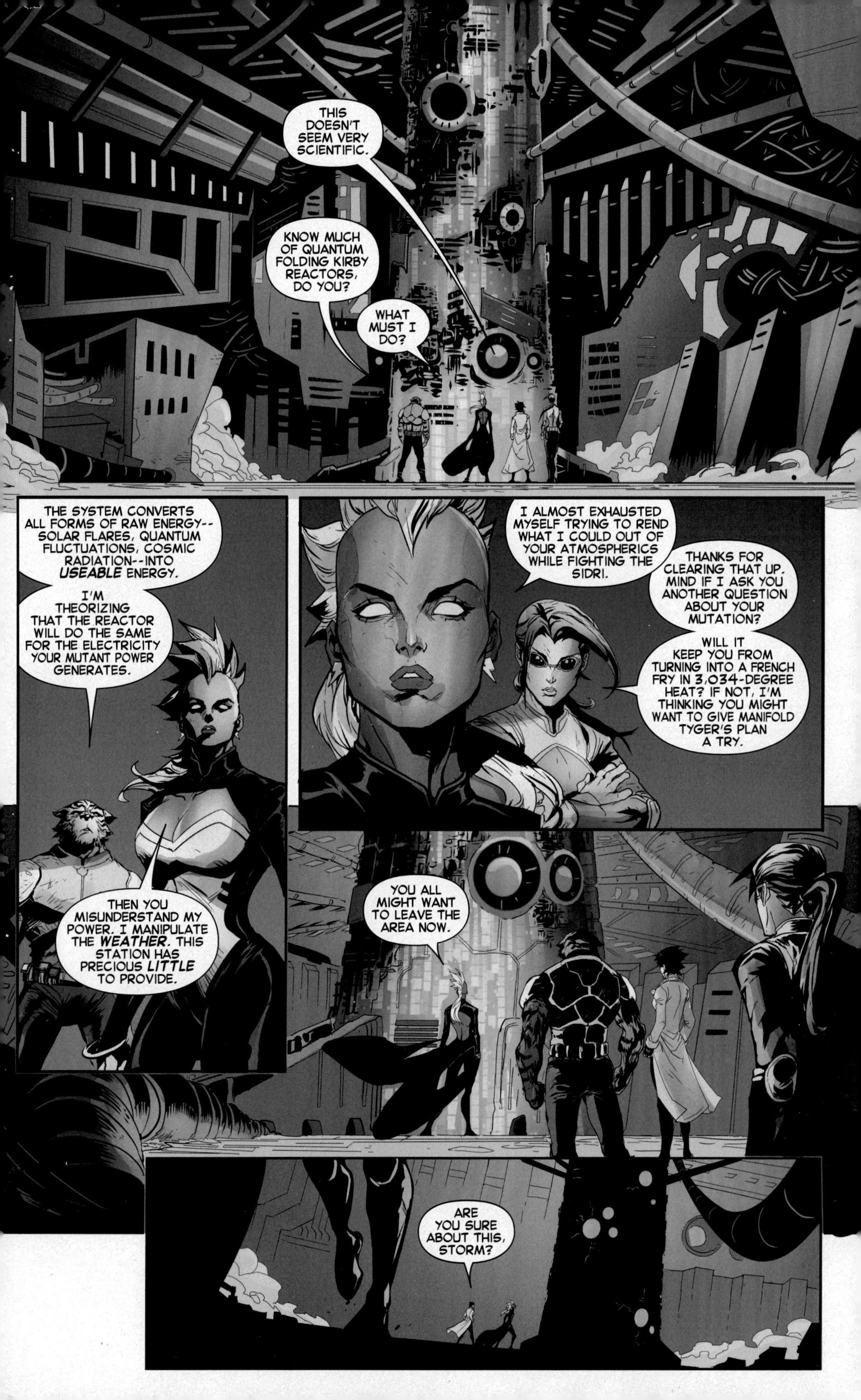
THIS DOESN'T SEEM VERY SCIENTIFIC.
KNOW MUCH OF QUANTUM FOLDING KIRBY REACTORS, DO YOU?
WHAT MUST I DO?
THE SYSTEM CONVERTS ALL FORMS OF RAW ENERGY-- SOLAR FLARES, QUANTUM FLUCTUATIONS, COSMIC RADIATION--INTO USEABLE ENERGY.
I'M THEORIZING THAT THE REACTOR WILL DO THE SAME FOR THE ELECTRICITY YOUR MUTANT POWER GENERATES.
THEN YOU MISUNDERSTAND MY POWER. I MANIPULATE THE WEATHER. THIS STATION HAS PRECIOUS LITTLE TO PROVIDE.
I ALMOST EXHAUSTED MYSELF TRYING TO REND WHAT I COULD OUT OF YOUR ATMOSPHERICS WHILE FIGHTING THE SIDRI.
THANKS FOR CLEARING THAT UP. MIND IF I ASK YOU ANOTHER QUESTION ABOUT YOUR MUTATION?
WILL IT KEEP YOU FROM TURNING INTO A FRENCH FRY IN 3,034-DEGREE HEAT? IF NOT, I'M THINKING YOU MIGHT WANT TO GIVE MANIFOLD TYGER'S PLAN A TRY.
YOU ALL MIGHT WANT TO LEAVE THE AREA NOW.
ARE YOU SURE ABOUT THIS, STORM?

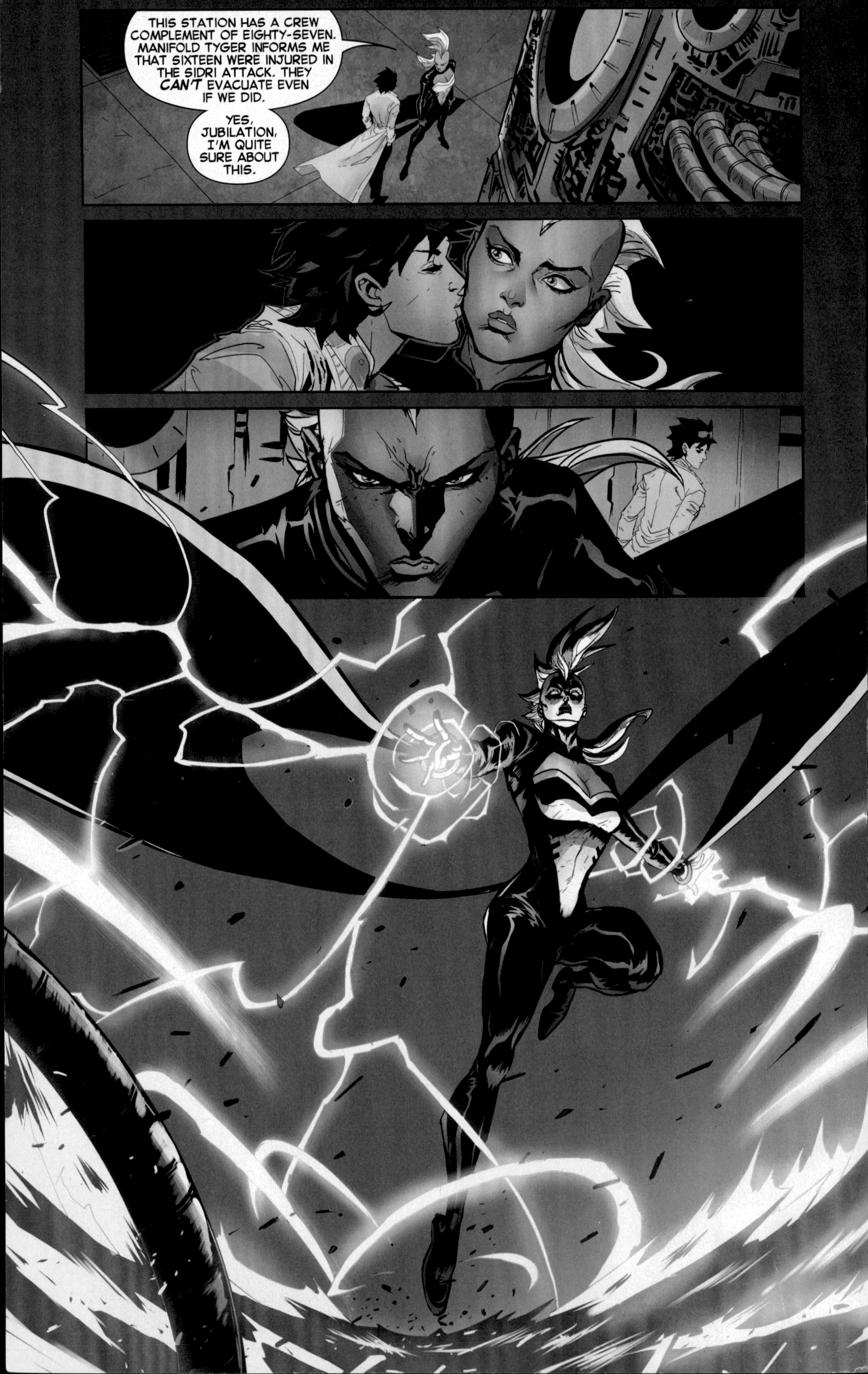

THIS STATION HAS A CREW COMPLEMENT OF EIGHTY-SEVEN. MANIFOLD TYGER INFORMS ME THAT SIXTEEN WERE INJURED IN THE SIDRI ATTACK. THEY *CAN'T* EVACUATE EVEN IF WE DID.
YES, JUBILATION, I'M QUITE SURE ABOUT THIS.

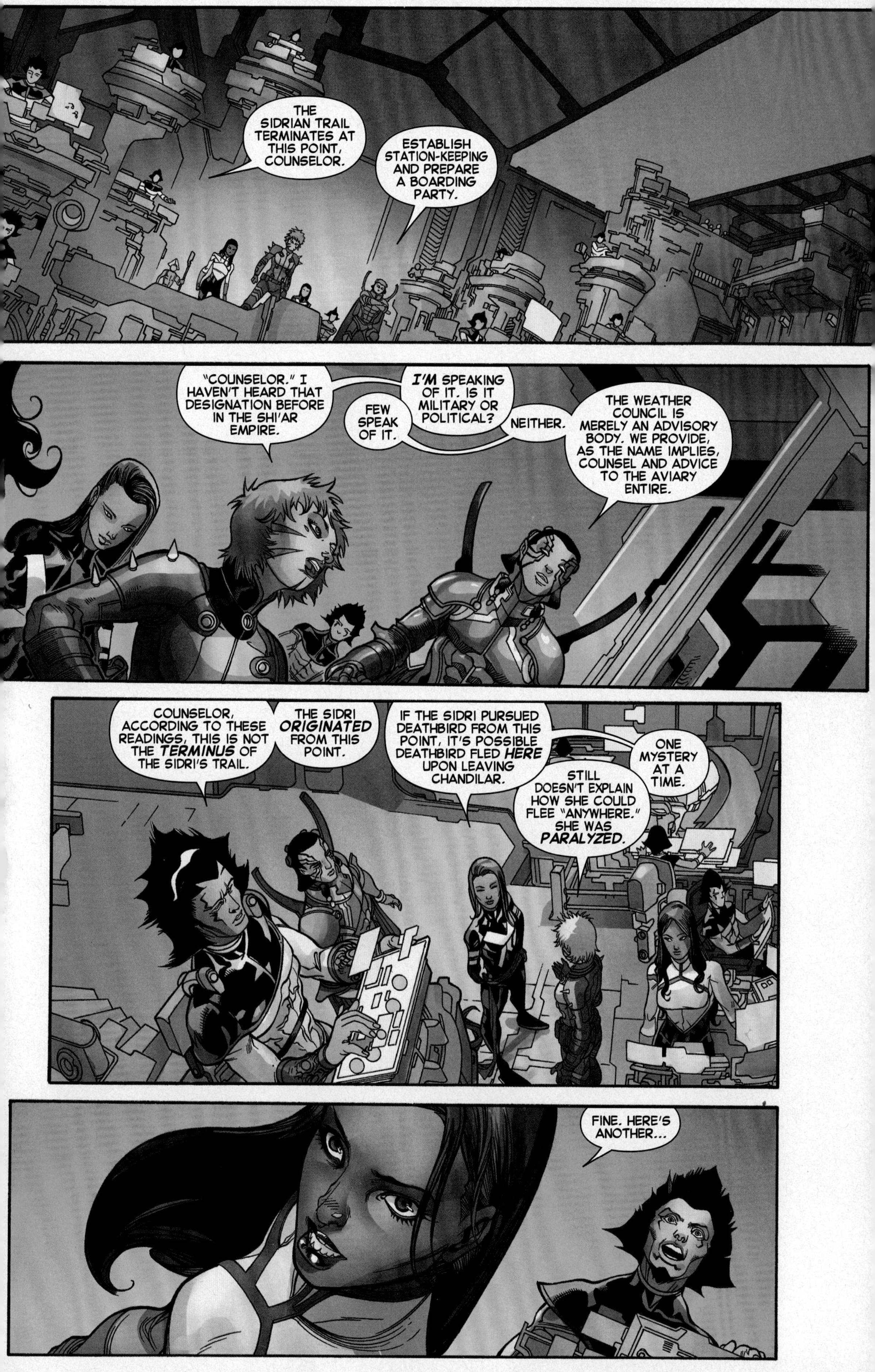

THE SIDRIAN TRAIL TERMINATES AT THIS POINT, COUNSELOR.
ESTABLISH STATION-KEEPING AND PREPARE A BOARDING PARTY.
"COUNSELOR." I HAVEN'T HEARD THAT DESIGNATION BEFORE IN THE SHI'AR EMPIRE.
FEW SPEAK OF IT.
I'M SPEAKING OF IT. IS IT MILITARY OR POLITICAL?
NEITHER.
THE WEATHER COUNCIL IS MERELY AN ADVISORY BODY. WE PROVIDE, AS THE NAME IMPLIES, COUNSEL AND ADVICE TO THE AVIARY ENTIRE.
COUNSELOR, ACCORDING TO THESE READINGS, THIS IS NOT THE TERMINUS OF THE SIDRI'S TRAIL.
THE SIDRI ORIGINATED FROM THIS POINT.
IF THE SIDRI PURSUED DEATHBIRD FROM THIS POINT, IT'S POSSIBLE DEATHBIRD FLED HERE UPON LEAVING CHANDILAR.
ONE MYSTERY AT A TIME.
STILL DOESN'T EXPLAIN HOW SHE COULD FLEE "ANYWHERE." SHE WAS PARALYZED.
FINE. HERE'S ANOTHER...

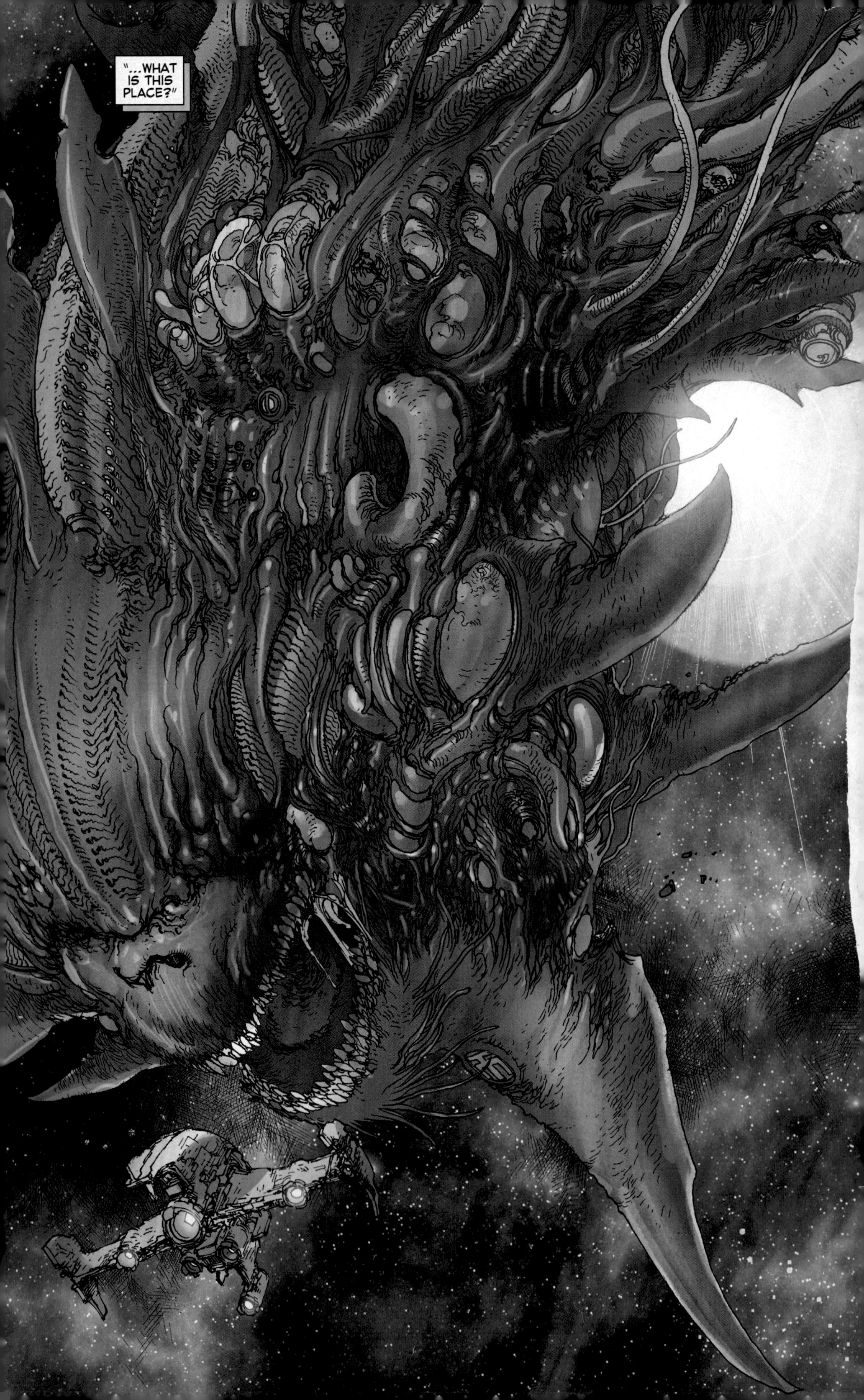
"...WHAT IS THIS PLACE?"

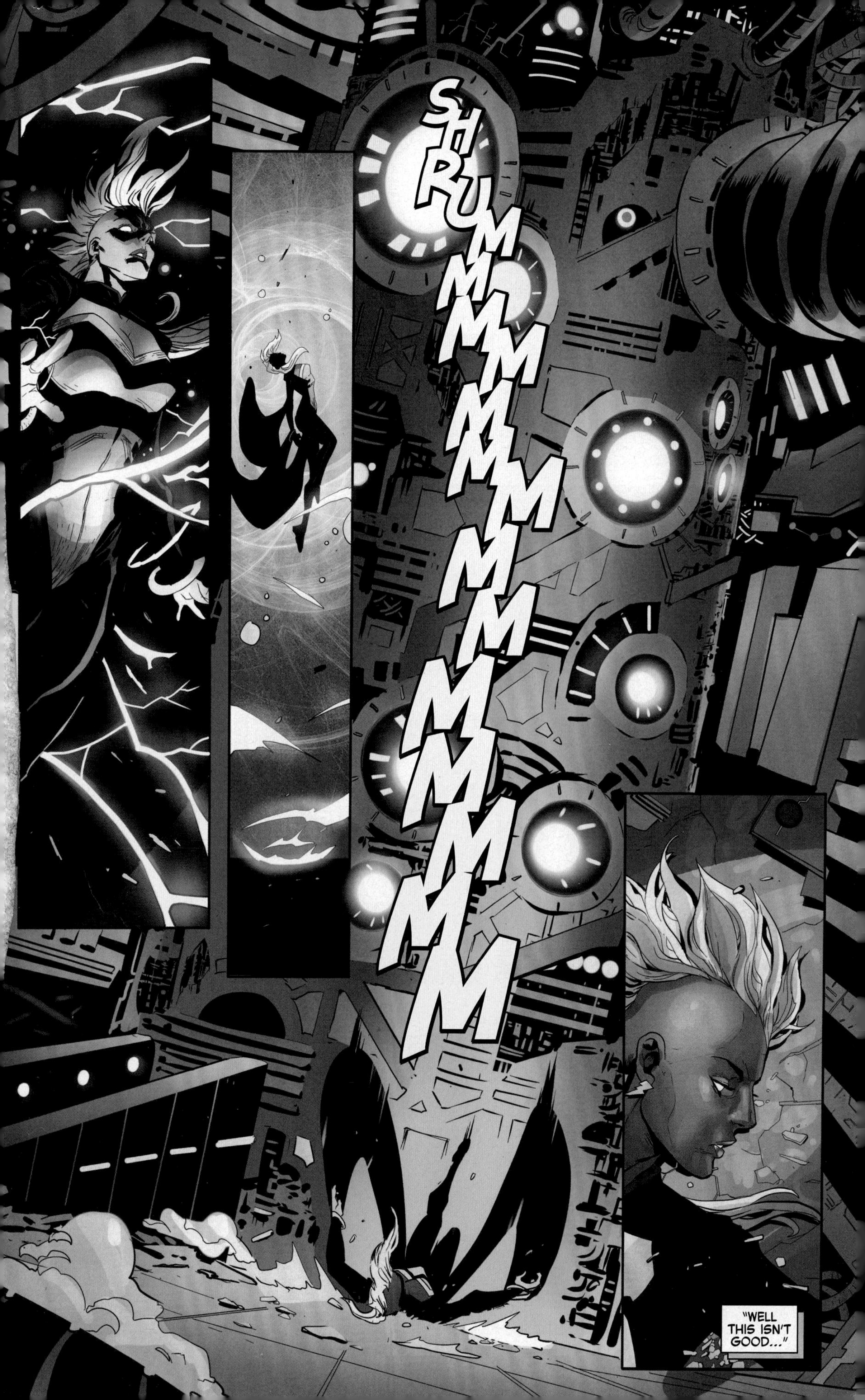
SHRUMMMMMMMMMMMMMMM
"WELL THIS ISN'T GOOD..."

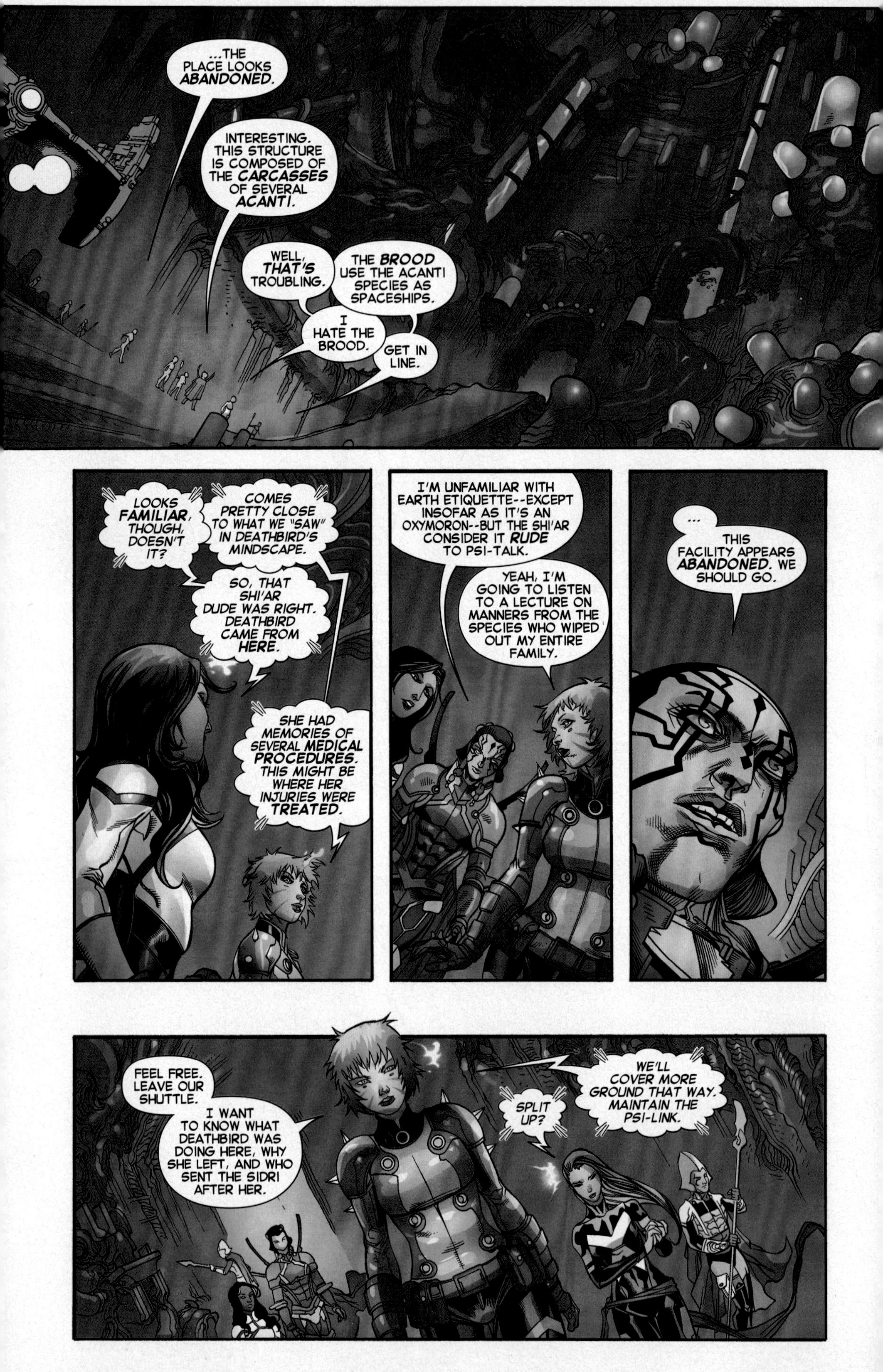
...THE PLACE LOOKS ABANDONED.
INTERESTING. THIS STRUCTURE IS COMPOSED OF THE CARCASSES OF SEVERAL ACANTI.
WELL, THAT'S TROUBLING.
THE BROOD USE THE ACANTI SPECIES AS SPACESHIPS.
I HATE THE BROOD.
GET IN LINE.
LOOKS FAMILIAR, THOUGH, DOESN'T IT?
COMES PRETTY CLOSE TO WHAT WE "SAW" IN DEATHBIRD'S MINDSCAPE.
SO, THAT SHI'AR DUDE WAS RIGHT. DEATHBIRD CAME FROM HERE.
SHE HAD MEMORIES OF SEVERAL MEDICAL PROCEDURES. THIS MIGHT BE WHERE HER INJURIES WERE TREATED.
I'M UNFAMILIAR WITH EARTH ETIQUETTE--EXCEPT INSOFAR AS IT'S AN OXYMORON--BUT THE SHI'AR CONSIDER IT RUDE TO PSI-TALK.
YEAH, I'M GOING TO LISTEN TO A LECTURE ON MANNERS FROM THE SPECIES WHO WIPED OUT MY ENTIRE FAMILY.
...
THIS FACILITY APPEARS ABANDONED. WE SHOULD GO.
FEEL FREE. LEAVE OUR SHUTTLE.
I WANT TO KNOW WHAT DEATHBIRD WAS DOING HERE, WHY SHE LEFT, AND WHO SENT THE SIDRI AFTER HER.
SPLIT UP?
WE'LL COVER MORE GROUND THAT WAY. MAINTAIN THE PSI-LINK.

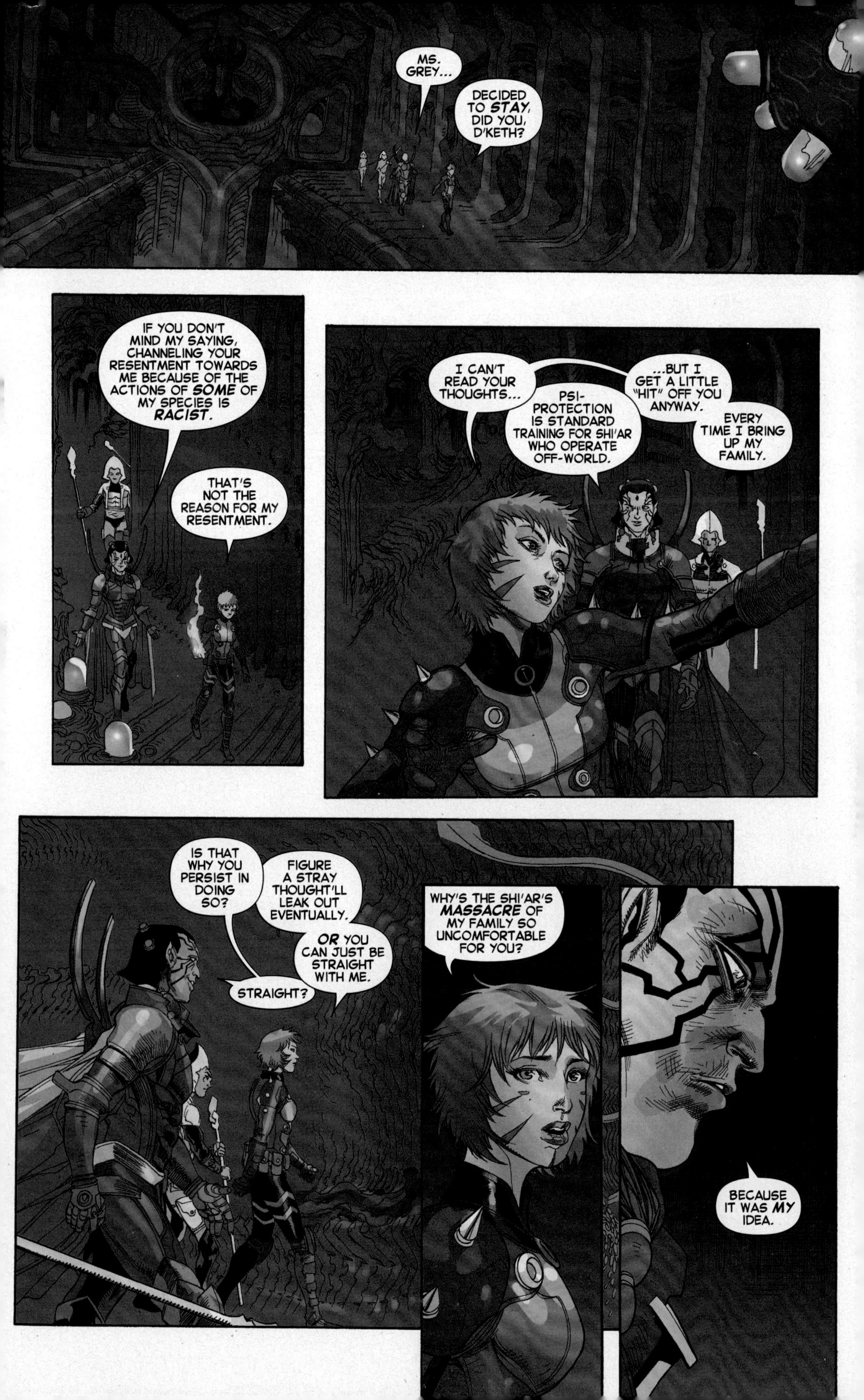
MS. GREY...
DECIDED TO STAY, DID YOU, D'KETH?
IF YOU DON'T MIND MY SAYING, CHANNELING YOUR RESENTMENT TOWARDS ME BECAUSE OF THE ACTIONS OF SOME OF MY SPECIES IS RACIST.
THAT'S NOT THE REASON FOR MY RESENTMENT.
I CAN'T READ YOUR THOUGHTS...
...BUT I GET A LITTLE "HIT" OFF YOU ANYWAY.
PSI-PROTECTION IS STANDARD TRAINING FOR SHI'AR WHO OPERATE OFF-WORLD.
EVERY TIME I BRING UP MY FAMILY.
IS THAT WHY YOU PERSIST IN DOING SO?
FIGURE A STRAY THOUGHT'LL LEAK OUT EVENTUALLY.
STRAIGHT?
OR YOU CAN JUST BE STRAIGHT WITH ME.
WHY'S THE SHI'AR'S MASSACRE OF MY FAMILY SO UNCOMFORTABLE FOR YOU?
BECAUSE IT WAS MY IDEA.

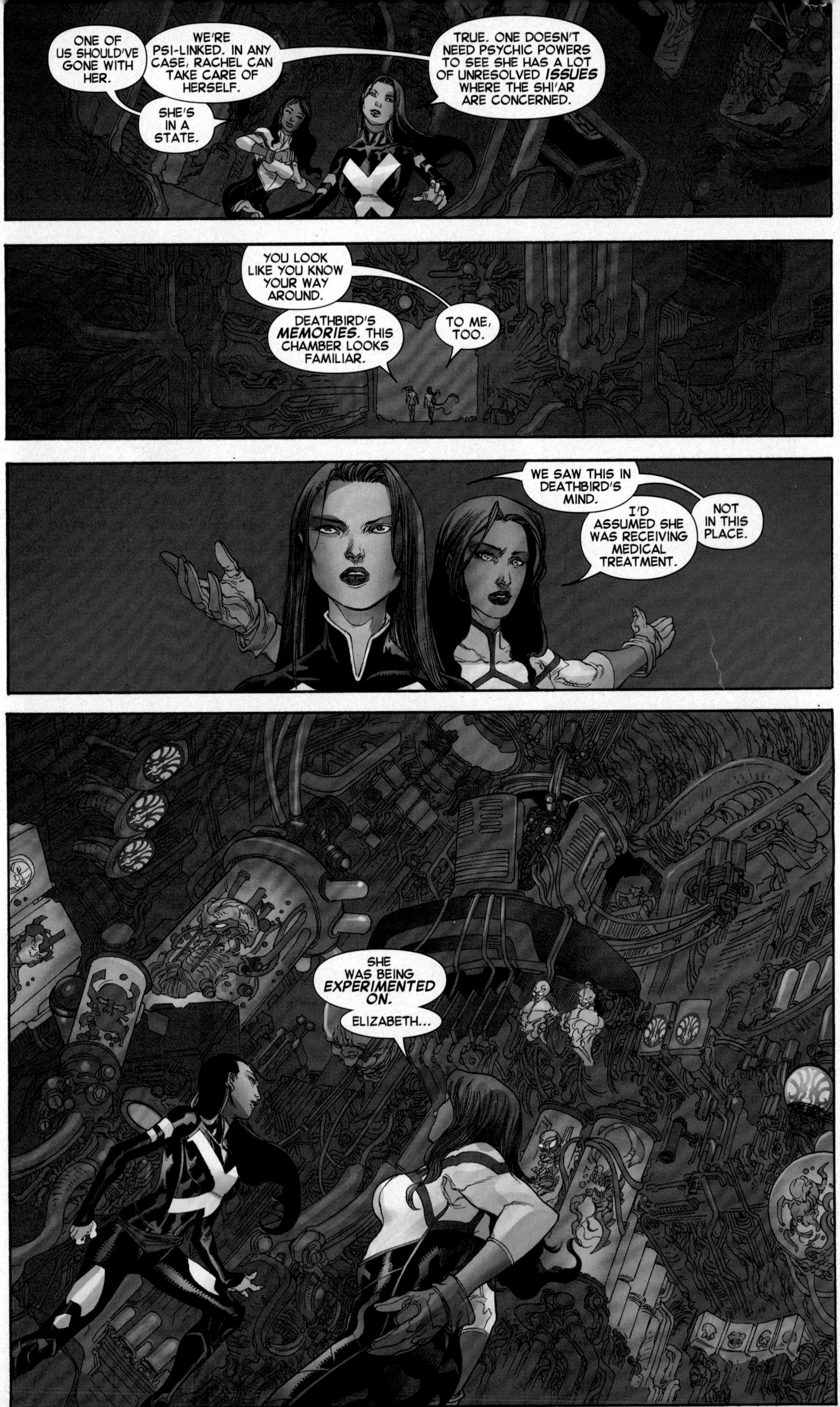
ONE OF US SHOULD'VE GONE WITH HER.
WE'RE PSI-LINKED. IN ANY CASE, RACHEL CAN TAKE CARE OF HERSELF.
SHE'S IN A STATE.
TRUE. ONE DOESN'T NEED PSYCHIC POWERS TO SEE SHE HAS A LOT OF UNRESOLVED ISSUES WHERE THE SHI'AR ARE CONCERNED.
YOU LOOK LIKE YOU KNOW YOUR WAY AROUND.
DEATHBIRD'S MEMORIES. THIS CHAMBER LOOKS FAMILIAR.
TO ME, TOO.
WE SAW THIS IN DEATHBIRD'S MIND.
I'D ASSUMED SHE WAS RECEIVING MEDICAL TREATMENT.
NOT IN THIS PLACE.
SHE WAS BEING EXPERIMENTED ON.
ELIZABETH...

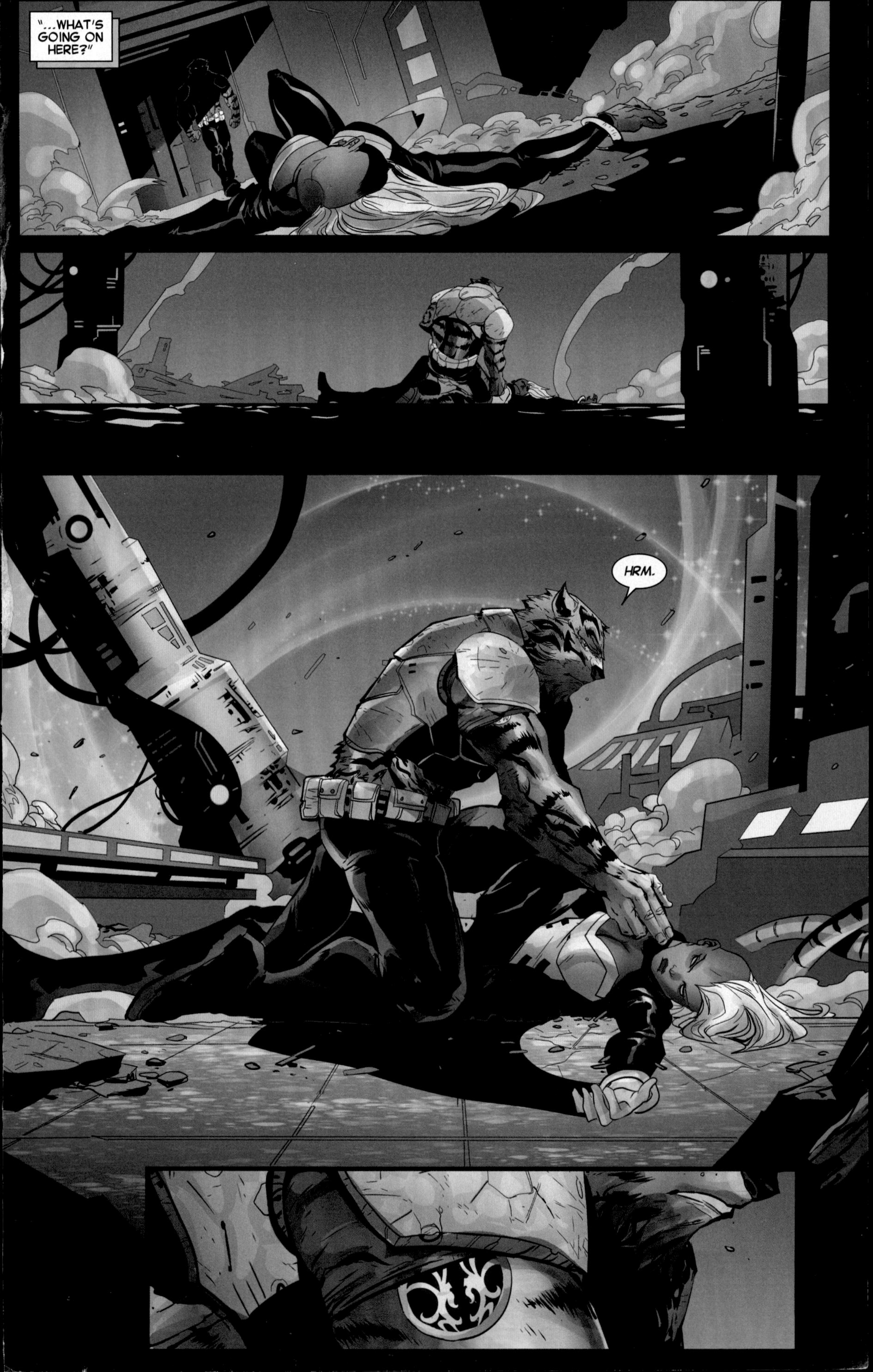
"...WHAT'S GOING ON HERE?"
HRM.

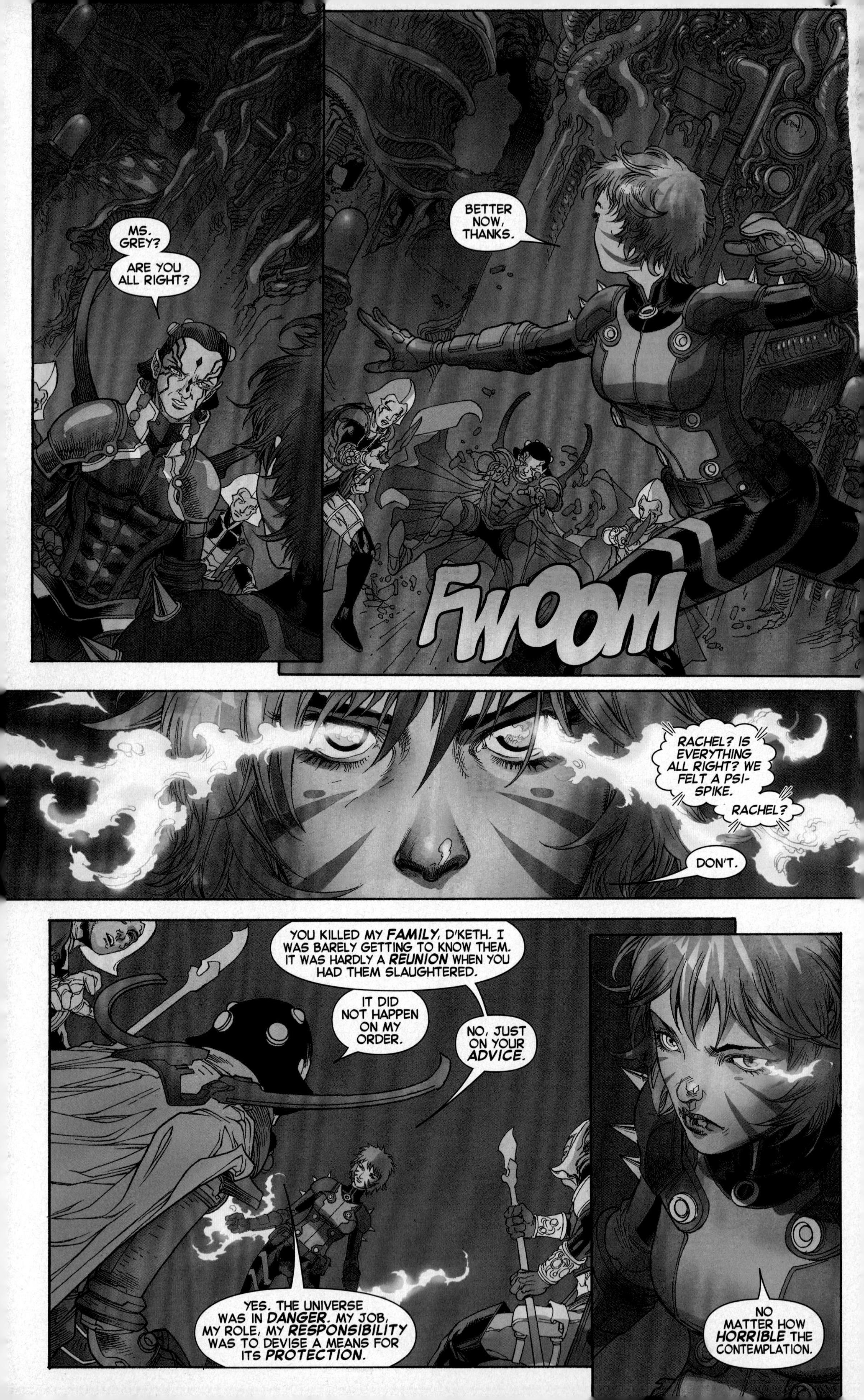
MS. GREY?
ARE YOU ALL RIGHT?
BETTER NOW, THANKS.
FWOOM
RACHEL? IS EVERYTHING ALL RIGHT? WE FELT A PSI-SPIKE.
RACHEL?
DON'T.
YOU KILLED MY FAMILY, D'KETH. I WAS BARELY GETTING TO KNOW THEM. IT WAS HARDLY A REUNION WHEN YOU HAD THEM SLAUGHTERED.
IT DID NOT HAPPEN ON MY ORDER.
NO, JUST ON YOUR ADVICE.
YES. THE UNIVERSE WAS IN DANGER. MY JOB, MY ROLE, MY RESPONSIBILITY WAS TO DEVISE A MEANS FOR ITS PROTECTION.
NO MATTER HOW HORRIBLE THE CONTEMPLATION.

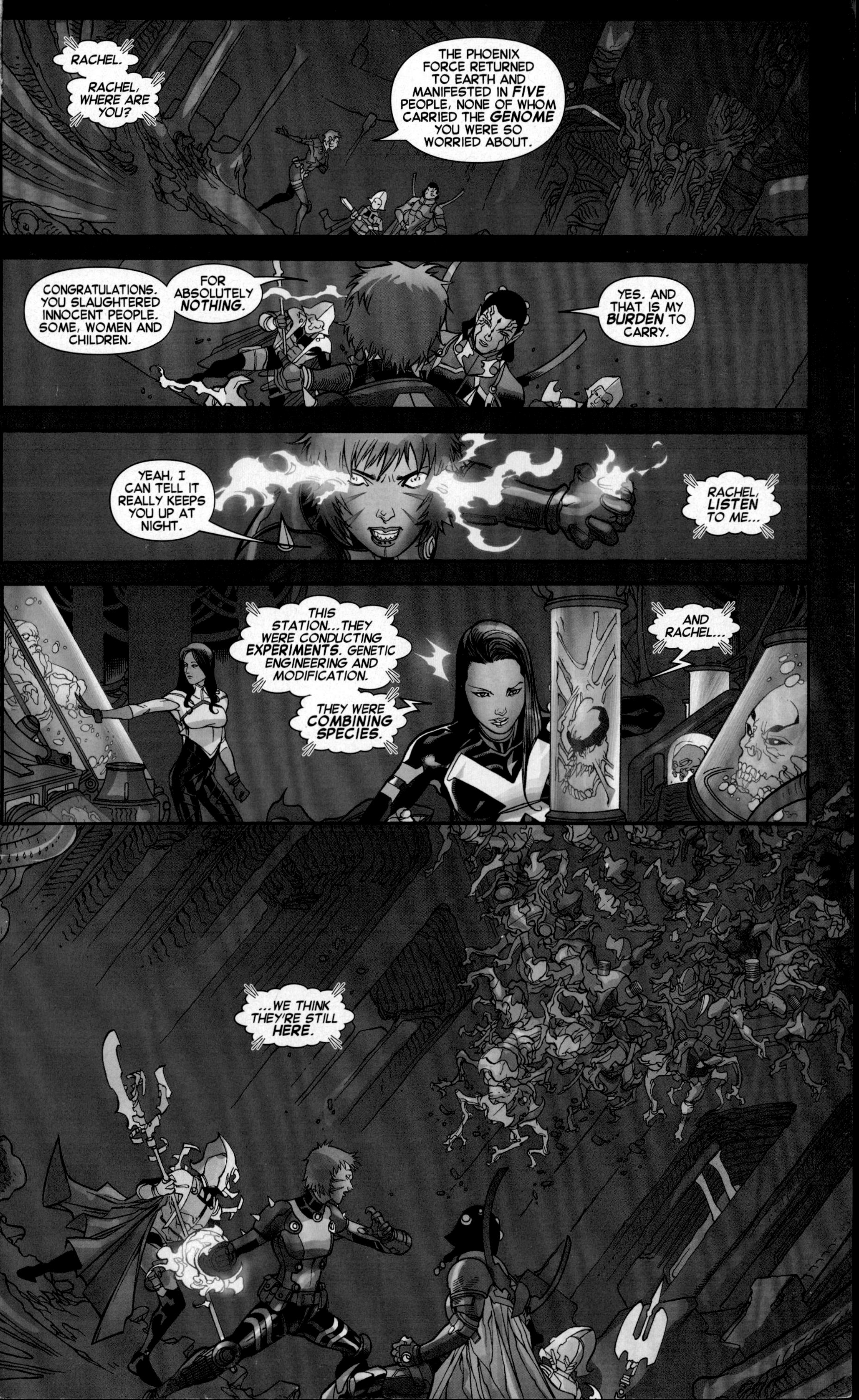
RACHEL.
RACHEL, WHERE ARE YOU?
THE PHOENIX FORCE RETURNED TO EARTH AND MANIFESTED IN *FIVE* PEOPLE, NONE OF WHOM CARRIED THE *GENOME* YOU WERE SO WORRIED ABOUT.
CONGRATULATIONS. YOU SLAUGHTERED INNOCENT PEOPLE. SOME, WOMEN AND CHILDREN.
FOR ABSOLUTELY *NOTHING*.
YES. AND THAT IS MY *BURDEN* TO CARRY.
YEAH, I CAN TELL IT REALLY KEEPS YOU UP AT NIGHT.
RACHEL, *LISTEN* TO ME...
THIS STATION...THEY WERE CONDUCTING *EXPERIMENTS*. GENETIC ENGINEERING AND MODIFICATION.
THEY WERE *COMBINING SPECIES*.
AND RACHEL...
...WE THINK THEY'RE STILL *HERE*.

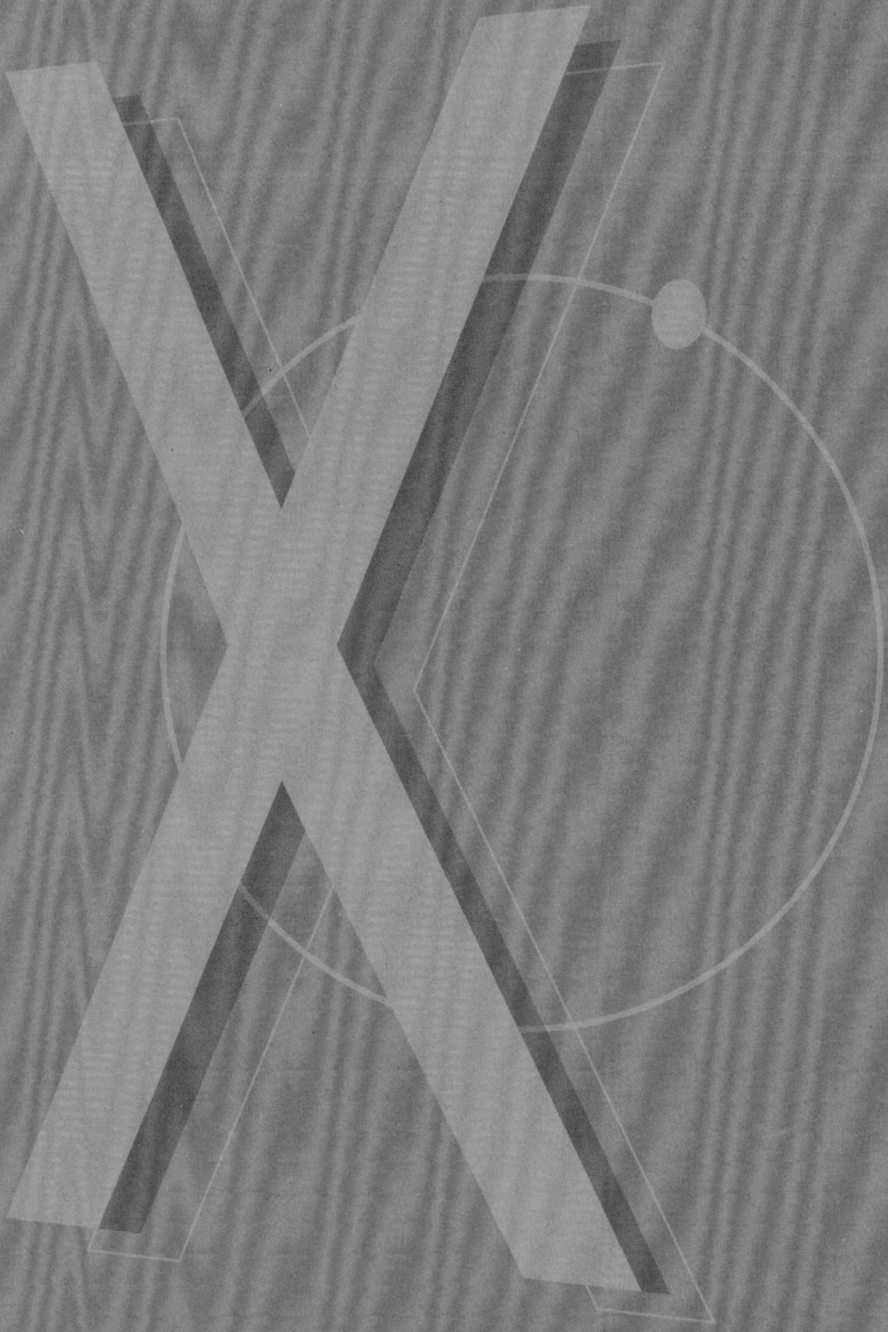

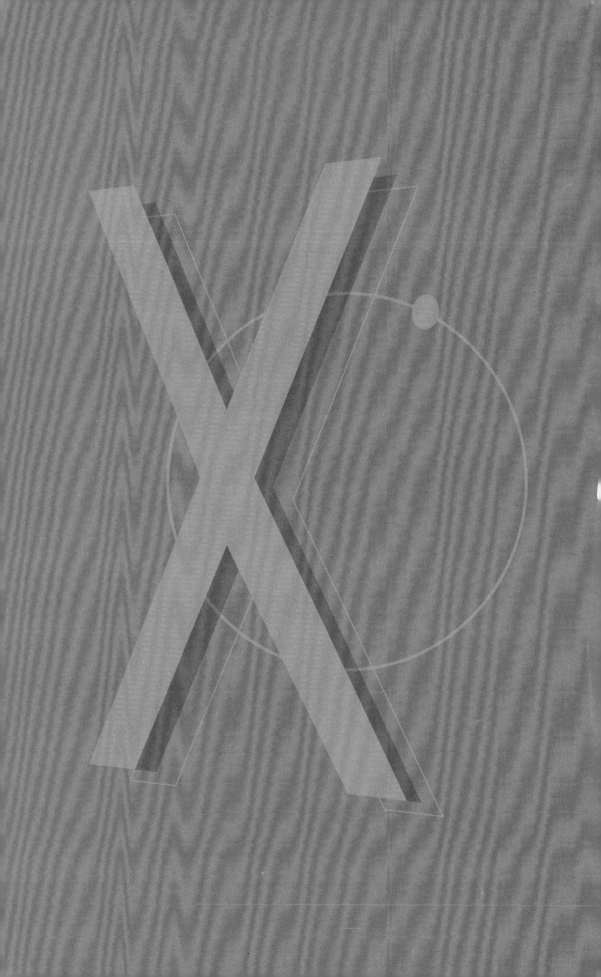

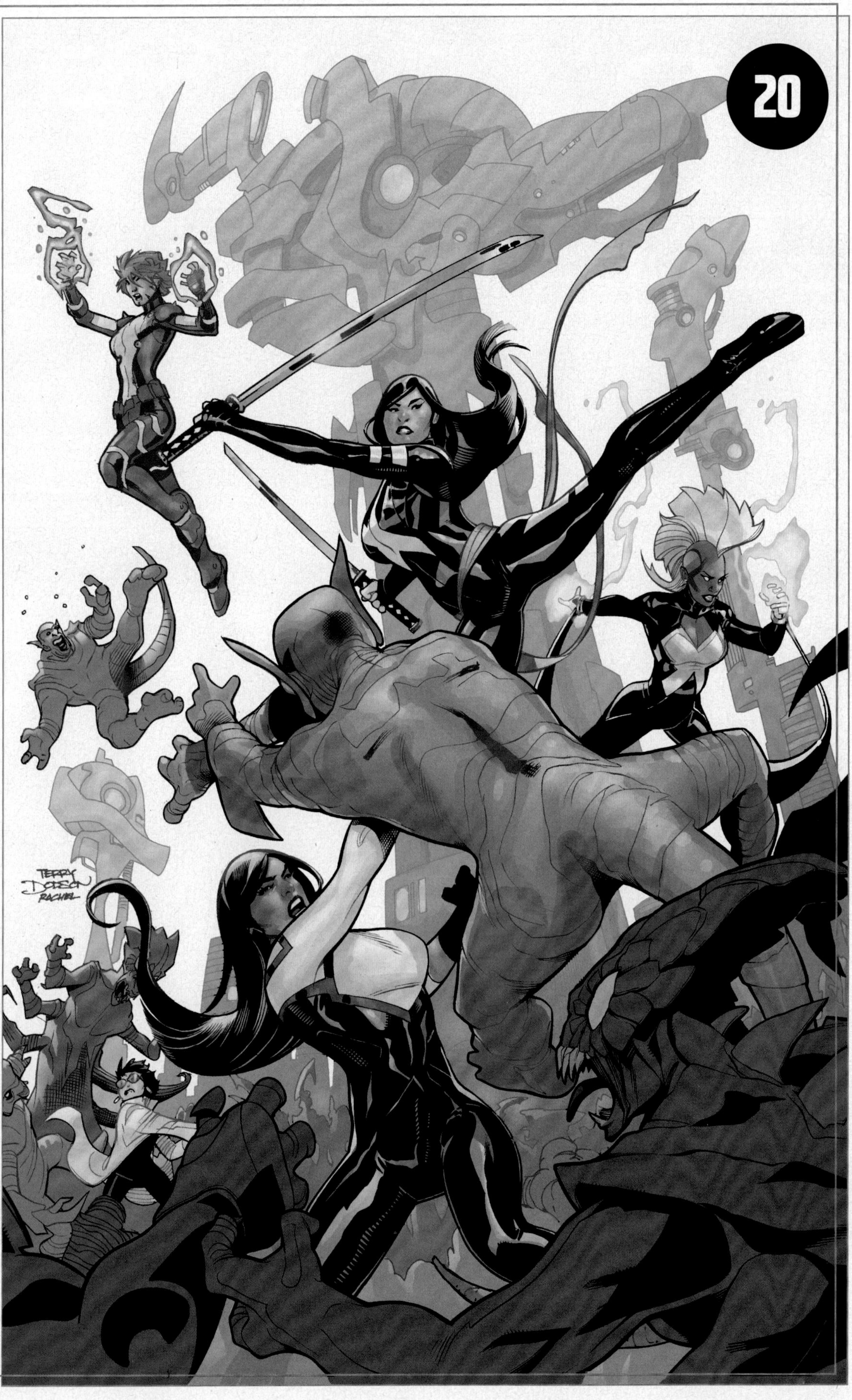
20
TERRY DODSON
RACHEL

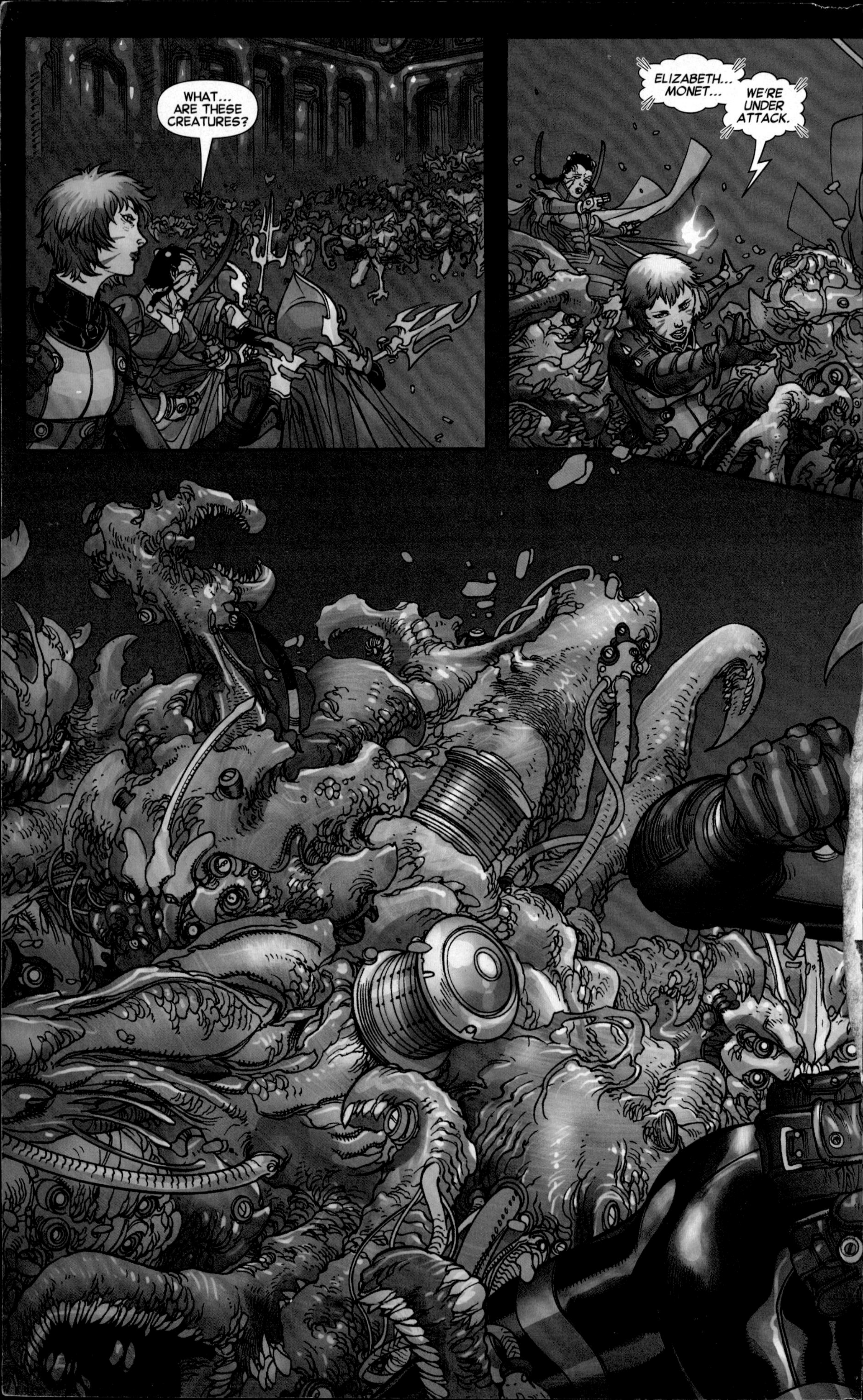
WHAT... ARE THESE CREATURES?
ELIZABETH... MONET...
WE'RE UNDER ATTACK.

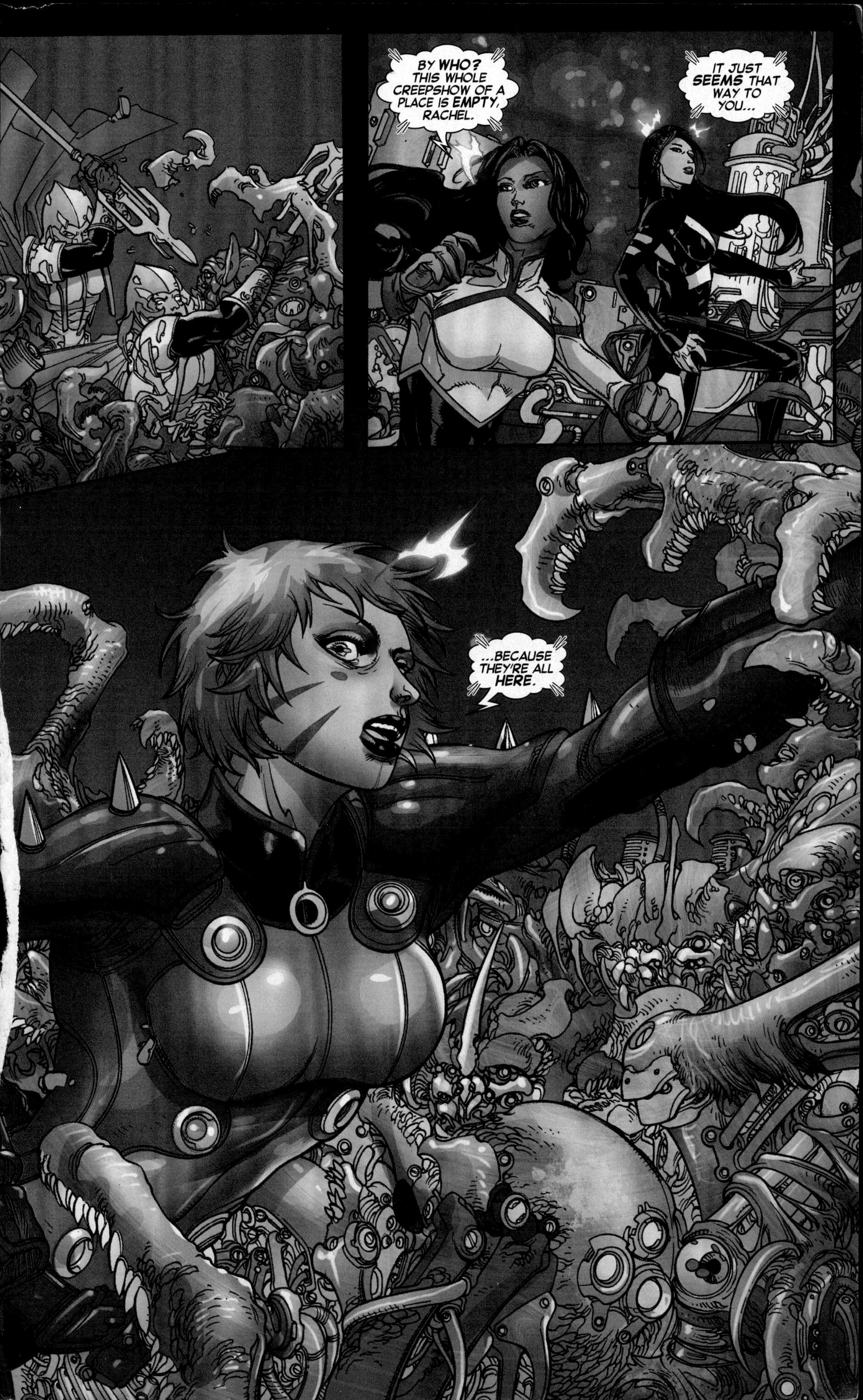
BY WHO? THIS WHOLE CREEPSHOW OF A PLACE IS EMPTY, RACHEL.
IT JUST SEEMS THAT WAY TO YOU...
...BECAUSE THEY'RE ALL HERE.

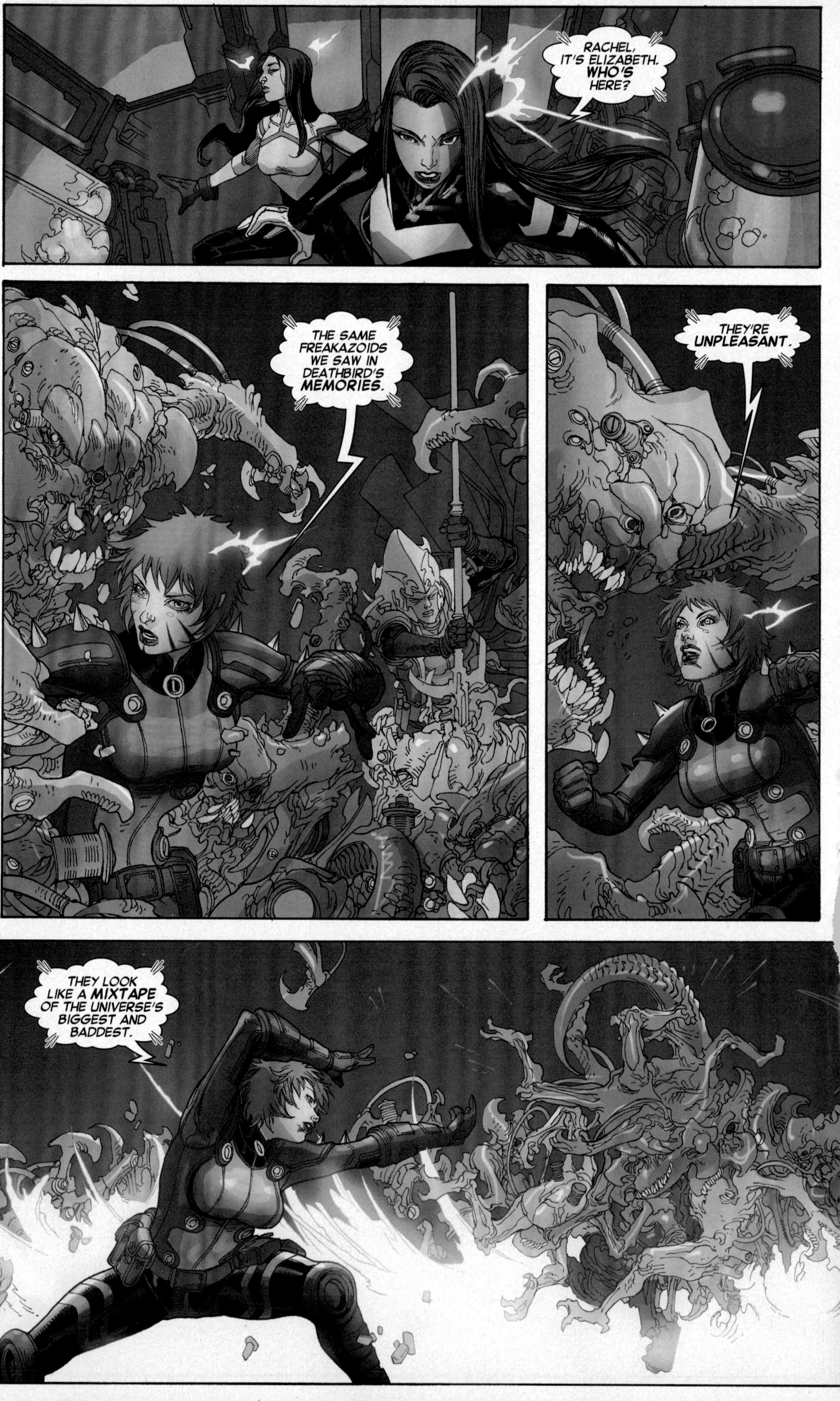
RACHEL, IT'S ELIZABETH. WHO'S HERE?
THE SAME FREAKAZOIDS WE SAW IN DEATHBIRD'S MEMORIES.
THEY'RE UNPLEASANT.
THEY LOOK LIKE A MIXTAPE OF THE UNIVERSE'S BIGGEST AND BADDEST.

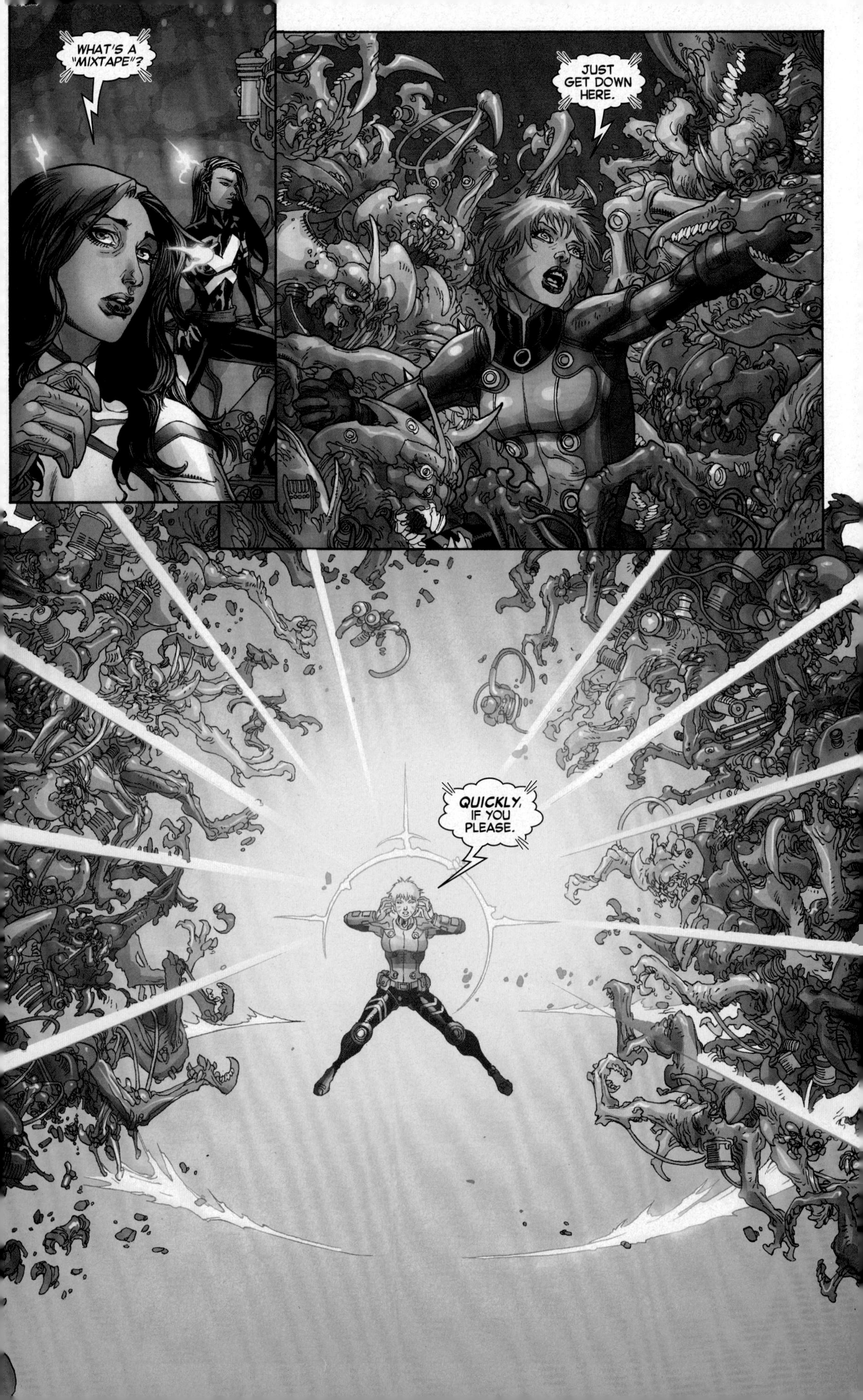
WHAT'S A "MIXTAPE"?
JUST GET DOWN HERE.
QUICKLY, IF YOU PLEASE.

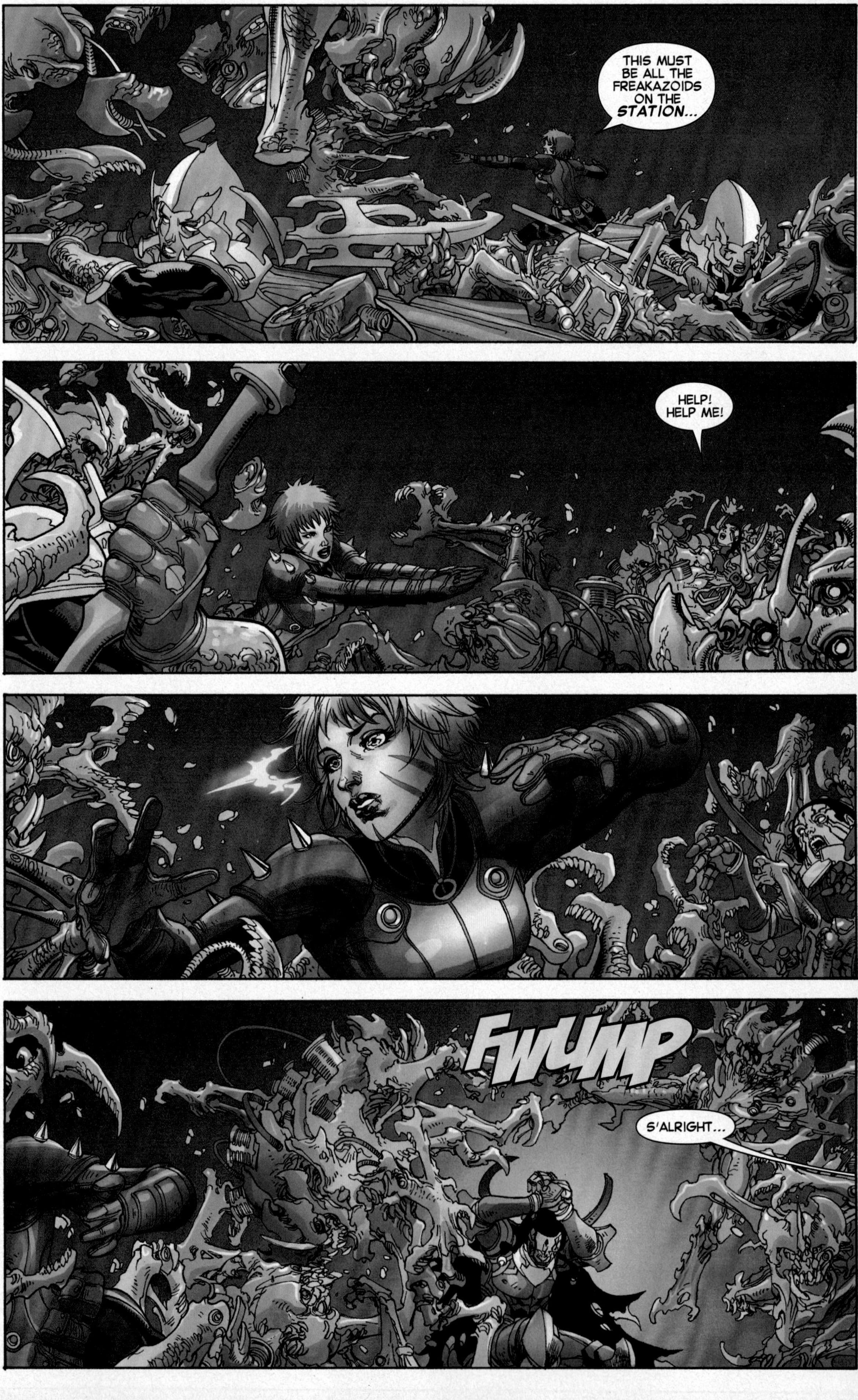
THIS MUST BE ALL THE FREAKAZOIDS ON THE STATION...
HELP! HELP ME!
FWUMP
S'ALRIGHT...

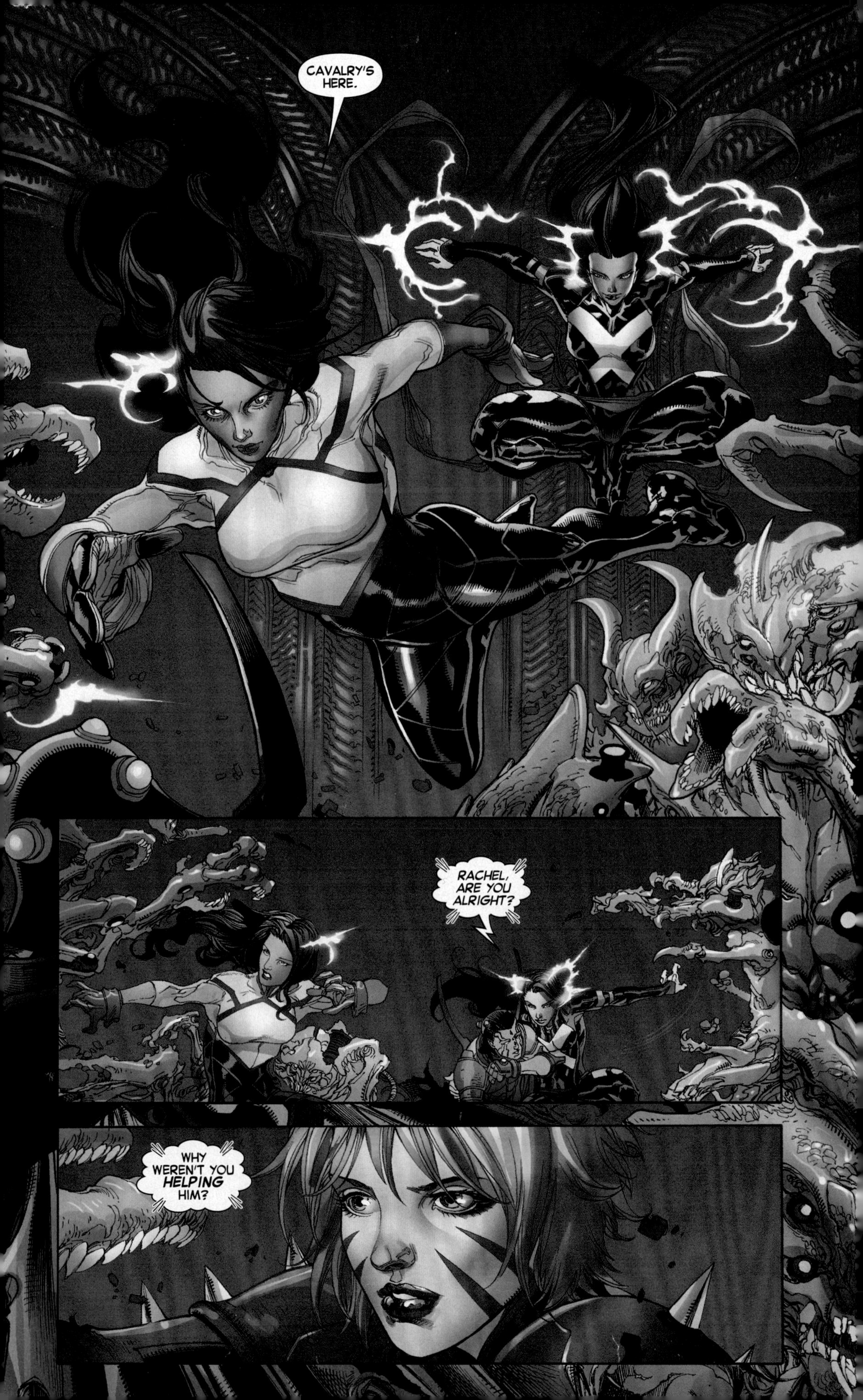
CAVALRY'S HERE.
RACHEL, ARE YOU ALRIGHT?
WHY WEREN'T YOU *HELPING* HIM?

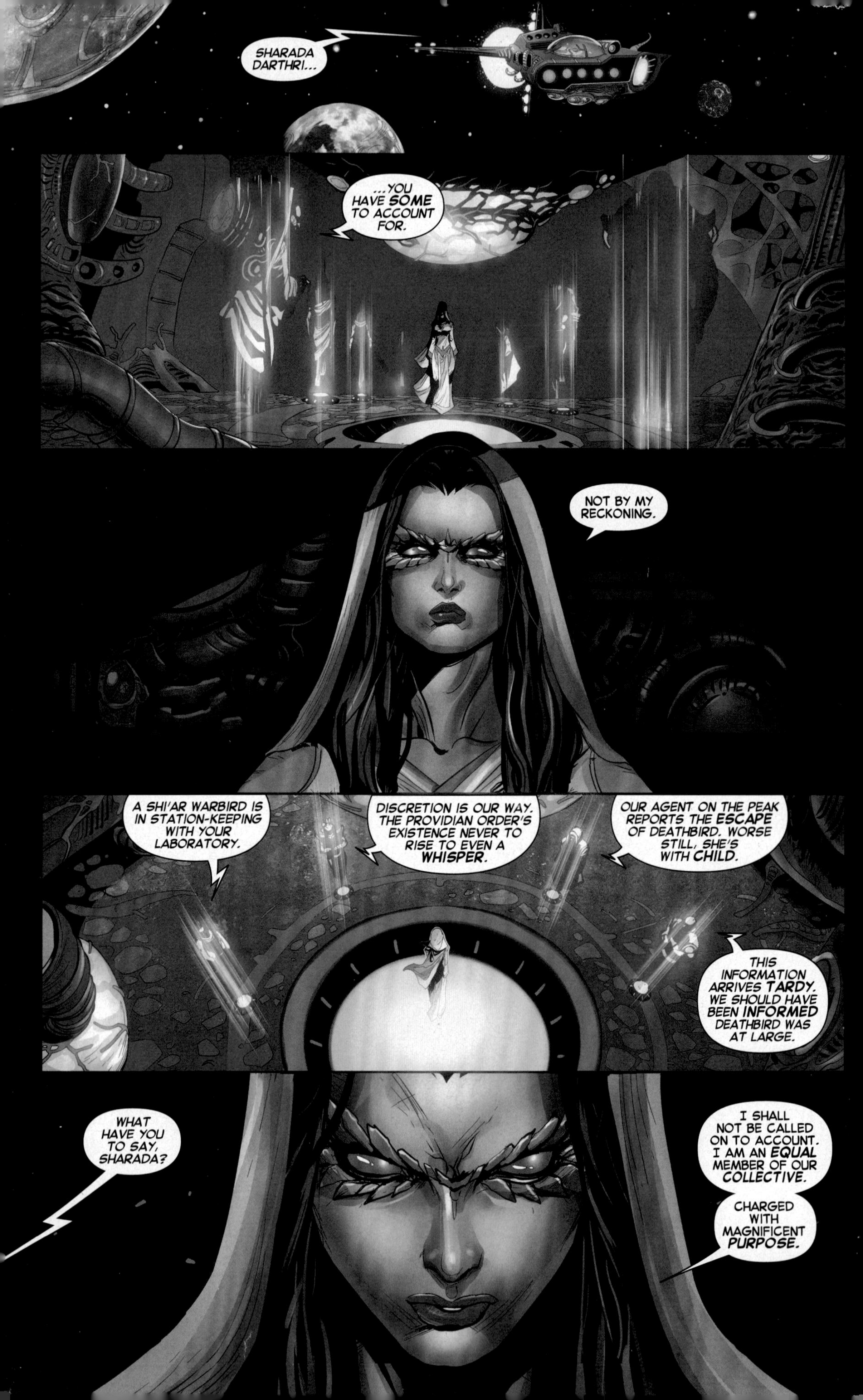
SHARADA DARTHRI...
...YOU HAVE SOME TO ACCOUNT FOR.
NOT BY MY RECKONING.
A SHI'AR WARBIRD IS IN STATION-KEEPING WITH YOUR LABORATORY.
DISCRETION IS OUR WAY. THE PROVIDIAN ORDER'S EXISTENCE NEVER TO RISE TO EVEN A WHISPER.
OUR AGENT ON THE PEAK REPORTS THE ESCAPE OF DEATHBIRD. WORSE STILL, SHE'S WITH CHILD.
THIS INFORMATION ARRIVES TARDY. WE SHOULD HAVE BEEN INFORMED DEATHBIRD WAS AT LARGE.
WHAT HAVE YOU TO SAY, SHARADA?
I SHALL NOT BE CALLED ON TO ACCOUNT. I AM AN EQUAL MEMBER OF OUR COLLECTIVE.
CHARGED WITH MAGNIFICENT PURPOSE.

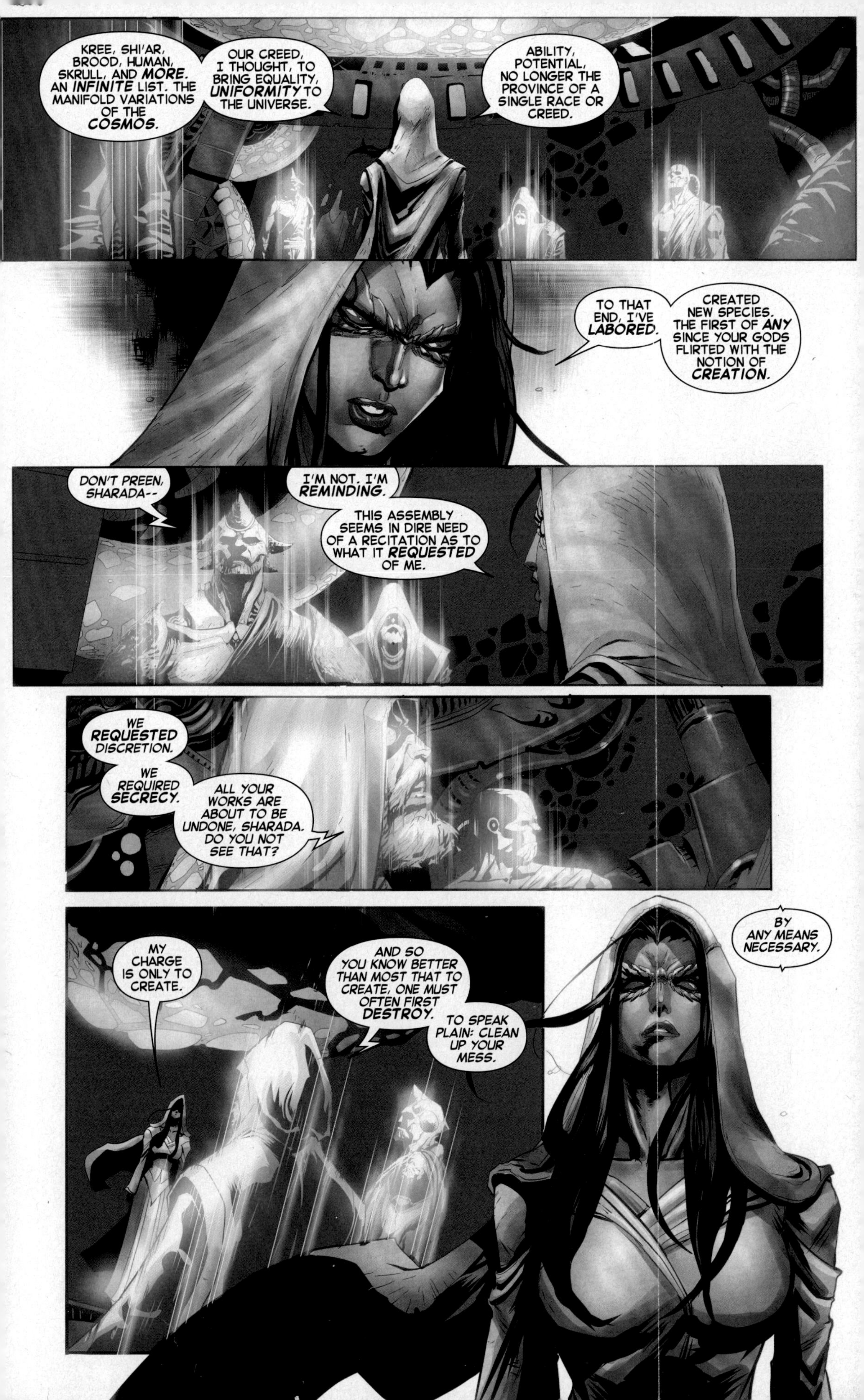

KREE, SHI'AR, BROOD, HUMAN, SKRULL, AND MORE. AN INFINITE LIST. THE MANIFOLD VARIATIONS OF THE COSMOS.
OUR CREED, I THOUGHT, TO BRING EQUALITY, UNIFORMITY TO THE UNIVERSE.
ABILITY, POTENTIAL, NO LONGER THE PROVINCE OF A SINGLE RACE OR CREED.
TO THAT END, I'VE LABORED.
CREATED NEW SPECIES. THE FIRST OF ANY SINCE YOUR GODS FLIRTED WITH THE NOTION OF CREATION.
DON'T PREEN, SHARADA--
I'M NOT. I'M REMINDING.
THIS ASSEMBLY SEEMS IN DIRE NEED OF A RECITATION AS TO WHAT IT REQUESTED OF ME.
WE REQUESTED DISCRETION.
WE REQUIRED SECRECY.
ALL YOUR WORKS ARE ABOUT TO BE UNDONE, SHARADA. DO YOU NOT SEE THAT?
MY CHARGE IS ONLY TO CREATE.
AND SO YOU KNOW BETTER THAN MOST THAT TO CREATE, ONE MUST OFTEN FIRST DESTROY.
TO SPEAK PLAIN: CLEAN UP YOUR MESS.
BY ANY MEANS NECESSARY.

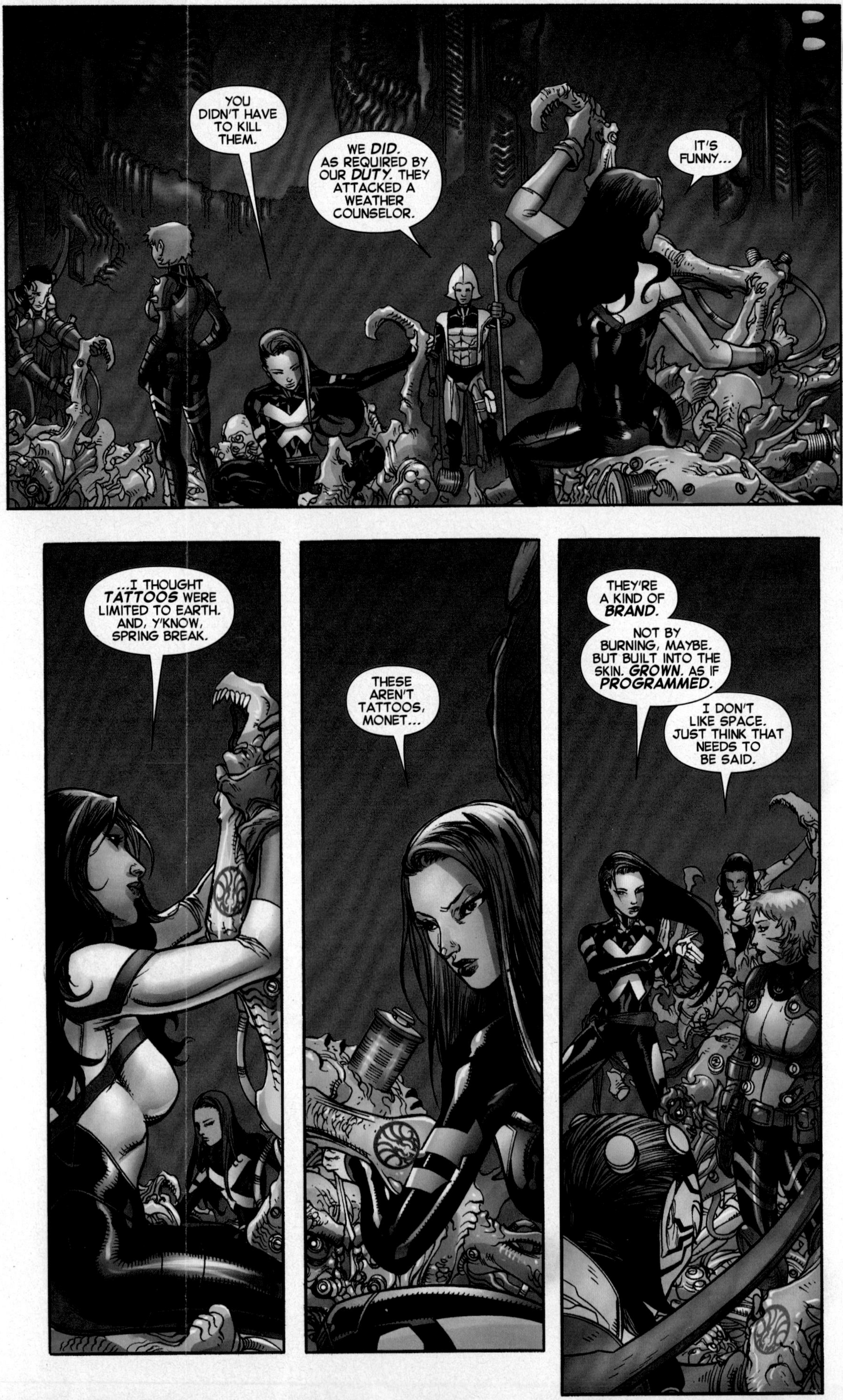

YOU DIDN'T HAVE TO KILL THEM.
WE DID. AS REQUIRED BY OUR DUTY. THEY ATTACKED A WEATHER COUNSELOR.
IT'S FUNNY...
...I THOUGHT TATTOOS WERE LIMITED TO EARTH. AND, Y'KNOW, SPRING BREAK.
THESE AREN'T TATTOOS, MONET...
THEY'RE A KIND OF BRAND.
NOT BY BURNING, MAYBE. BUT BUILT INTO THE SKIN. GROWN. AS IF PROGRAMMED.
I DON'T LIKE SPACE. JUST THINK THAT NEEDS TO BE SAID.

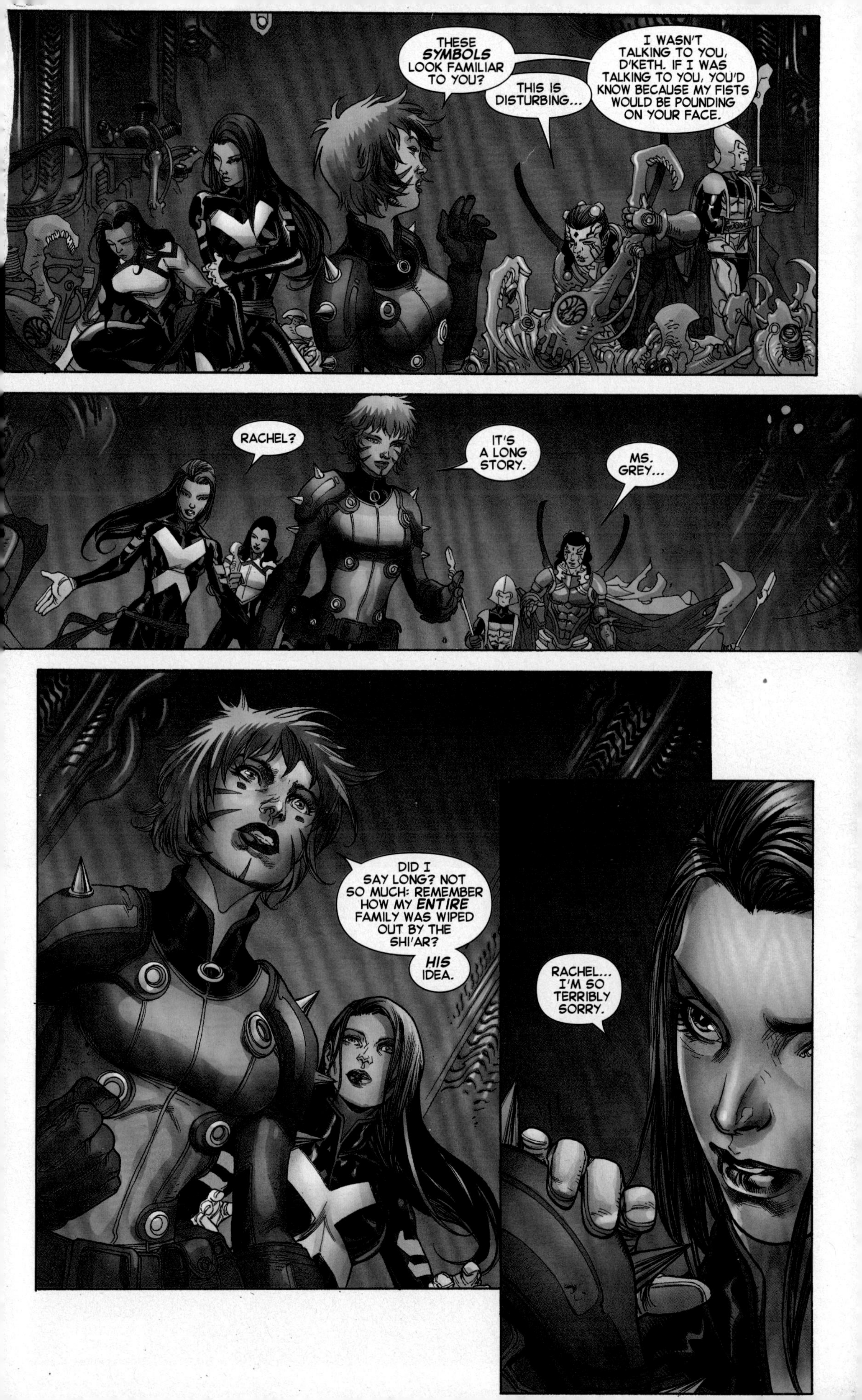
THESE SYMBOLS LOOK FAMILIAR TO YOU?
THIS IS DISTURBING...
I WASN'T TALKING TO YOU, D'KETH. IF I WAS TALKING TO YOU, YOU'D KNOW BECAUSE MY FISTS WOULD BE POUNDING ON YOUR FACE.
RACHEL?
IT'S A LONG STORY.
MS. GREY...
DID I SAY LONG? NOT SO MUCH: REMEMBER HOW MY ENTIRE FAMILY WAS WIPED OUT BY THE SHI'AR?
HIS IDEA.
RACHEL... I'M SO TERRIBLY SORRY.

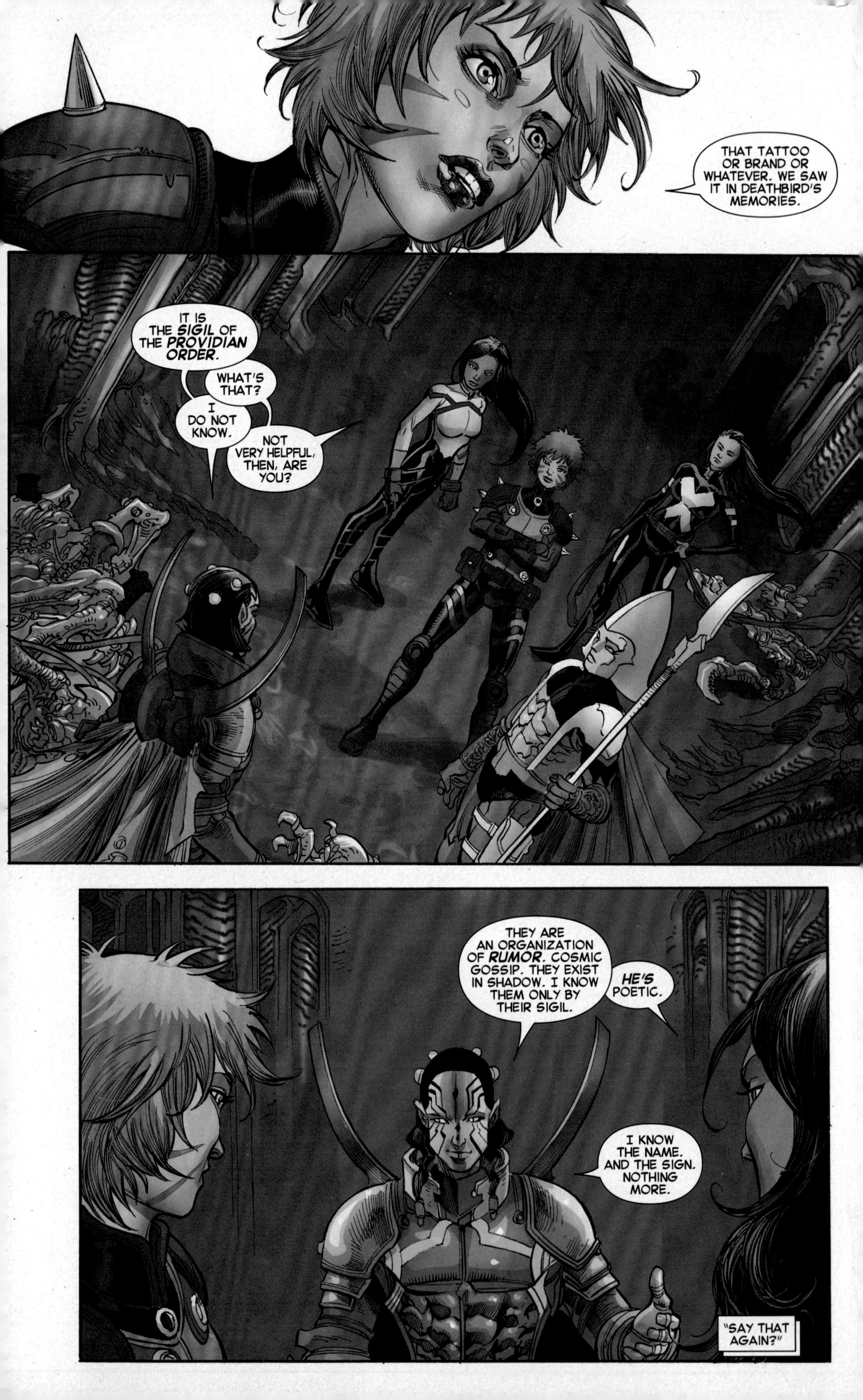

THAT TATTOO OR BRAND OR WHATEVER. WE SAW IT IN DEATHBIRD'S MEMORIES.
IT IS THE SIGIL OF THE PROVIDIAN ORDER.
WHAT'S THAT?
I DO NOT KNOW.
NOT VERY HELPFUL, THEN, ARE YOU?
THEY ARE AN ORGANIZATION OF RUMOR. COSMIC GOSSIP. THEY EXIST IN SHADOW. I KNOW THEM ONLY BY THEIR SIGIL.
HE'S POETIC.
I KNOW THE NAME. AND THE SIGN. NOTHING MORE.
"SAY THAT AGAIN?"

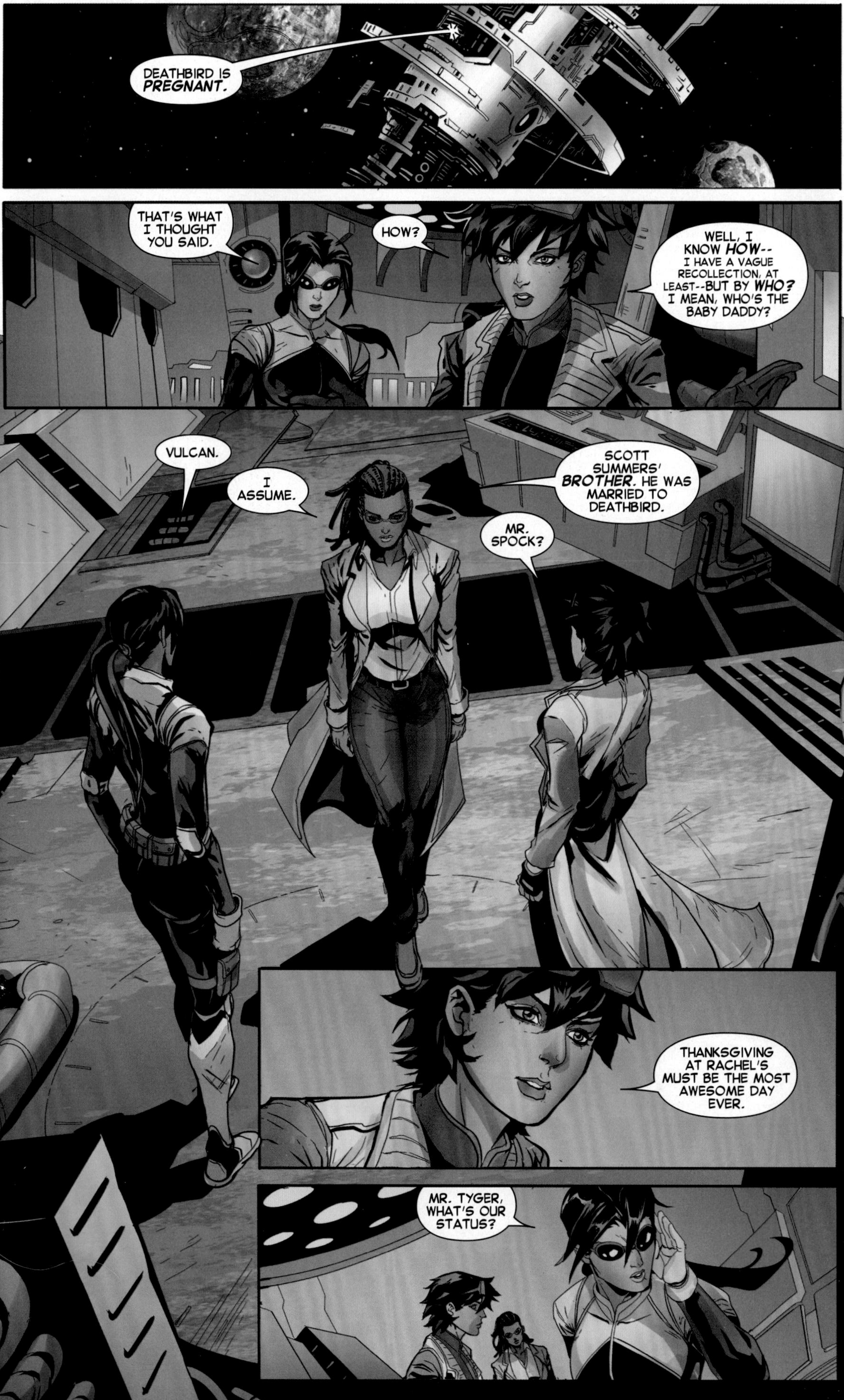
DEATHBIRD IS PREGNANT.
THAT'S WHAT I THOUGHT YOU SAID.
HOW?
WELL, I KNOW HOW--I HAVE A VAGUE RECOLLECTION, AT LEAST--BUT BY WHO? I MEAN, WHO'S THE BABY DADDY?
VULCAN.
I ASSUME.
SCOTT SUMMERS' BROTHER. HE WAS MARRIED TO DEATHBIRD.
MR. SPOCK?
THANKSGIVING AT RACHEL'S MUST BE THE MOST AWESOME DAY EVER.
MR. TYGER, WHAT'S OUR STATUS?

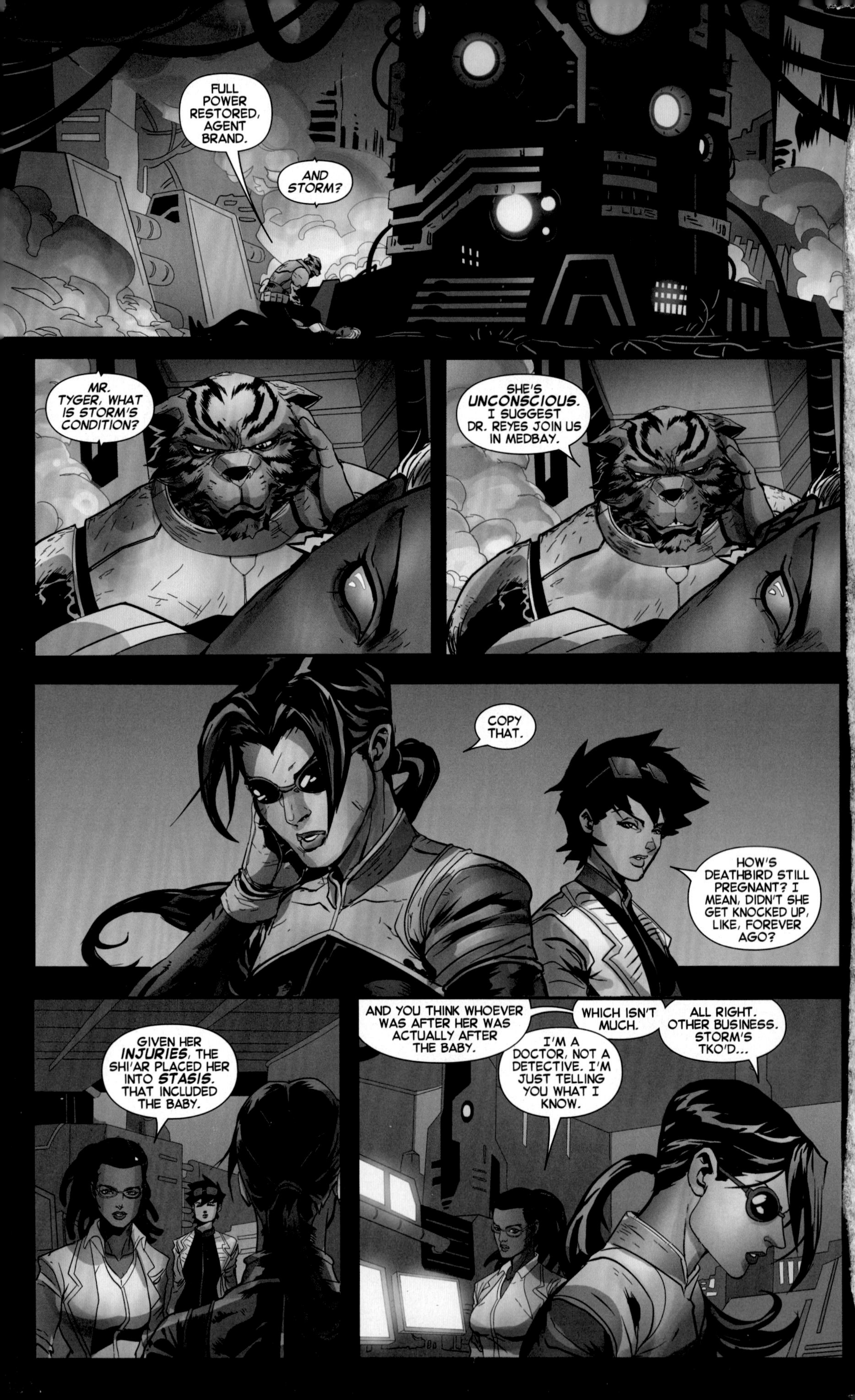
FULL POWER RESTORED, AGENT BRAND.
AND STORM?
MR. TYGER, WHAT IS STORM'S CONDITION?
SHE'S UNCONSCIOUS. I SUGGEST DR. REYES JOIN US IN MEDBAY.
COPY THAT.
HOW'S DEATHBIRD STILL PREGNANT? I MEAN, DIDN'T SHE GET KNOCKED UP, LIKE, FOREVER AGO?
GIVEN HER INJURIES, THE SHI'AR PLACED HER INTO STASIS. THAT INCLUDED THE BABY.
AND YOU THINK WHOEVER WAS AFTER HER WAS ACTUALLY AFTER THE BABY.
I'M A DOCTOR, NOT A DETECTIVE. I'M JUST TELLING YOU WHAT I KNOW.
WHICH ISN'T MUCH.
ALL RIGHT. OTHER BUSINESS. STORM'S TKO'D...

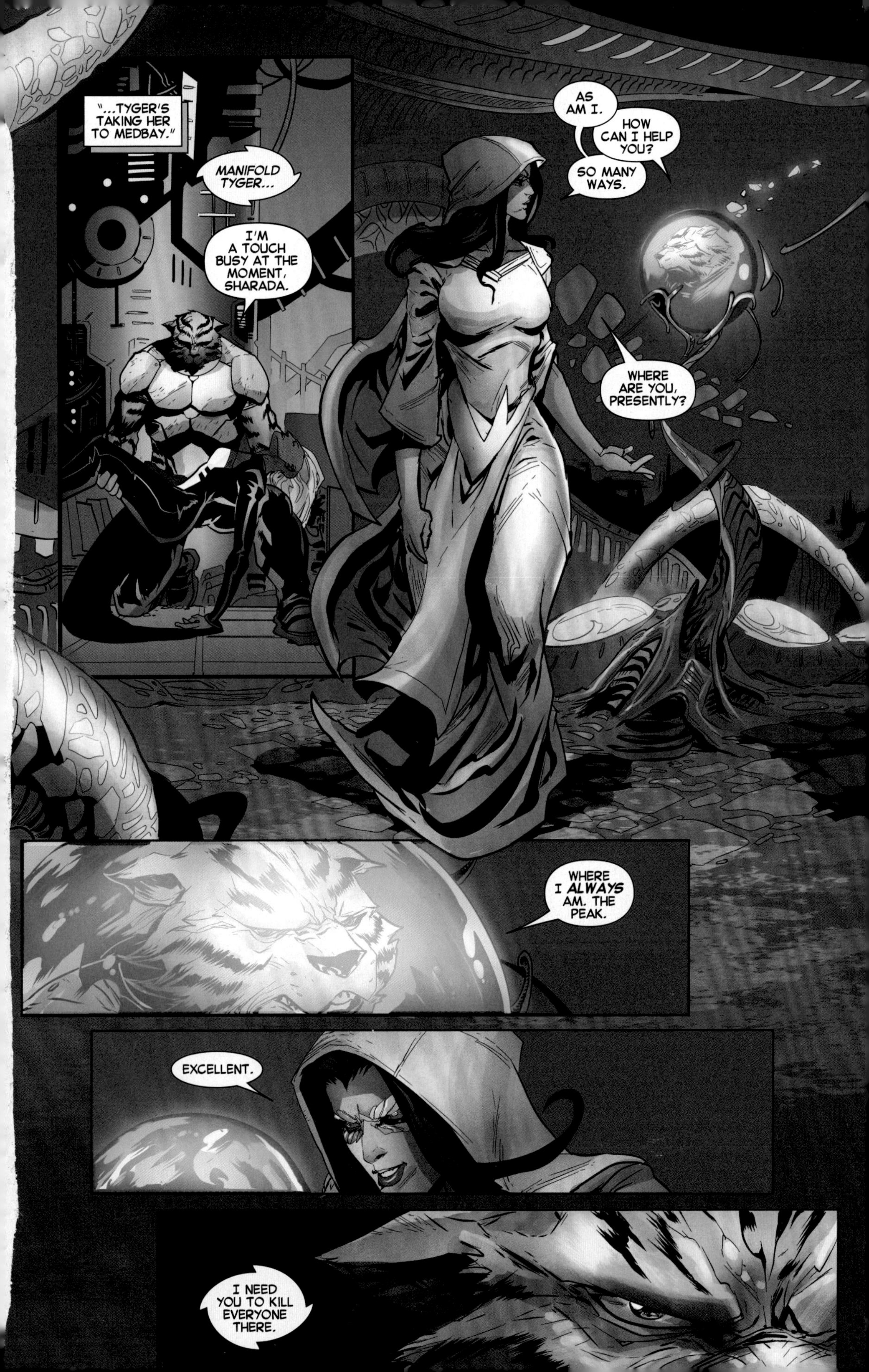
"...TYGER'S TAKING HER TO MEDBAY."
MANIFOLD TYGER...
I'M A TOUCH BUSY AT THE MOMENT, SHARADA.
AS AM I.
HOW CAN I HELP YOU?
SO MANY WAYS.
WHERE ARE YOU, PRESENTLY?
WHERE I ALWAYS AM. THE PEAK.
EXCELLENT.
I NEED YOU TO KILL EVERYONE THERE.

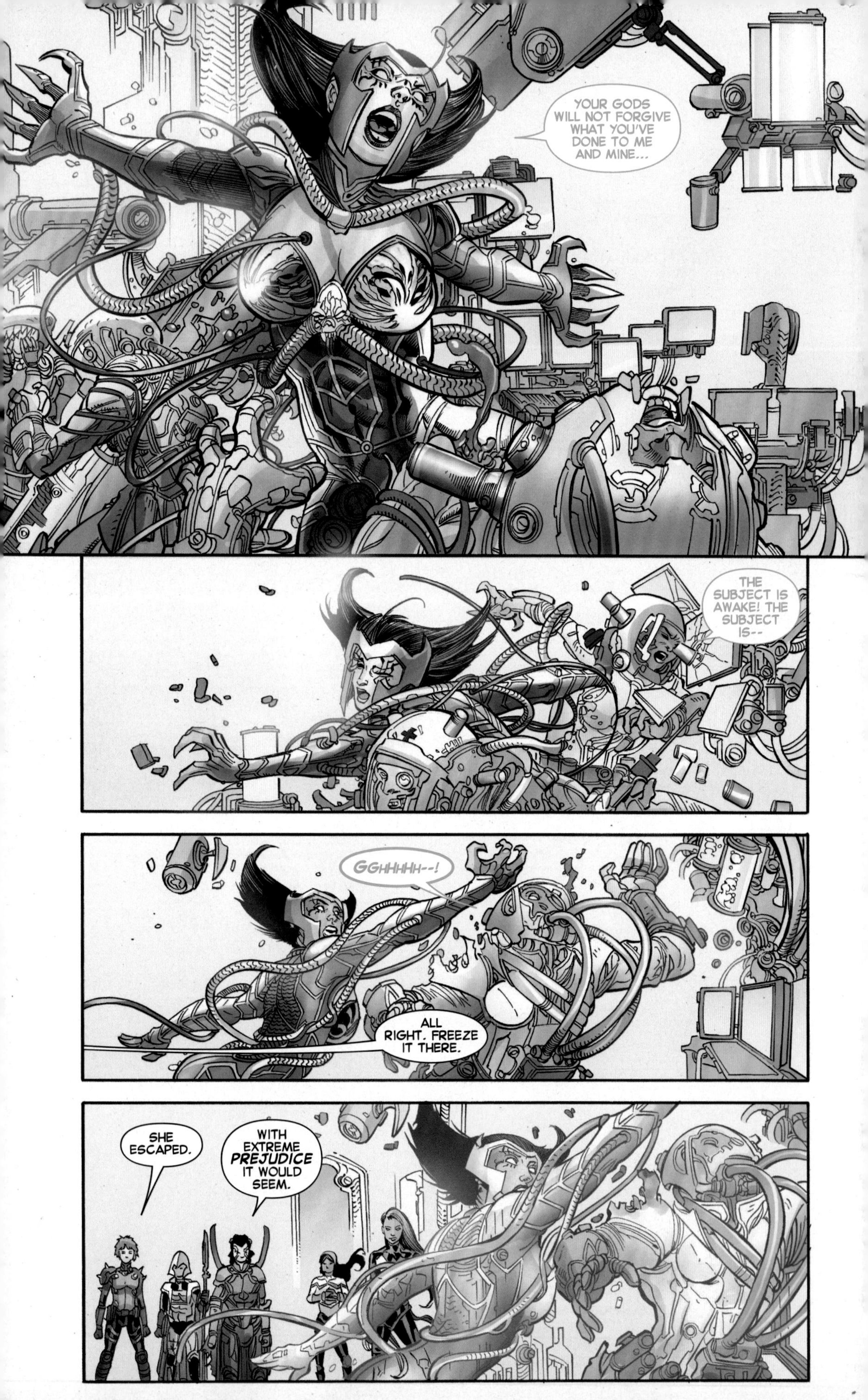

YOUR GODS WILL NOT FORGIVE WHAT YOU'VE DONE TO ME AND MINE...
THE SUBJECT IS AWAKE! THE SUBJECT IS--
GGHHHHH--!
ALL RIGHT. FREEZE IT THERE.
SHE ESCAPED.
WITH EXTREME *PREJUDICE* IT WOULD SEEM.

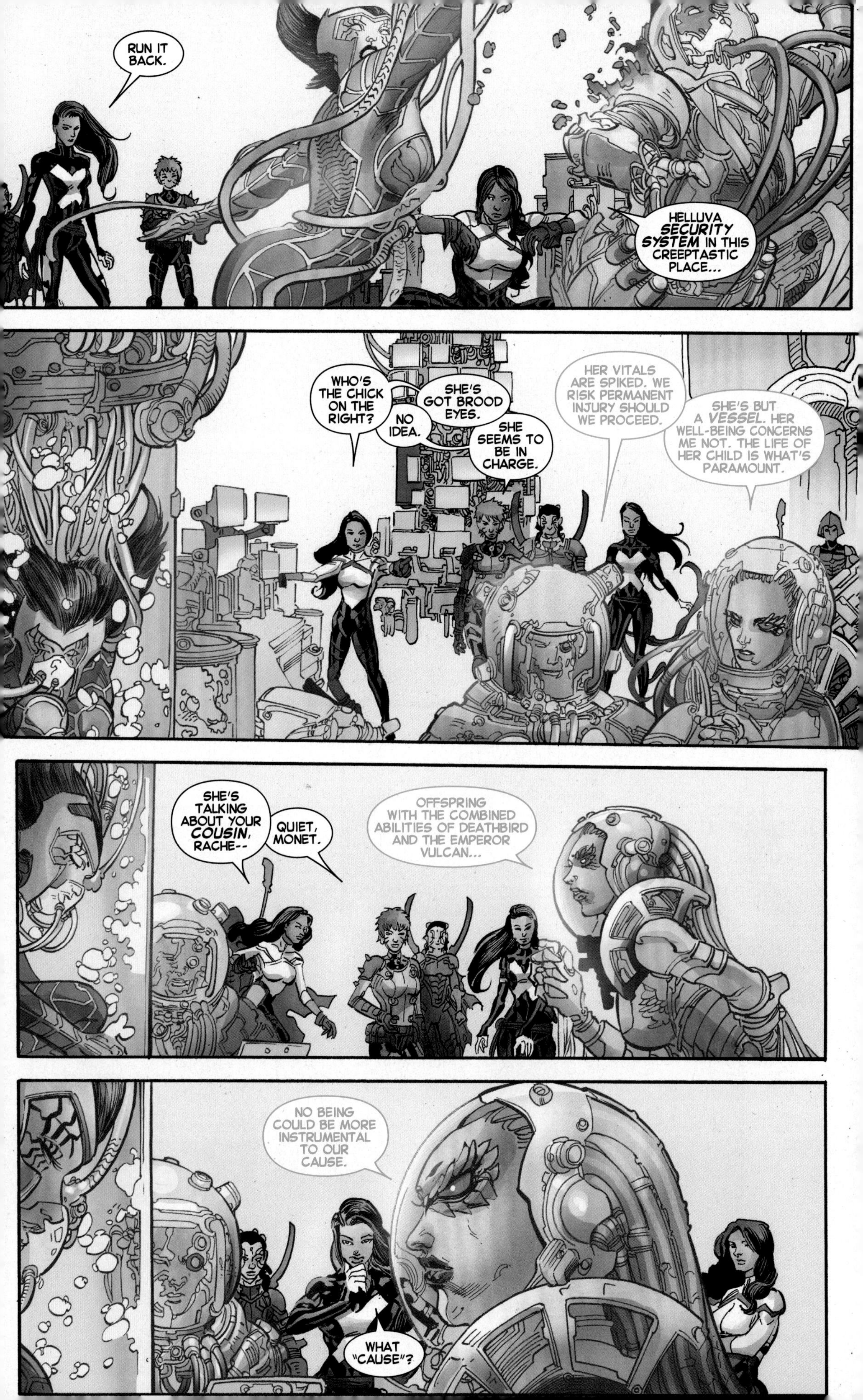
RUN IT BACK.
HELLUVA SECURITY SYSTEM IN THIS CREEPTASTIC PLACE...
WHO'S THE CHICK ON THE RIGHT?
SHE'S GOT BROOD EYES.
NO IDEA.
SHE SEEMS TO BE IN CHARGE.
HER VITALS ARE SPIKED. WE RISK PERMANENT INJURY SHOULD WE PROCEED.
SHE'S BUT A VESSEL. HER WELL-BEING CONCERNS ME NOT. THE LIFE OF HER CHILD IS WHAT'S PARAMOUNT.
SHE'S TALKING ABOUT YOUR COUSIN, RACHE--
QUIET, MONET.
OFFSPRING WITH THE COMBINED ABILITIES OF DEATHBIRD AND THE EMPEROR VULCAN...
NO BEING COULD BE MORE INSTRUMENTAL TO OUR CAUSE.
WHAT "CAUSE"?

RUN IT *FORWARD.* JUMP A FEW DAYS.

I AM TRYING. THIS SYSTEM'S CONTROLS ARE NOT INTUITIVE...

MS. GREY...IT WOULD APPEAR WE HAVE UNFINISHED BUSINESS...

NOT THE PLACE. *DEFINITELY* NOT THE TIME.

YOU SHOULD KNOW THAT MY *COUNSEL*--I ACTED IN ACCORDANCE WITH WHAT I CONSIDERED TO BE THE BEST INTERESTS OF THE EMPIRE AND, I BELIEVE, THE UNIVERSE *ENTIRE.*

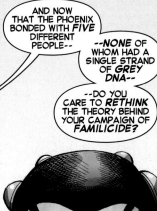

AND NOW THAT THE PHOENIX BONDED WITH *FIVE* DIFFERENT PEOPLE--

--*NONE* OF WHOM HAD A SINGLE STRAND OF *GREY* DNA--

--DO YOU CARE TO *RETHINK* THE THEORY BEHIND YOUR CAMPAIGN OF *FAMILICIDE?*

YEAH. YOU KILLED MY *FAMILY* BECAUSE YOU *THOUGHT* THE PHOENIX COULD ONLY SYMBIOTE WITH MY GENELINE. GOT IT.

I BELIEVE I'VE ISOLATED THE MOMENT OF DEATHBIRD'S *AWAKENING*...

CEREBRAL FUNCTIONS STILL NOMINAL...

PREPARING GENETIC INFLUX MODULE...

KREE.

GENELINE?

SHI'AR...MUTANT...*AND* KREE...

THIS WILL BE SOMETHING OF EXCEPTIONAL SWAY...

LADY SHARADA WILL BE *PLEASED*.

THE FETUS IS TAKING THE INFLUX WELL...

ALL BASELINES READING GREEN...

WAIT. I'M GETTING A CORTEX SPIKE...

THE FETUS' CORTEX ISN'T SUFFICIENTLY DEVELOPED--

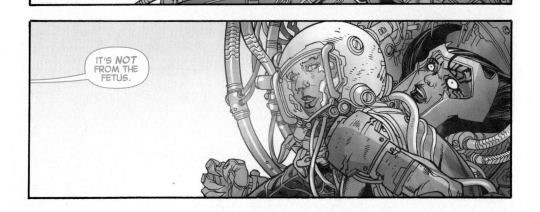

IT'S *NOT* FROM THE FETUS.

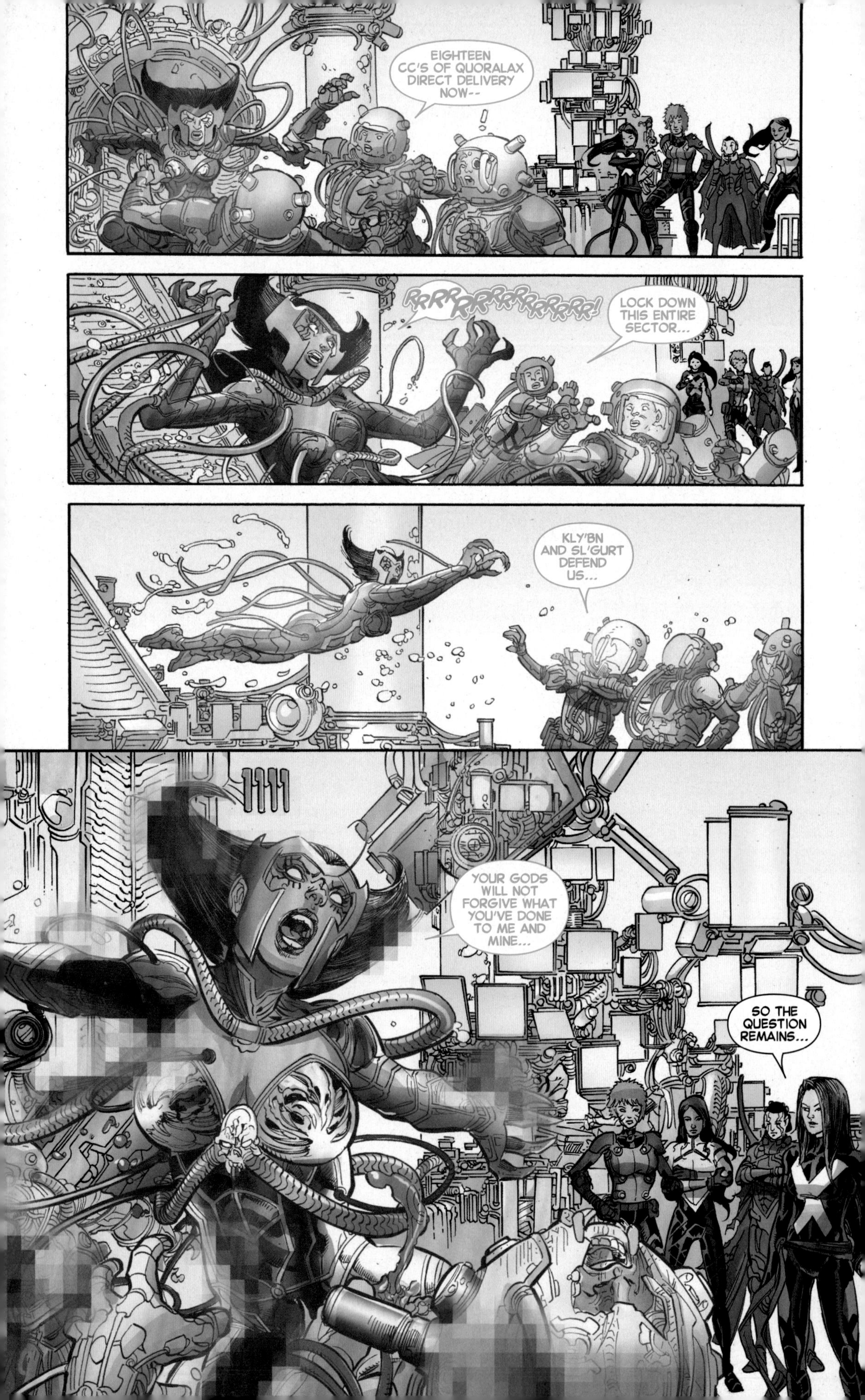
EIGHTEEN CC'S OF QUORALAX DIRECT DELIVERY NOW--
!
RRRRRRRRRRRRRR!
LOCK DOWN THIS ENTIRE SECTOR...
KLY'BN AND SL'GURT DEFEND US...
YOUR GODS WILL NOT FORGIVE WHAT YOU'VE DONE TO ME AND MINE...
SO THE QUESTION REMAINS...

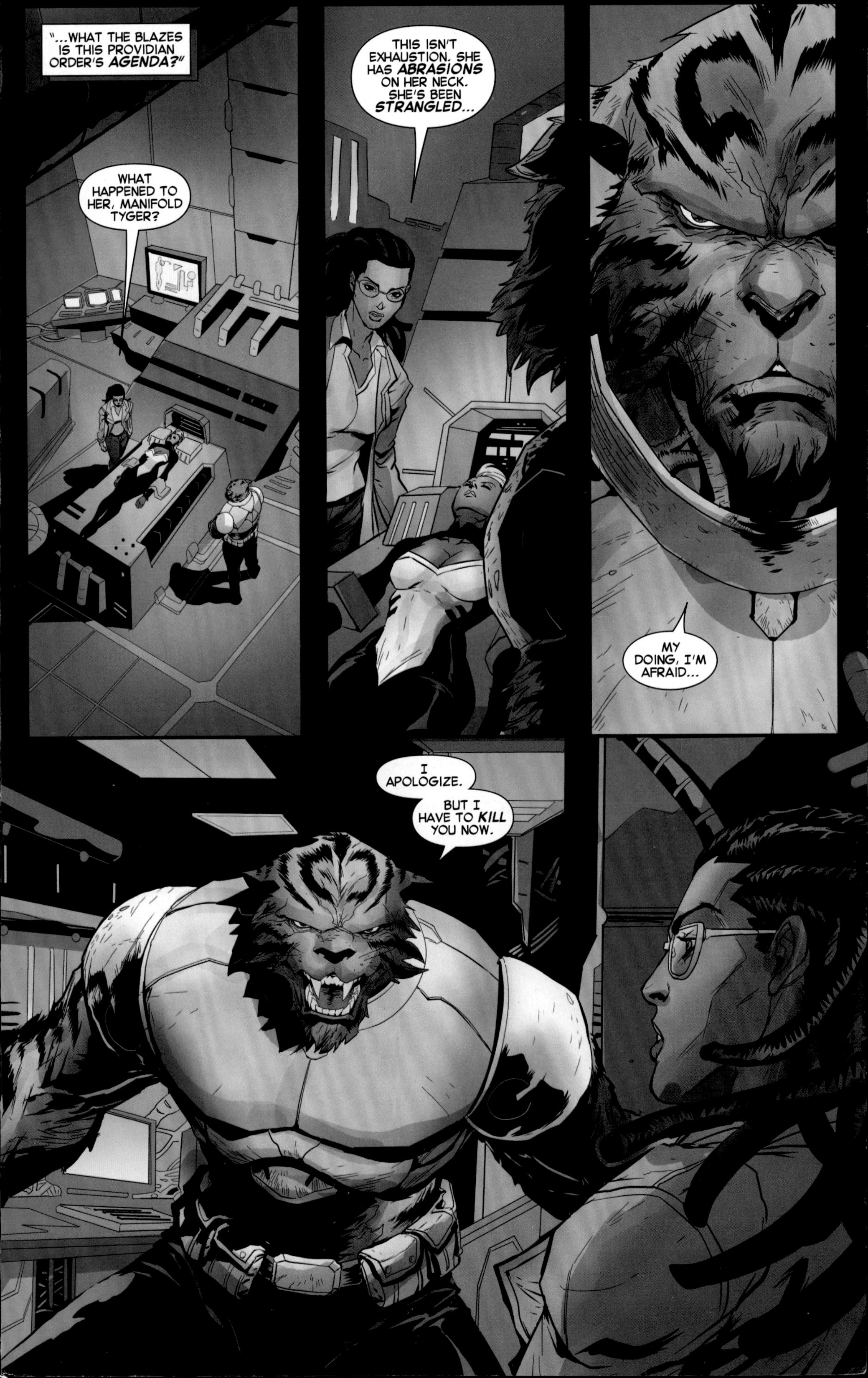
"...WHAT THE BLAZES IS THIS PROVIDIAN ORDER'S AGENDA?"
WHAT HAPPENED TO HER, MANIFOLD TYGER?
THIS ISN'T EXHAUSTION. SHE HAS ABRASIONS ON HER NECK. SHE'S BEEN STRANGLED...
MY DOING, I'M AFRAID...
I APOLOGIZE.
BUT I HAVE TO KILL YOU NOW.

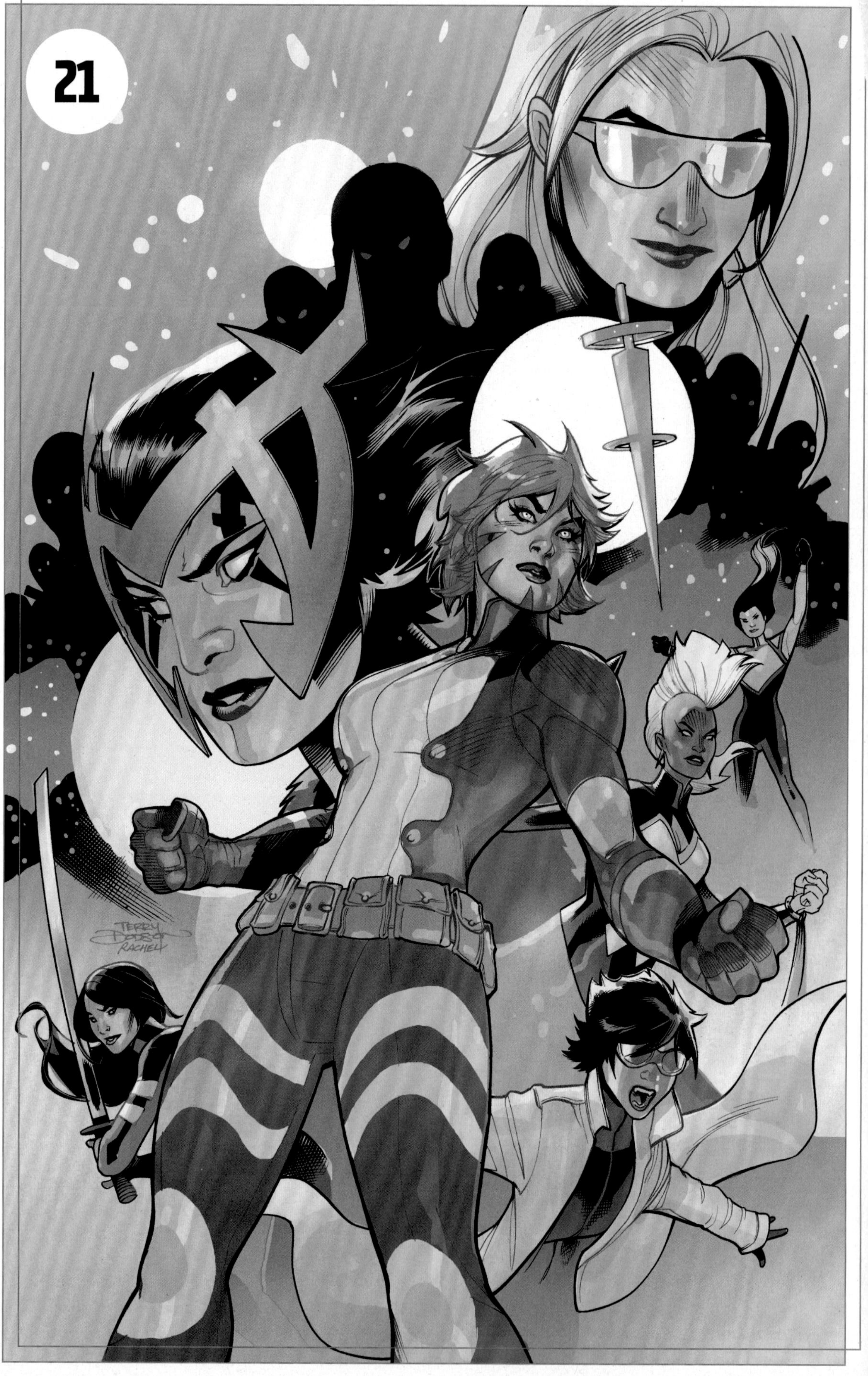
21
TERRY DODSON RACHEL

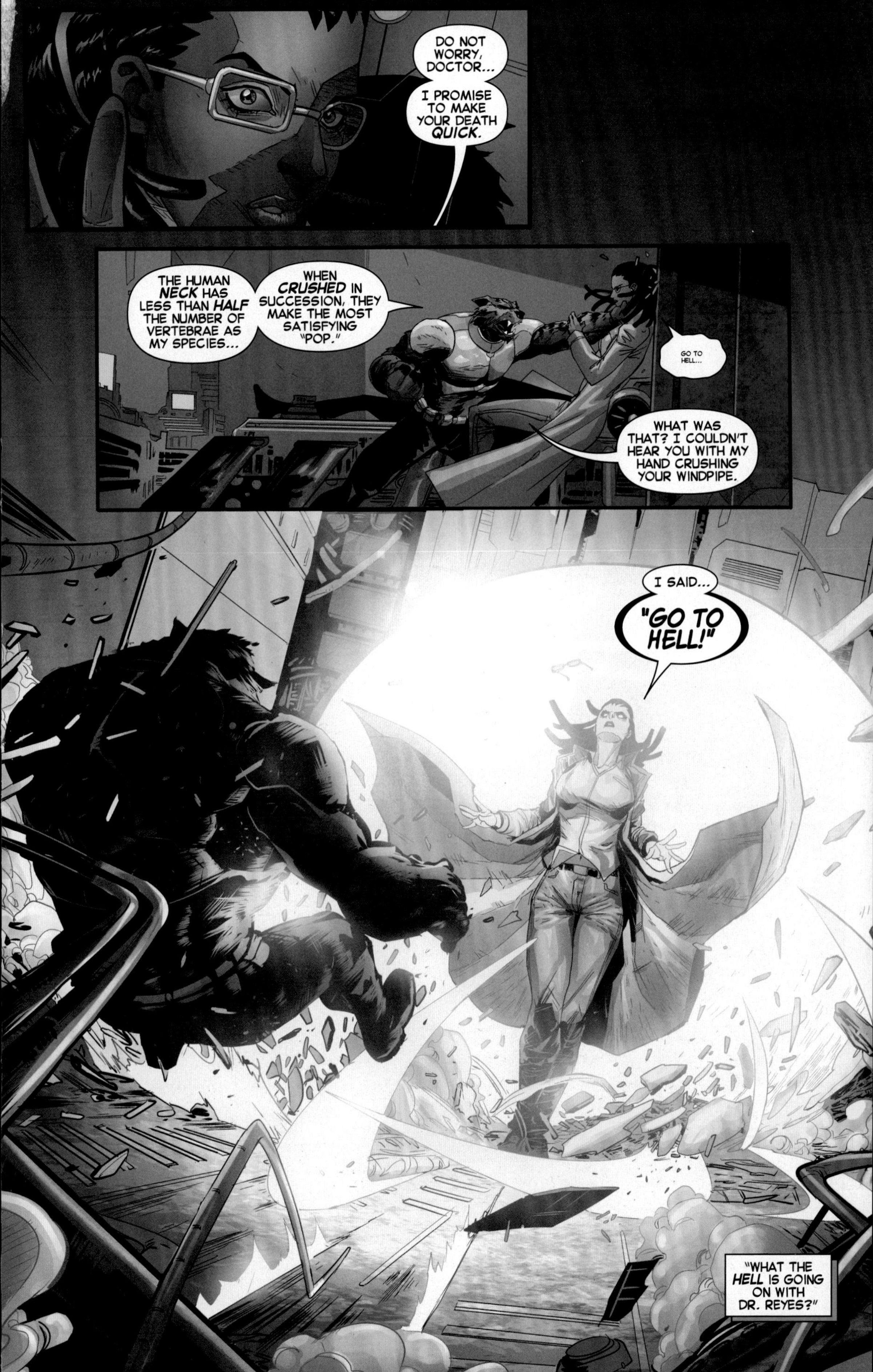
DO NOT WORRY, DOCTOR...
I PROMISE TO MAKE YOUR DEATH QUICK.
THE HUMAN NECK HAS LESS THAN HALF THE NUMBER OF VERTEBRAE AS MY SPECIES...
WHEN CRUSHED IN SUCCESSION, THEY MAKE THE MOST SATISFYING "POP."
GO TO HELL...
WHAT WAS THAT? I COULDN'T HEAR YOU WITH MY HAND CRUSHING YOUR WINDPIPE.
I SAID...
"GO TO HELL!"
"WHAT THE HELL IS GOING ON WITH DR. REYES?"

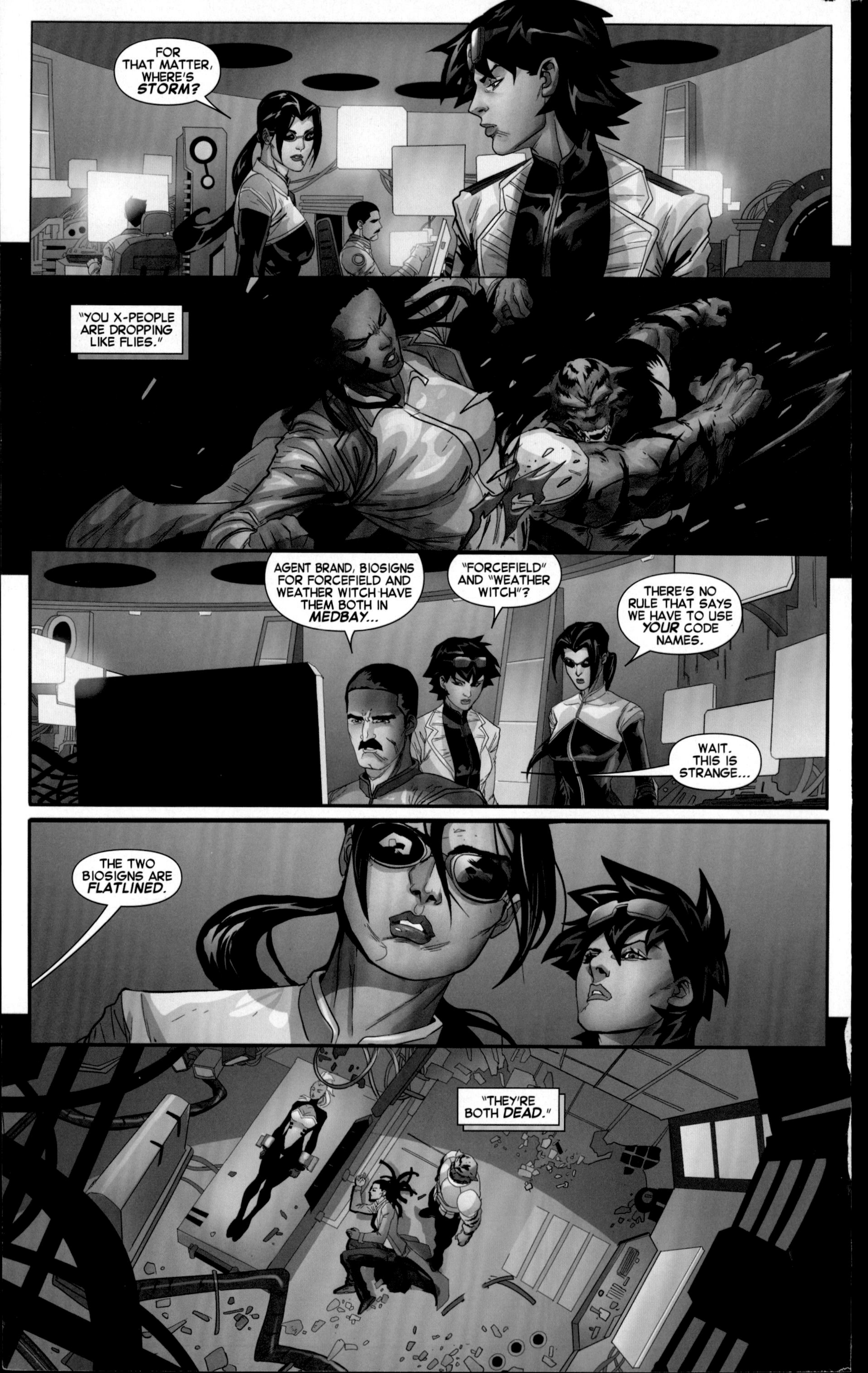
FOR THAT MATTER, WHERE'S STORM?
"YOU X-PEOPLE ARE DROPPING LIKE FLIES."
AGENT BRAND, BIOSIGNS FOR FORCEFIELD AND WEATHER WITCH HAVE THEM BOTH IN MEDBAY...
"FORCEFIELD" AND "WEATHER WITCH"?
THERE'S NO RULE THAT SAYS WE HAVE TO USE YOUR CODE NAMES.
WAIT. THIS IS STRANGE...
THE TWO BIOSIGNS ARE FLATLINED.
"THEY'RE BOTH DEAD."

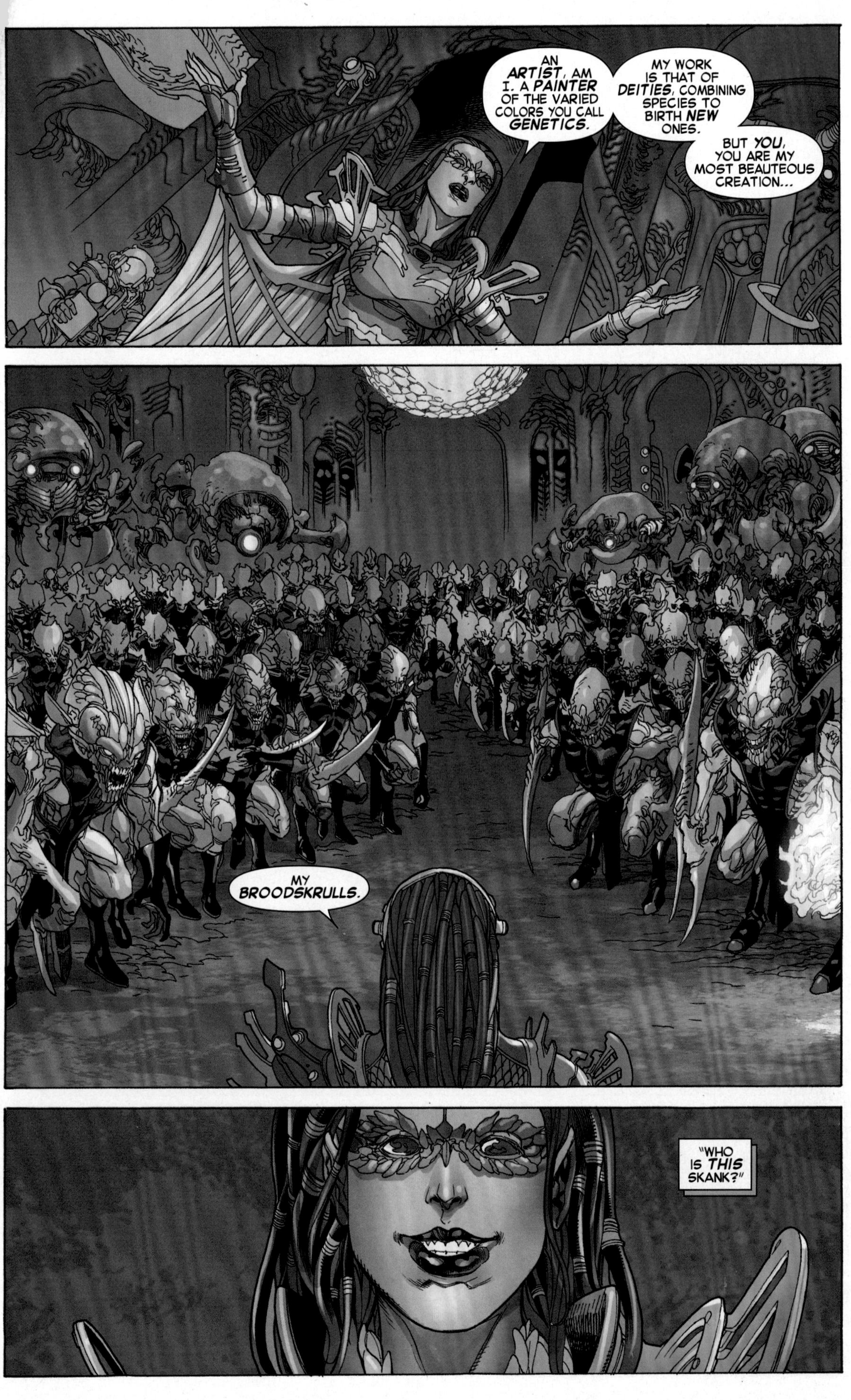
AN ARTIST, AM I. A PAINTER OF THE VARIED COLORS YOU CALL GENETICS.
MY WORK IS THAT OF DEITIES, COMBINING SPECIES TO BIRTH NEW ONES.
BUT YOU, YOU ARE MY MOST BEAUTEOUS CREATION...
MY BROODSKRULLS.
"WHO IS THIS SKANK?"

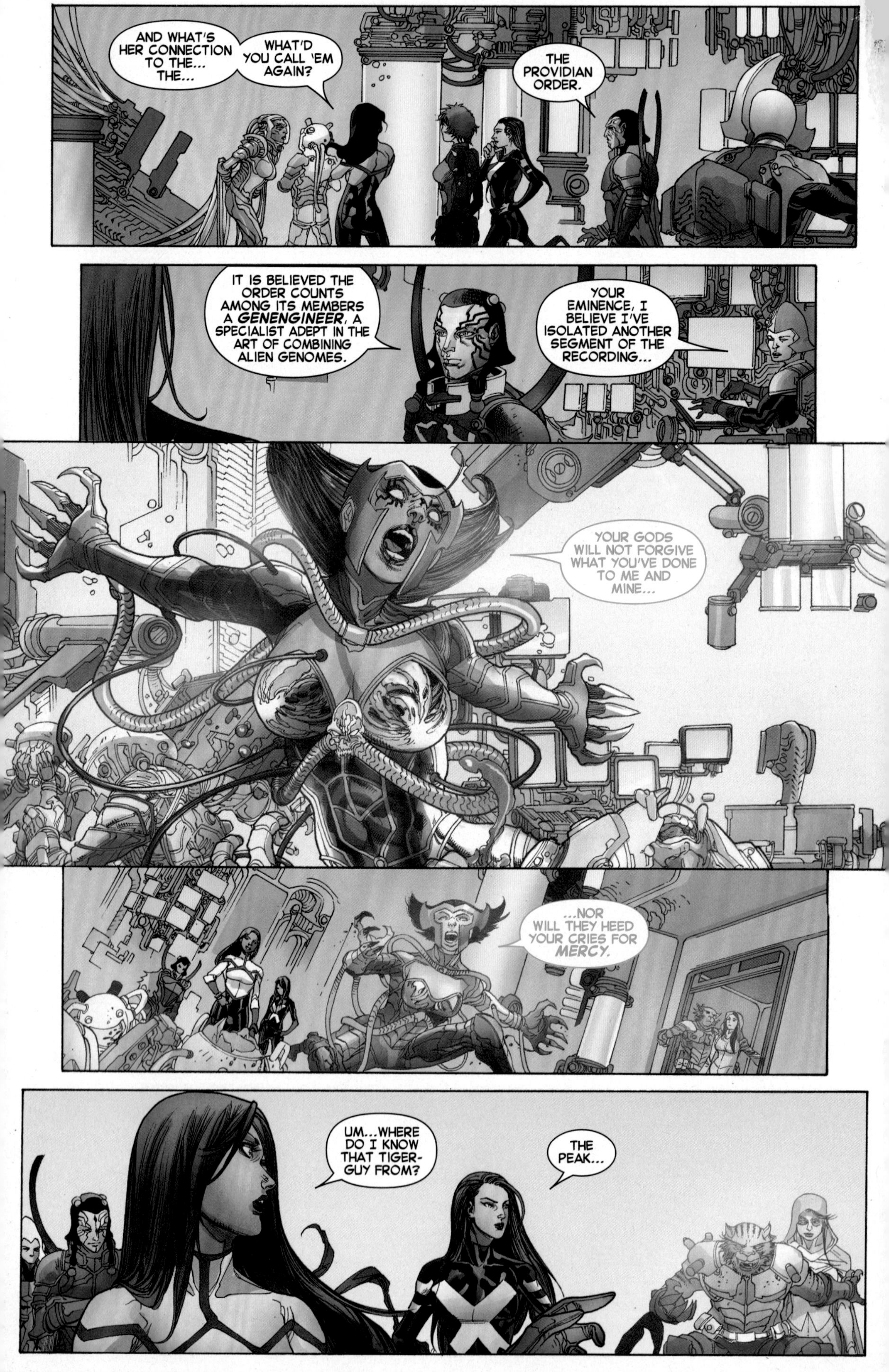

AND WHAT'S HER CONNECTION TO THE... THE...
WHAT'D YOU CALL 'EM AGAIN?
THE PROVIDIAN ORDER.
IT IS BELIEVED THE ORDER COUNTS AMONG ITS MEMBERS A GENENGINEER, A SPECIALIST ADEPT IN THE ART OF COMBINING ALIEN GENOMES.
YOUR EMINENCE, I BELIEVE I'VE ISOLATED ANOTHER SEGMENT OF THE RECORDING...
YOUR GODS WILL NOT FORGIVE WHAT YOU'VE DONE TO ME AND MINE...
...NOR WILL THEY HEED YOUR CRIES FOR MERCY.
UM...WHERE DO I KNOW THAT TIGER-GUY FROM?
THE PEAK...

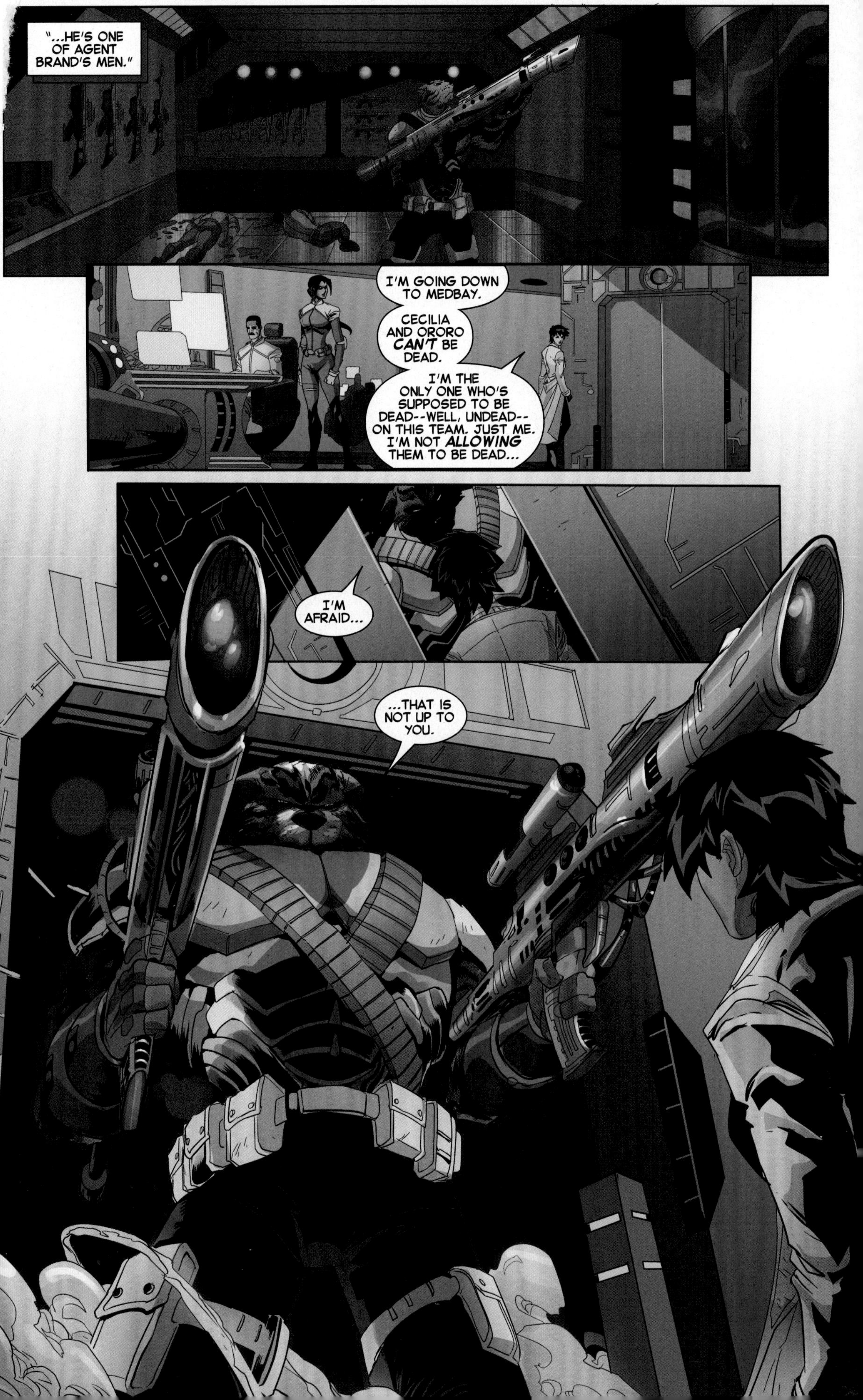
"...HE'S ONE OF AGENT BRAND'S MEN."
I'M GOING DOWN TO MEDBAY.
CECILIA AND ORORO CAN'T BE DEAD.
I'M THE ONLY ONE WHO'S SUPPOSED TO BE DEAD--WELL, UNDEAD--ON THIS TEAM. JUST ME. I'M NOT ALLOWING THEM TO BE DEAD...
I'M AFRAID...
...THAT IS NOT UP TO YOU.

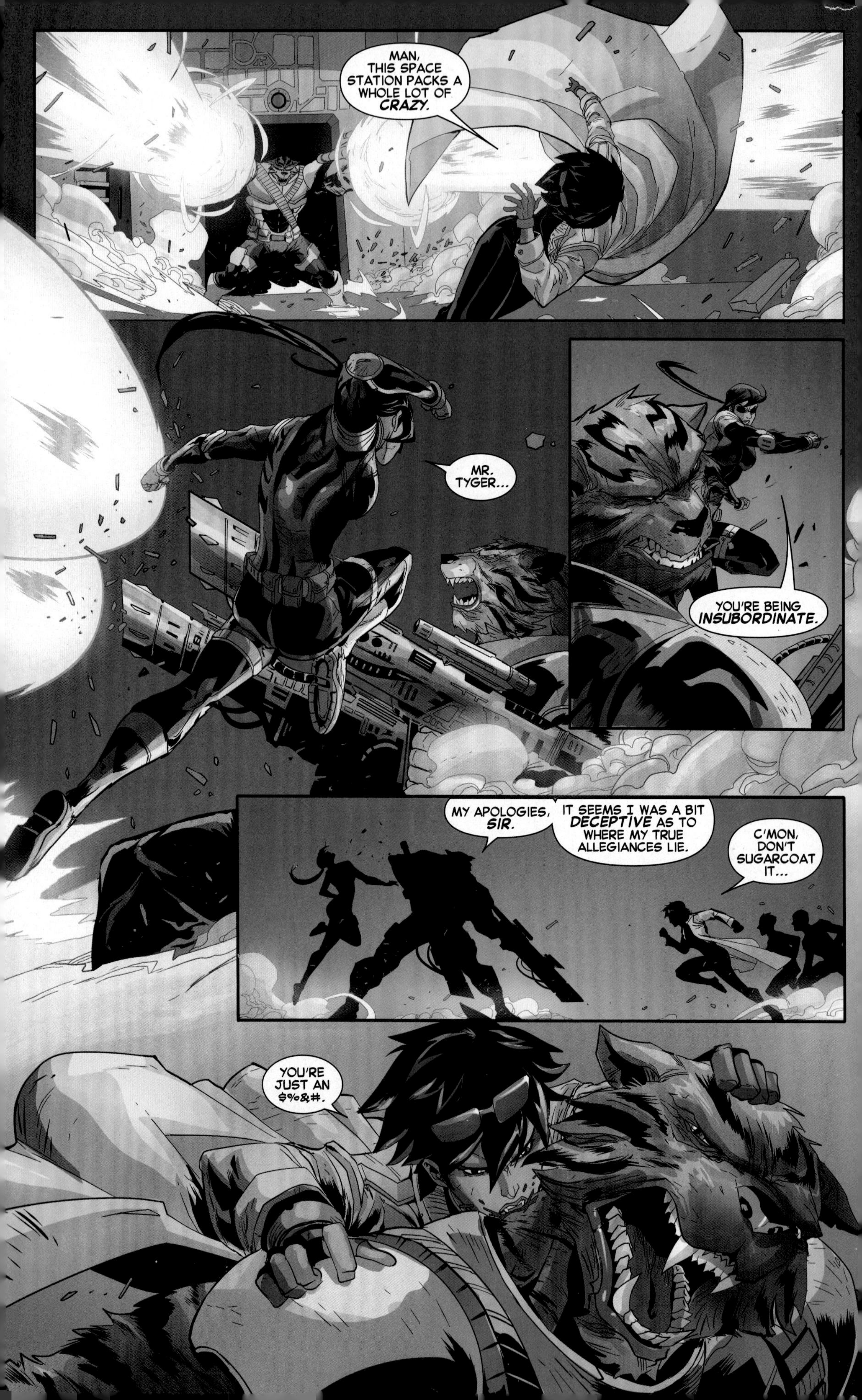
MAN, THIS SPACE STATION PACKS A WHOLE LOT OF CRAZY.
MR. TYGER...
YOU'RE BEING INSUBORDINATE.
MY APOLOGIES, SIR.
IT SEEMS I WAS A BIT DECEPTIVE AS TO WHERE MY TRUE ALLEGIANCES LIE.
C'MON, DON'T SUGARCOAT IT...
YOU'RE JUST AN $%&#.

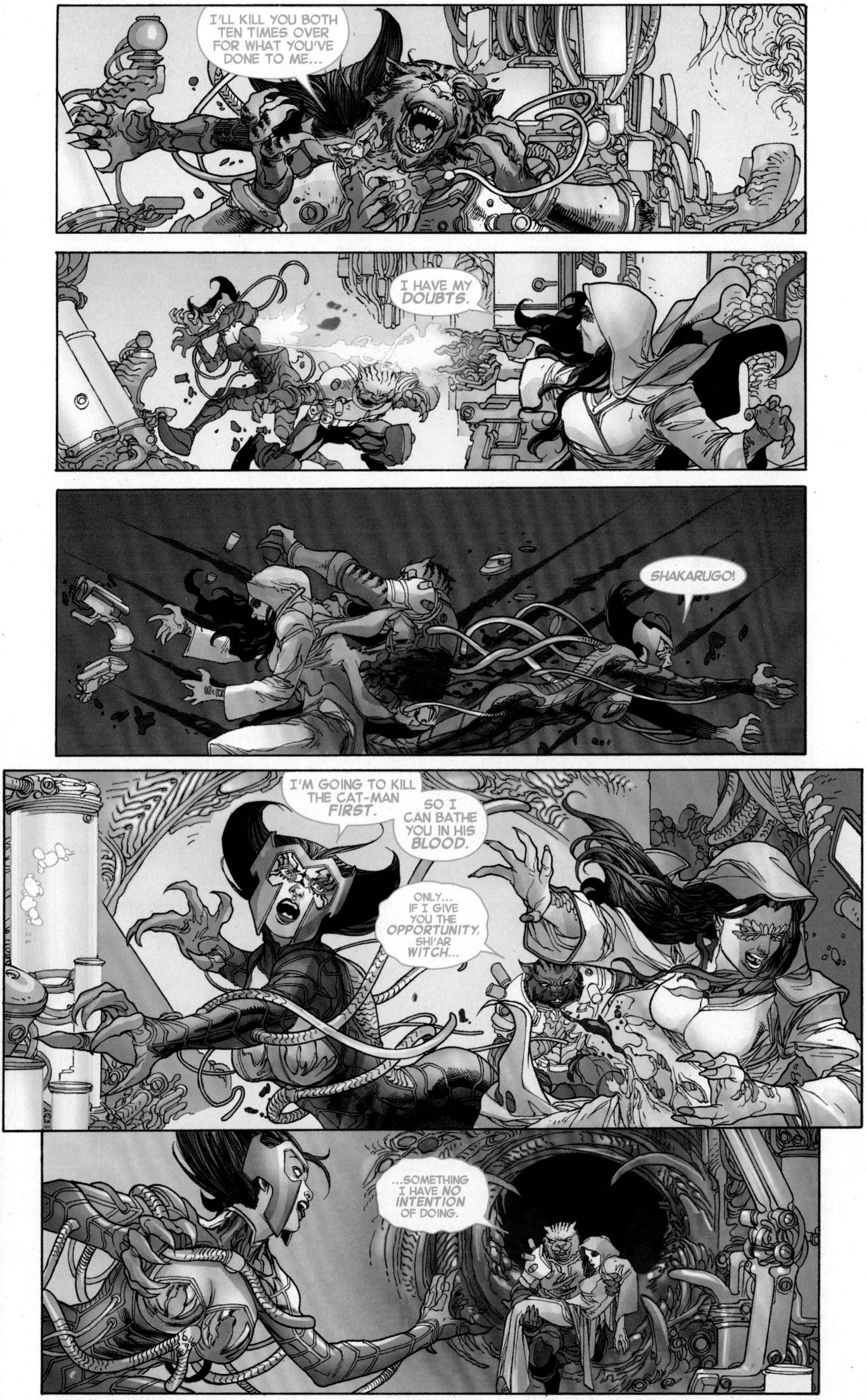
I'LL KILL YOU BOTH TEN TIMES OVER FOR WHAT YOU'VE DONE TO ME...
I HAVE MY DOUBTS.
SHAKARUGO!
I'M GOING TO KILL THE CAT-MAN FIRST.
SO I CAN BATHE YOU IN HIS BLOOD.
ONLY... IF I GIVE YOU THE OPPORTUNITY, SHI'AR WITCH...
...SOMETHING I HAVE NO INTENTION OF DOING.

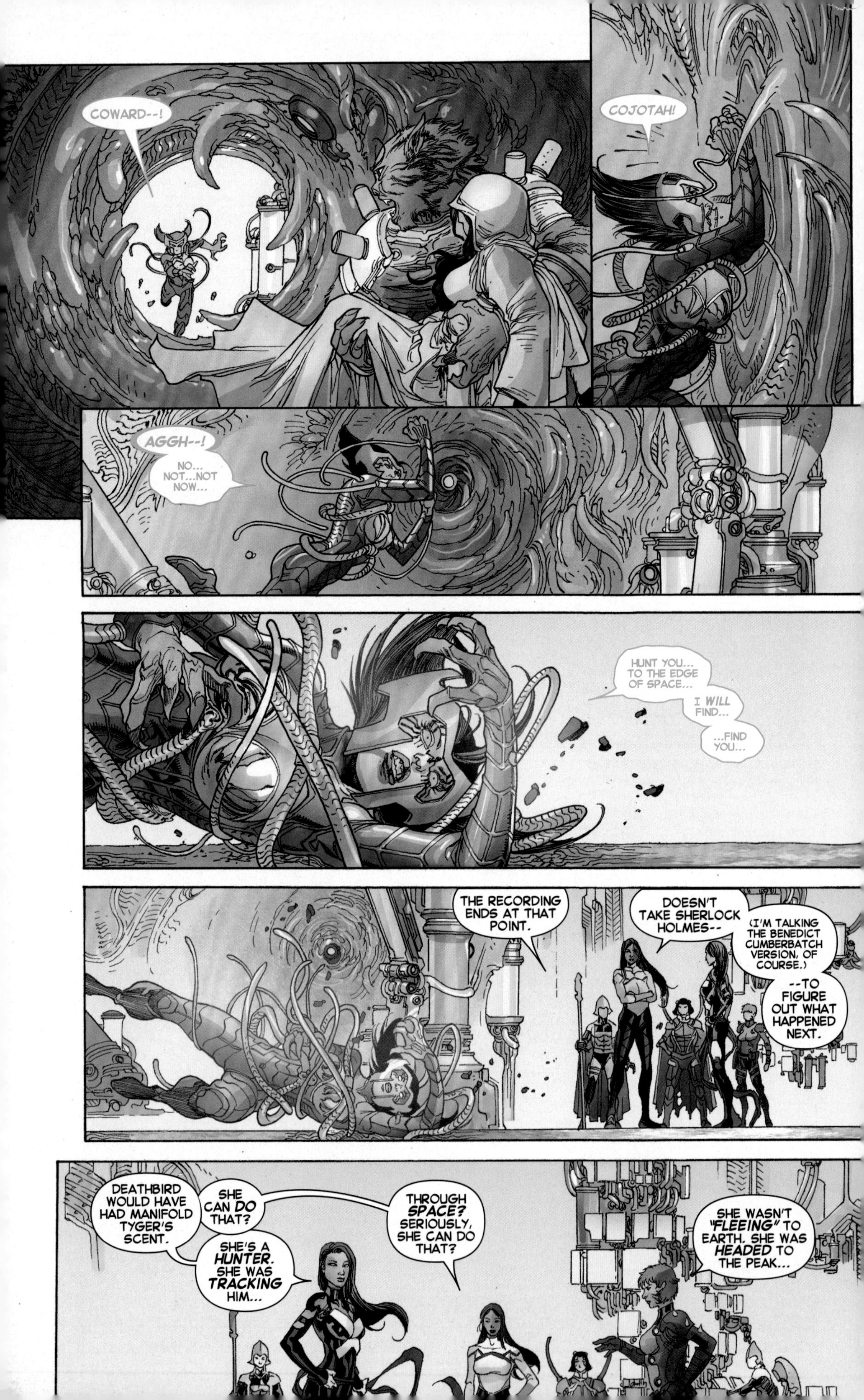
COWARD--!
COJOTAH!
AGGH--!
NO... NOT...NOT NOW...
HUNT YOU... TO THE EDGE OF SPACE...
I WILL FIND...
...FIND YOU...
THE RECORDING ENDS AT THAT POINT.
DOESN'T TAKE SHERLOCK HOLMES--
(I'M TALKING THE BENEDICT CUMBERBATCH VERSION, OF COURSE.)
--TO FIGURE OUT WHAT HAPPENED NEXT.
DEATHBIRD WOULD HAVE HAD MANIFOLD TYGER'S SCENT.
SHE CAN DO THAT?
SHE'S A HUNTER. SHE WAS TRACKING HIM...
THROUGH SPACE? SERIOUSLY, SHE CAN DO THAT?
SHE WASN'T "FLEEING" TO EARTH. SHE WAS HEADED TO THE PEAK...

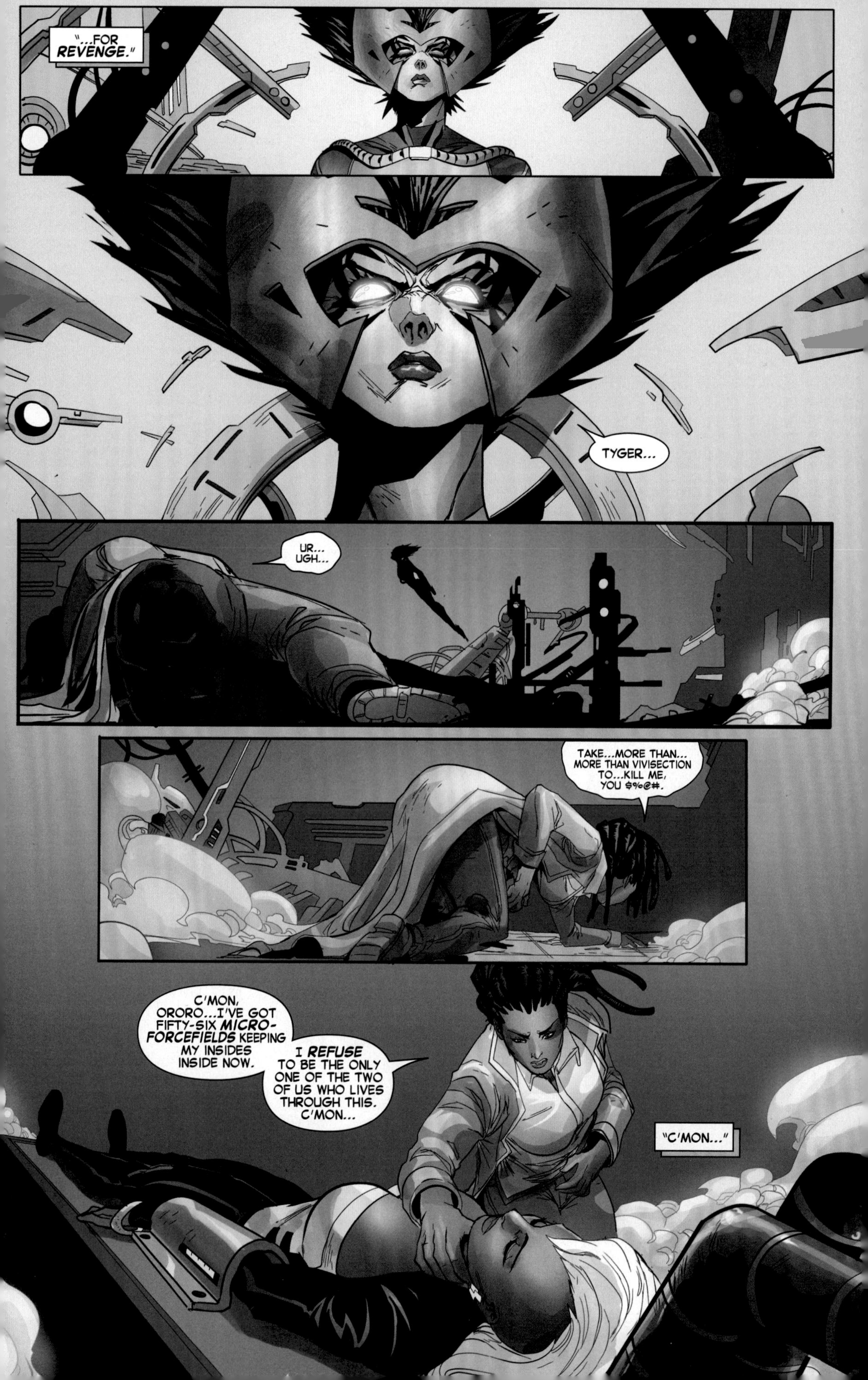
"...FOR REVENGE."
TYGER...
UR... UGH...
TAKE...MORE THAN... MORE THAN VIVISECTION TO...KILL ME, YOU $%@#.
C'MON, ORORO...I'VE GOT FIFTY-SIX MICRO-FORCEFIELDS KEEPING MY INSIDES INSIDE NOW.
I REFUSE TO BE THE ONLY ONE OF THE TWO OF US WHO LIVES THROUGH THIS. C'MON...
"C'MON..."

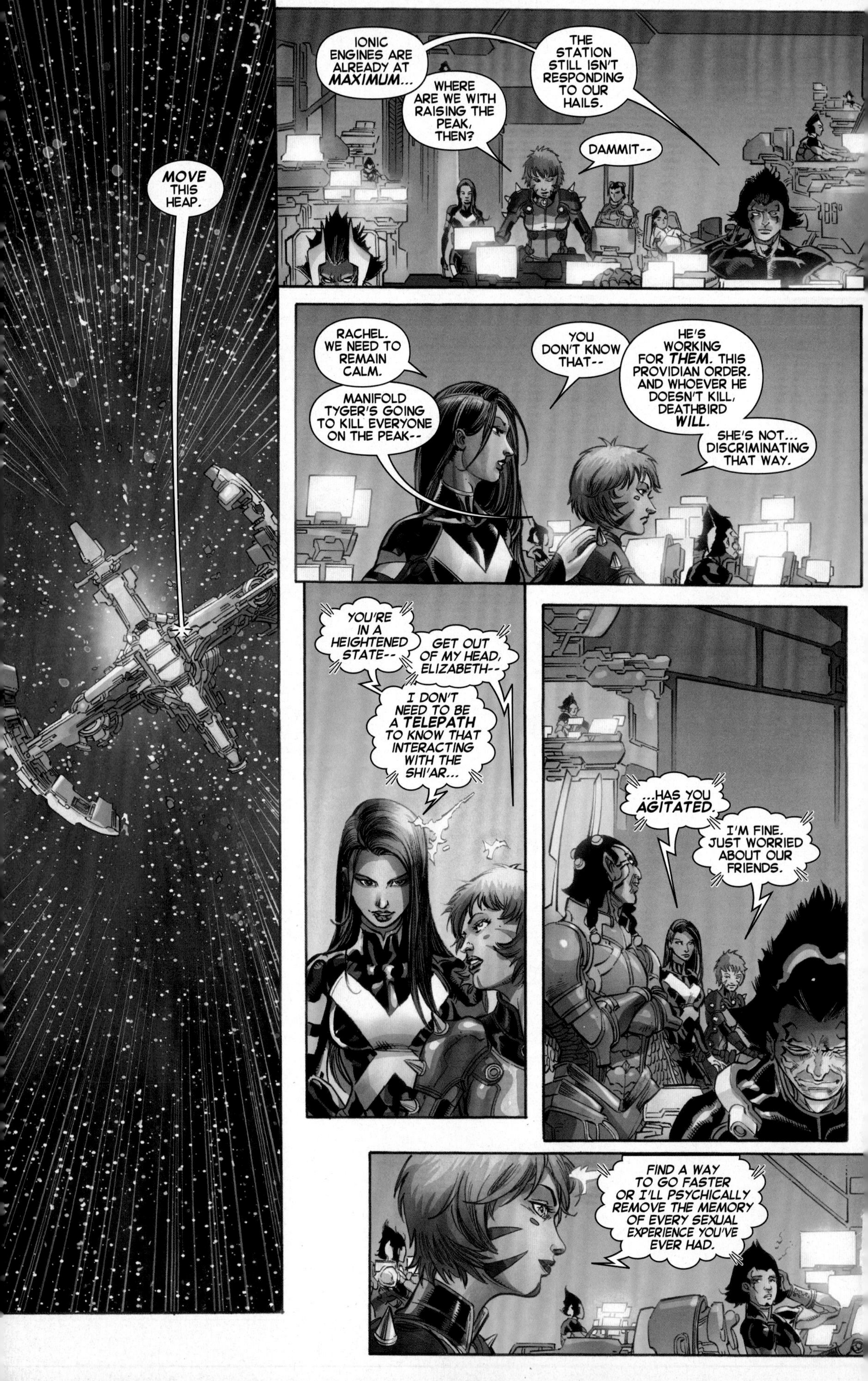
MOVE THIS HEAP.
IONIC ENGINES ARE ALREADY AT MAXIMUM...
THE STATION STILL ISN'T RESPONDING TO OUR HAILS.
WHERE ARE WE WITH RAISING THE PEAK, THEN?
DAMMIT--
RACHEL. WE NEED TO REMAIN CALM.
MANIFOLD TYGER'S GOING TO KILL EVERYONE ON THE PEAK--
YOU DON'T KNOW THAT--
HE'S WORKING FOR THEM. THIS PROVIDIAN ORDER. AND WHOEVER HE DOESN'T KILL, DEATHBIRD WILL.
SHE'S NOT... DISCRIMINATING THAT WAY.
YOU'RE IN A HEIGHTENED STATE--
GET OUT OF MY HEAD, ELIZABETH--
I DON'T NEED TO BE A TELEPATH TO KNOW THAT INTERACTING WITH THE SHI'AR...
...HAS YOU AGITATED.
I'M FINE. JUST WORRIED ABOUT OUR FRIENDS.
FIND A WAY TO GO FASTER OR I'LL PSYCHICALLY REMOVE THE MEMORY OF EVERY SEXUAL EXPERIENCE YOU'VE EVER HAD.

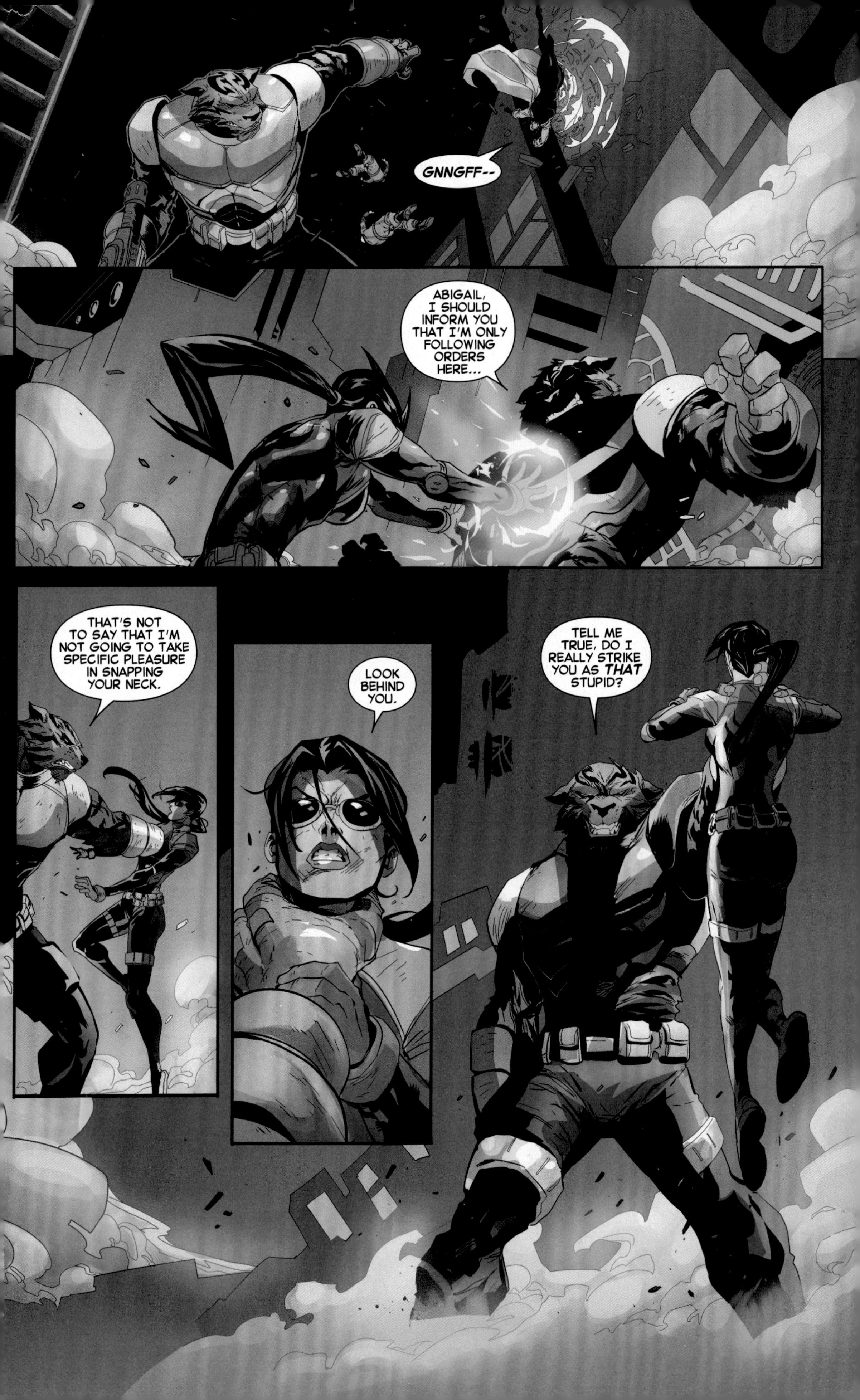
GNNGFF--
ABIGAIL, I SHOULD INFORM YOU THAT I'M ONLY FOLLOWING ORDERS HERE...
THAT'S NOT TO SAY THAT I'M NOT GOING TO TAKE SPECIFIC PLEASURE IN SNAPPING YOUR NECK.
LOOK BEHIND YOU.
TELL ME TRUE, DO I REALLY STRIKE YOU AS THAT STUPID?

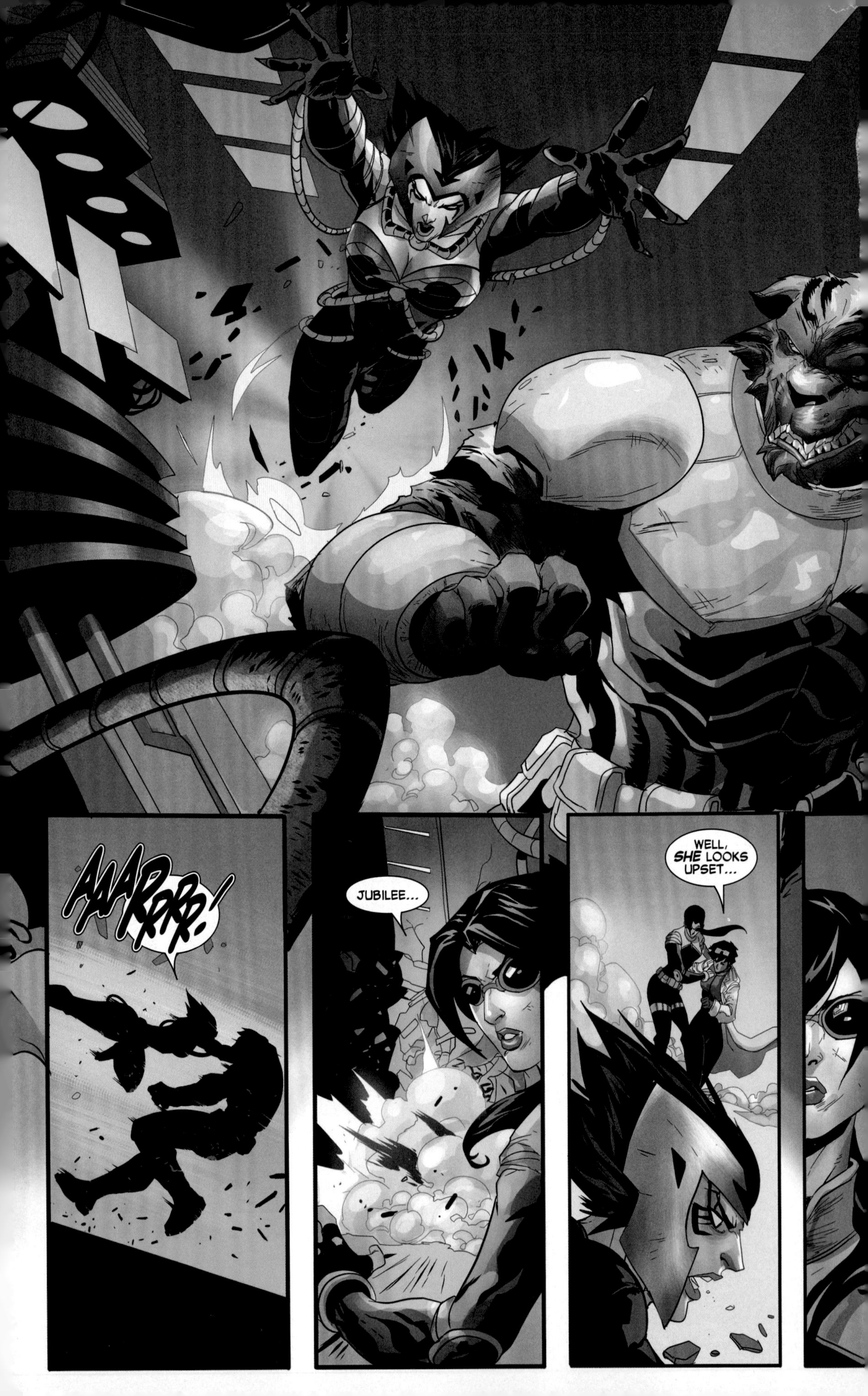
AAARRRR!
JUBILEE...
WELL, SHE LOOKS UPSET...

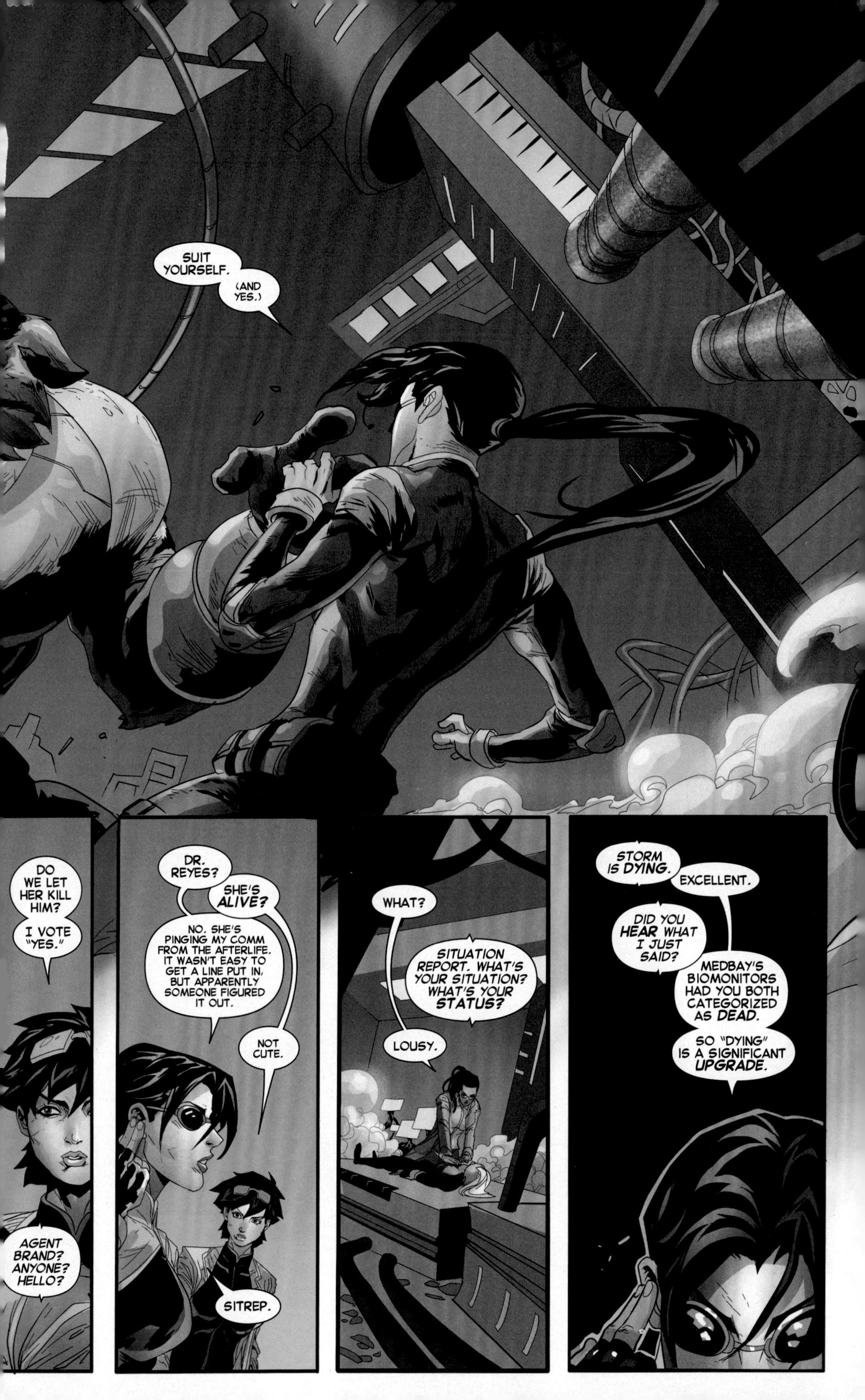
SUIT YOURSELF.
(AND YES.)
DO WE LET HER KILL HIM?
I VOTE "YES."
AGENT BRAND? ANYONE? HELLO?
DR. REYES?
SHE'S ALIVE?
NO. SHE'S PINGING MY COMM FROM THE AFTERLIFE. IT WASN'T EASY TO GET A LINE PUT IN, BUT APPARENTLY SOMEONE FIGURED IT OUT.
NOT CUTE.
SITREP.
WHAT?
SITUATION REPORT. WHAT'S YOUR SITUATION? WHAT'S YOUR STATUS?
LOUSY.
STORM IS DYING.
EXCELLENT.
DID YOU HEAR WHAT I JUST SAID?
MEDBAY'S BIOMONITORS HAD YOU BOTH CATEGORIZED AS DEAD.
SO "DYING" IS A SIGNIFICANT UPGRADE.

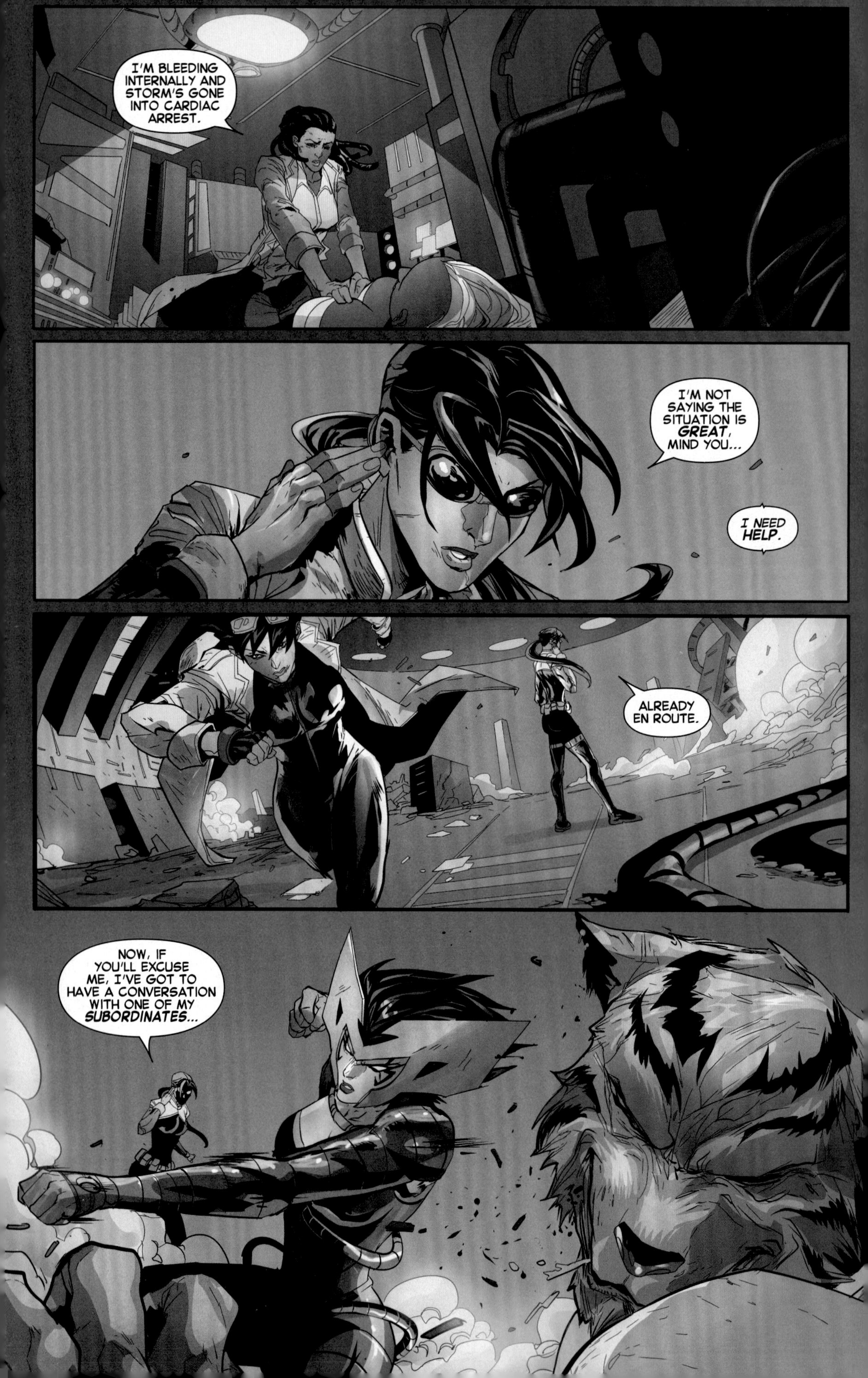
I'M BLEEDING INTERNALLY AND STORM'S GONE INTO CARDIAC ARREST.
I'M NOT SAYING THE SITUATION IS *GREAT*, MIND YOU...
I NEED HELP.
ALREADY EN ROUTE.
NOW, IF YOU'LL EXCUSE ME, I'VE GOT TO HAVE A CONVERSATION WITH ONE OF MY *SUBORDINATES*...

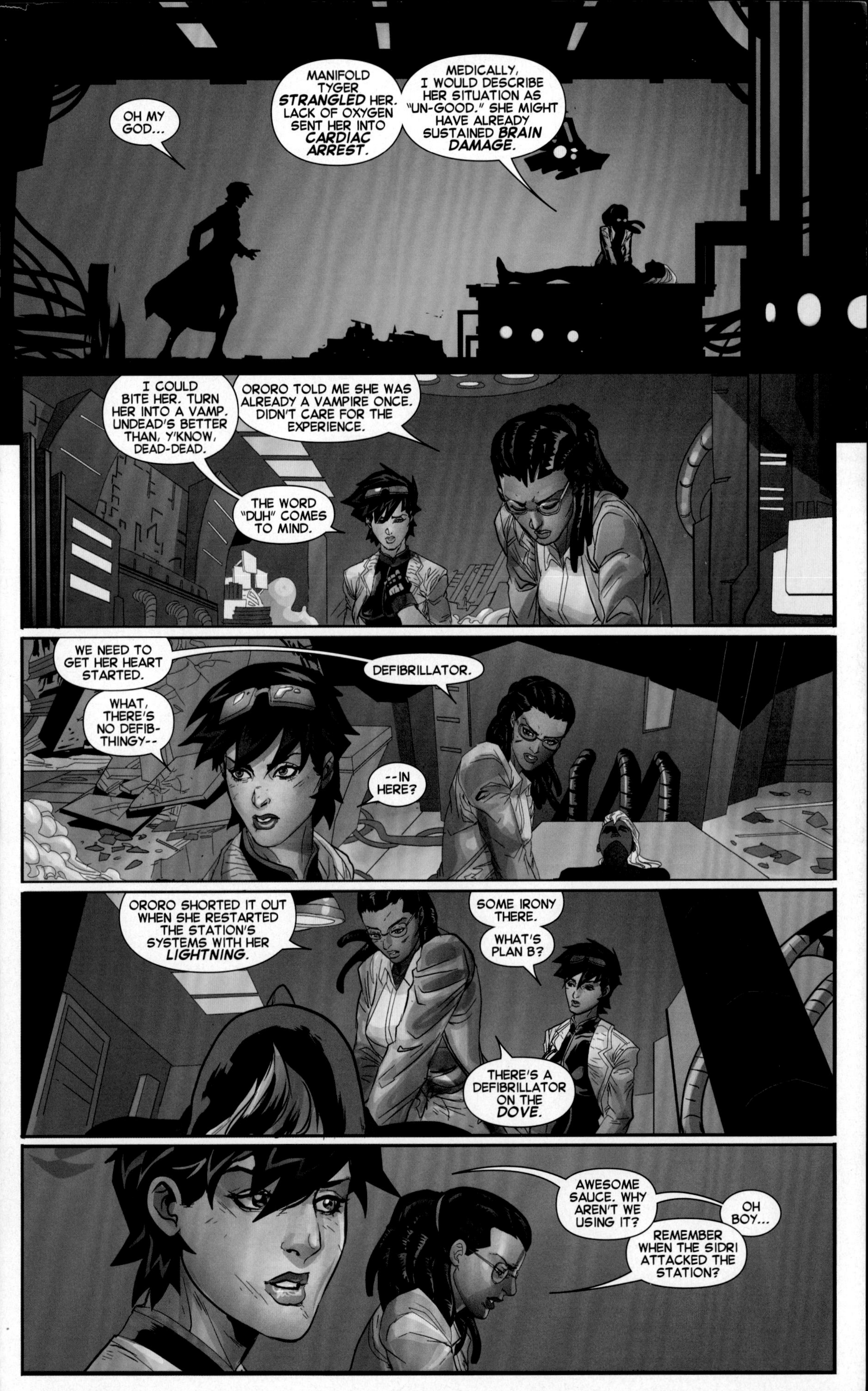
OH MY GOD...
MANIFOLD TYGER STRANGLED HER. LACK OF OXYGEN SENT HER INTO CARDIAC ARREST.
MEDICALLY, I WOULD DESCRIBE HER SITUATION AS "UN-GOOD." SHE MIGHT HAVE ALREADY SUSTAINED BRAIN DAMAGE.
I COULD BITE HER. TURN HER INTO A VAMP. UNDEAD'S BETTER THAN, Y'KNOW, DEAD-DEAD.
ORORO TOLD ME SHE WAS ALREADY A VAMPIRE ONCE. DIDN'T CARE FOR THE EXPERIENCE.
THE WORD "DUH" COMES TO MIND.
WE NEED TO GET HER HEART STARTED.
DEFIBRILLATOR.
WHAT, THERE'S NO DEFIB-THINGY--
--IN HERE?
ORORO SHORTED IT OUT WHEN SHE RESTARTED THE STATION'S SYSTEMS WITH HER LIGHTNING.
SOME IRONY THERE.
WHAT'S PLAN B?
THERE'S A DEFIBRILLATOR ON THE DOVE.
AWESOME SAUCE. WHY AREN'T WE USING IT?
OH BOY...
REMEMBER WHEN THE SIDRI ATTACKED THE STATION?

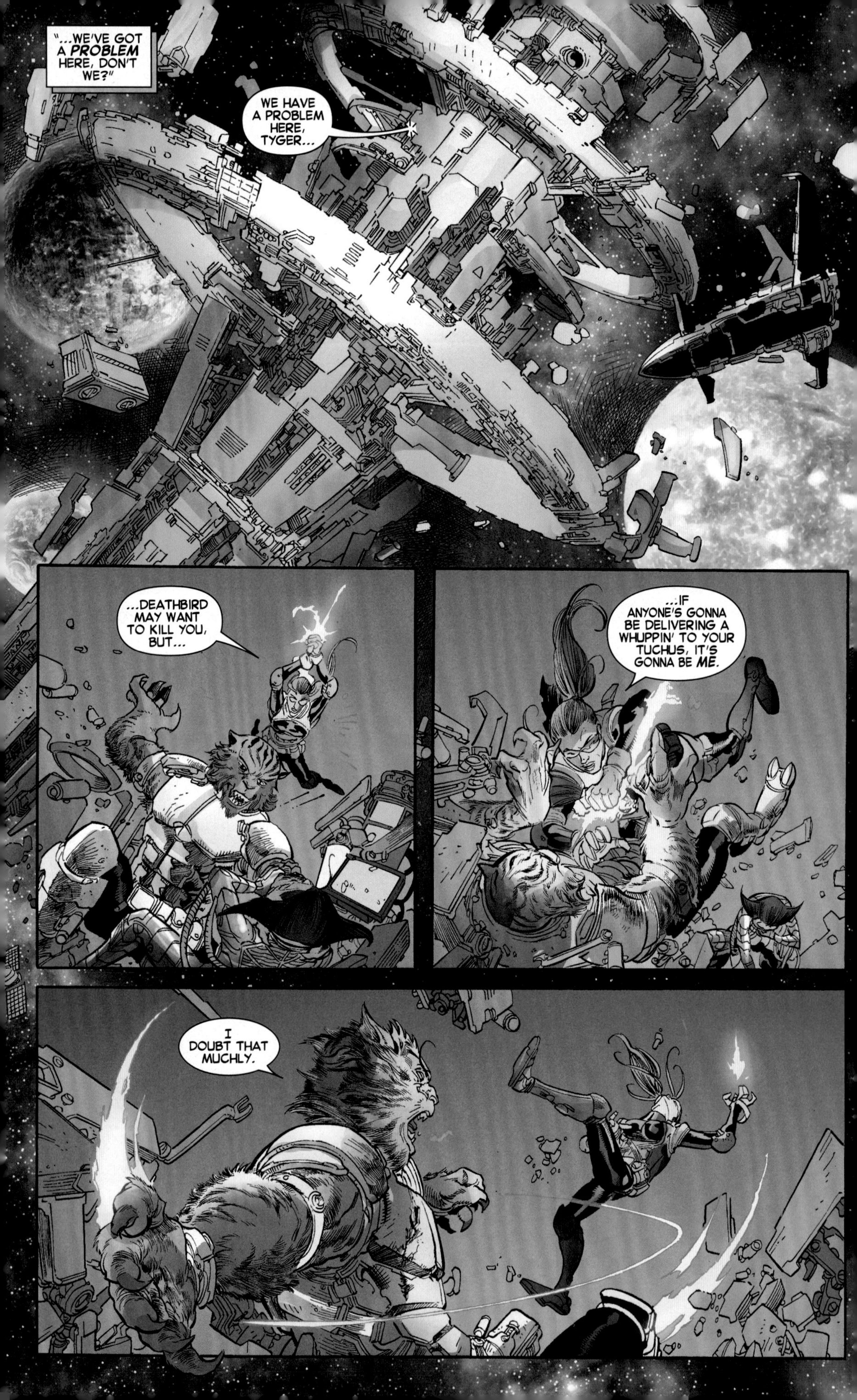
"...WE'VE GOT A PROBLEM HERE, DON'T WE?"
WE HAVE A PROBLEM HERE, TYGER...
...DEATHBIRD MAY WANT TO KILL YOU, BUT...
...IF ANYONE'S GONNA BE DELIVERING A WHUPPIN' TO YOUR TUCHUS, IT'S GONNA BE ME.
I DOUBT THAT MUCHLY.

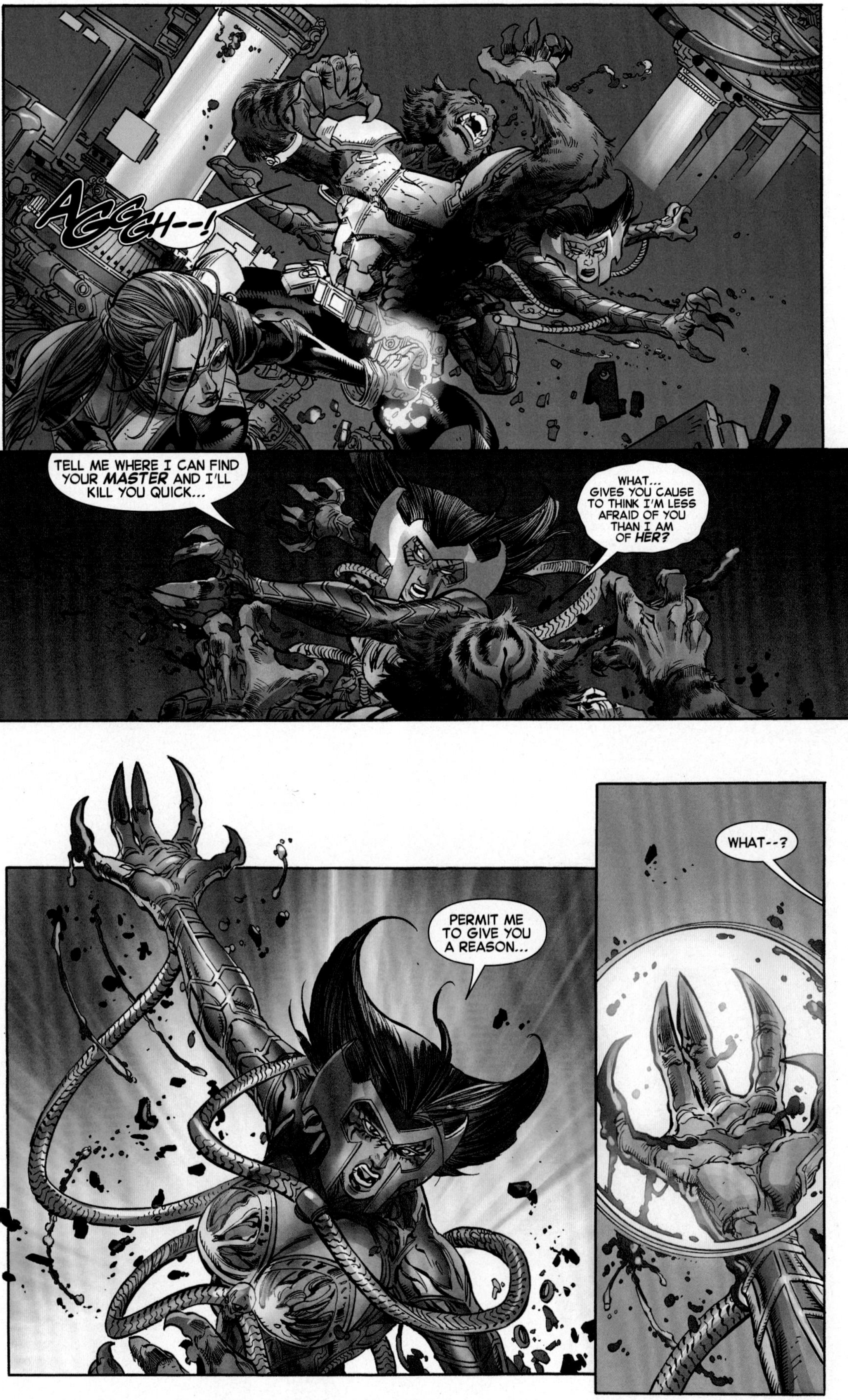
AGGGH--!
TELL ME WHERE I CAN FIND YOUR MASTER AND I'LL KILL YOU QUICK...
WHAT... GIVES YOU CAUSE TO THINK I'M LESS AFRAID OF YOU THAN I AM OF HER?
PERMIT ME TO GIVE YOU A REASON...
WHAT--?

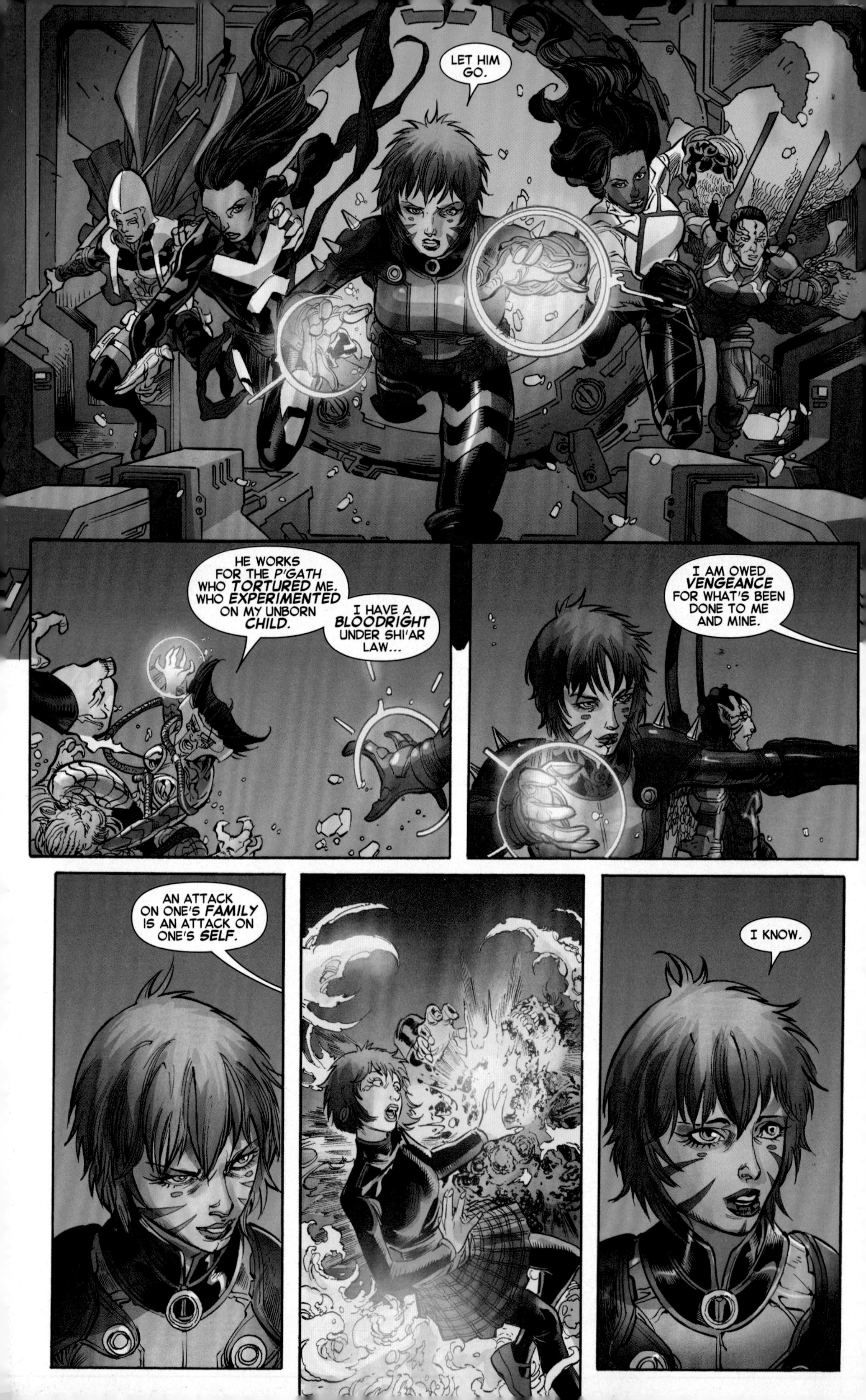
LET HIM GO.
HE WORKS FOR THE P'GATH WHO TORTURED ME. WHO EXPERIMENTED ON MY UNBORN CHILD.
I HAVE A BLOODRIGHT UNDER SHI'AR LAW...
I AM OWED VENGEANCE FOR WHAT'S BEEN DONE TO ME AND MINE.
AN ATTACK ON ONE'S FAMILY IS AN ATTACK ON ONE'S SELF.
I KNOW.

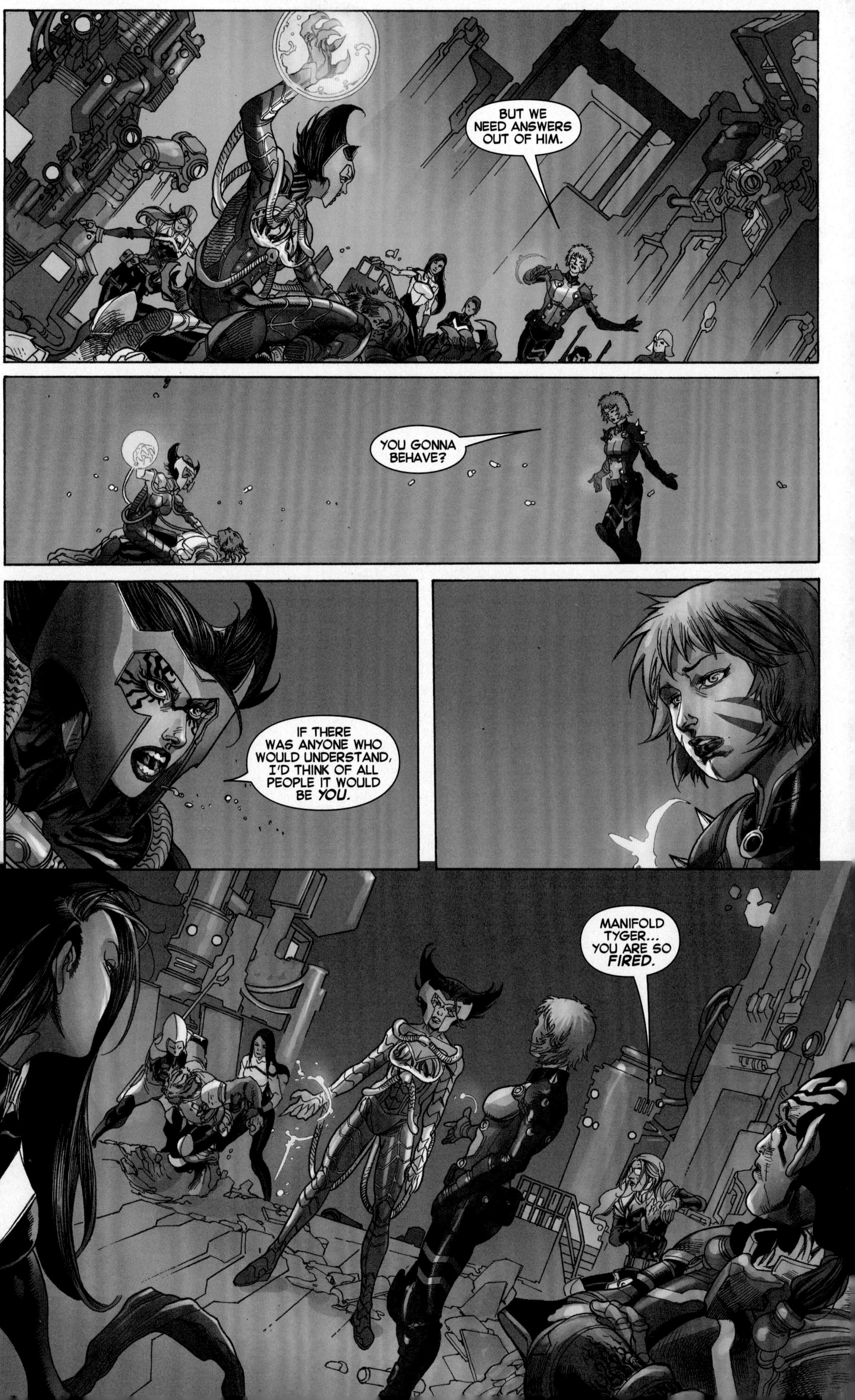
BUT WE NEED ANSWERS OUT OF HIM.
YOU GONNA BEHAVE?
IF THERE WAS ANYONE WHO WOULD UNDERSTAND, I'D THINK OF ALL PEOPLE IT WOULD BE *YOU.*
MANIFOLD TYGER... YOU ARE SO *FIRED.*

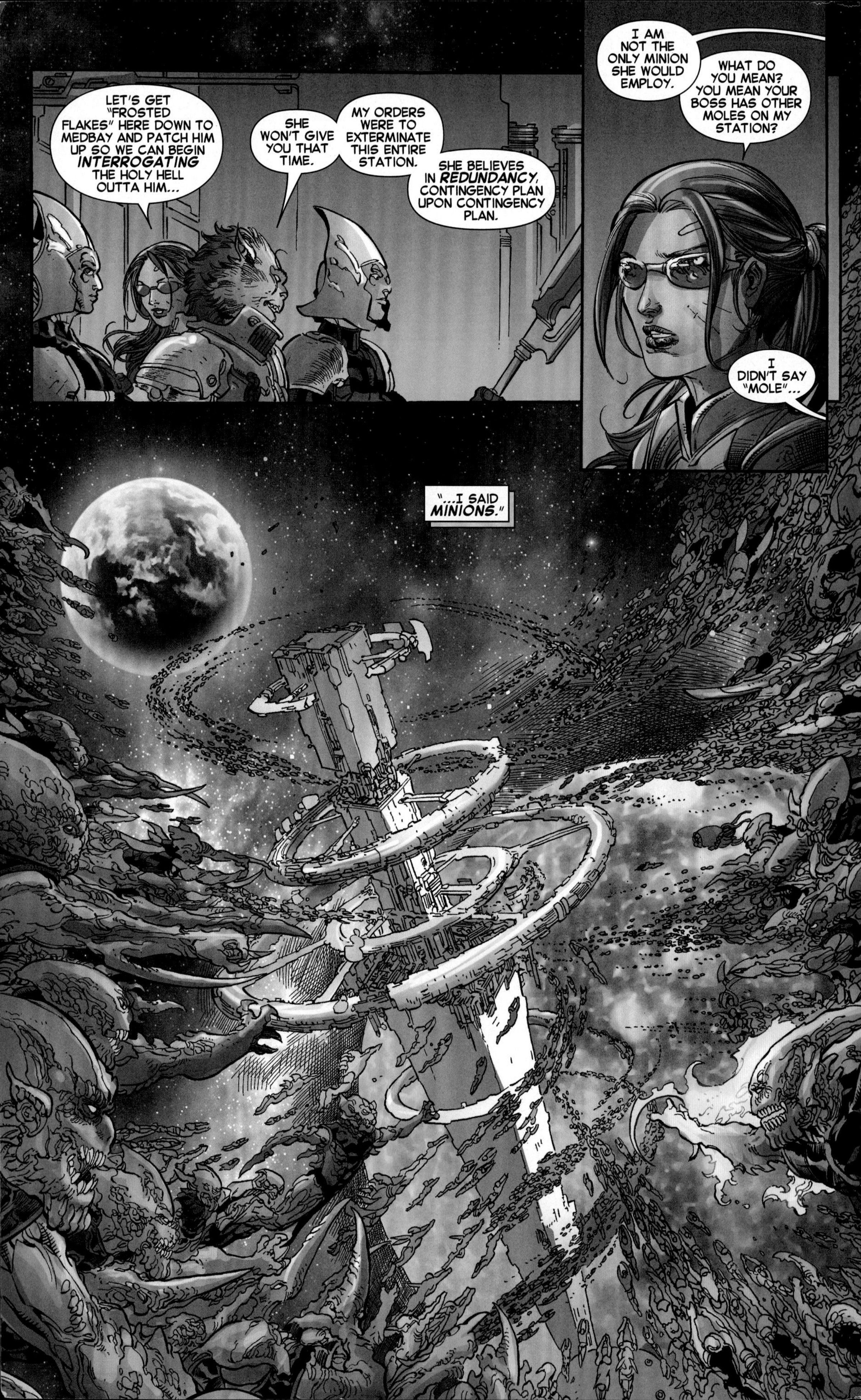
LET'S GET "FROSTED FLAKES" HERE DOWN TO MEDBAY AND PATCH HIM UP SO WE CAN BEGIN *INTERROGATING* THE HOLY HELL OUTTA HIM...
SHE WON'T GIVE YOU THAT TIME.
MY ORDERS WERE TO EXTERMINATE THIS ENTIRE STATION.
SHE BELIEVES IN *REDUNDANCY*, CONTINGENCY PLAN UPON CONTINGENCY PLAN.
I AM NOT THE ONLY MINION SHE WOULD EMPLOY.
WHAT DO YOU MEAN? YOU MEAN YOUR BOSS HAS OTHER MOLES ON MY STATION?
I DIDN'T SAY "MOLE"...
"...I SAID *MINIONS*."

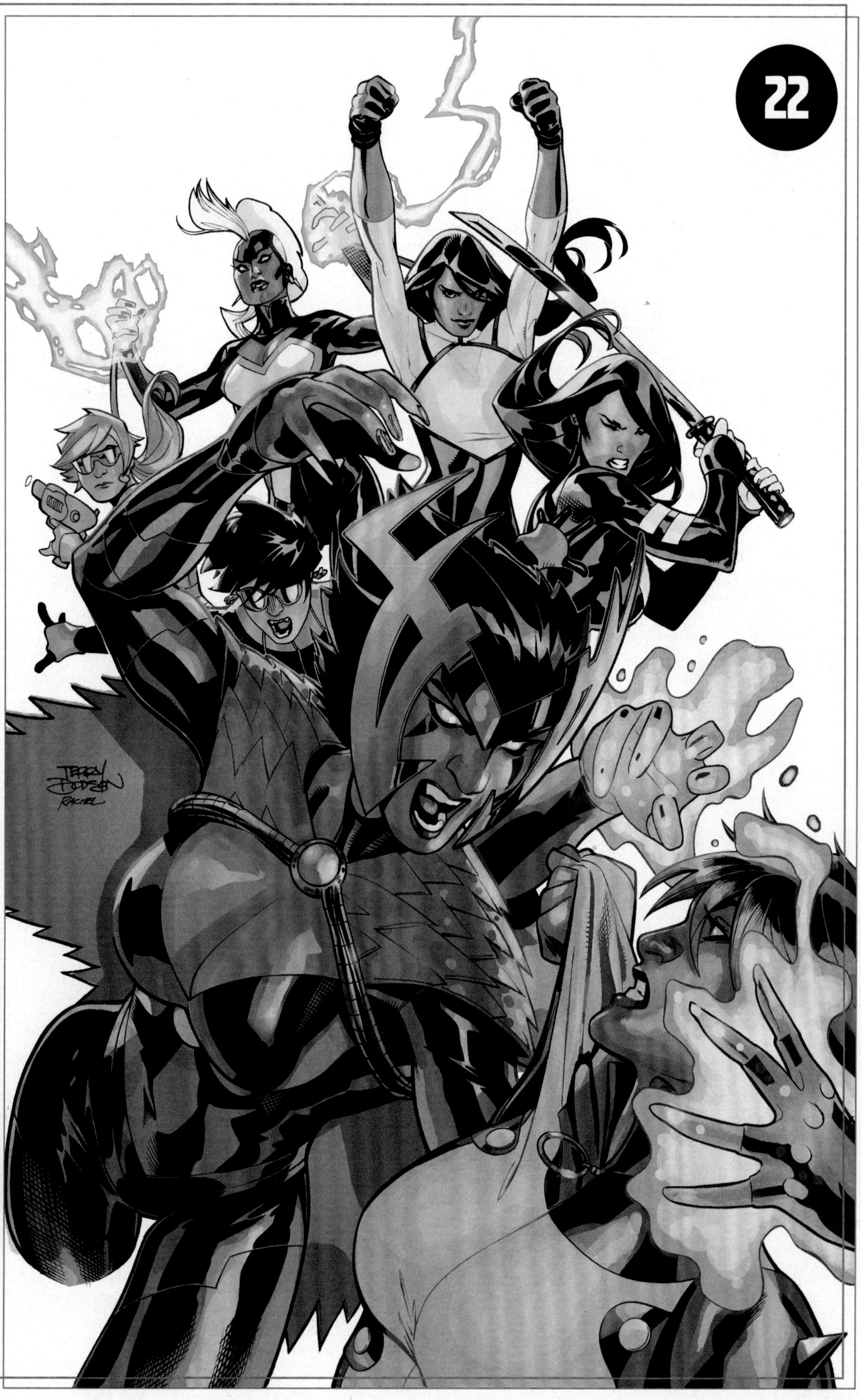
22
TERRY DODSON
RACHEL

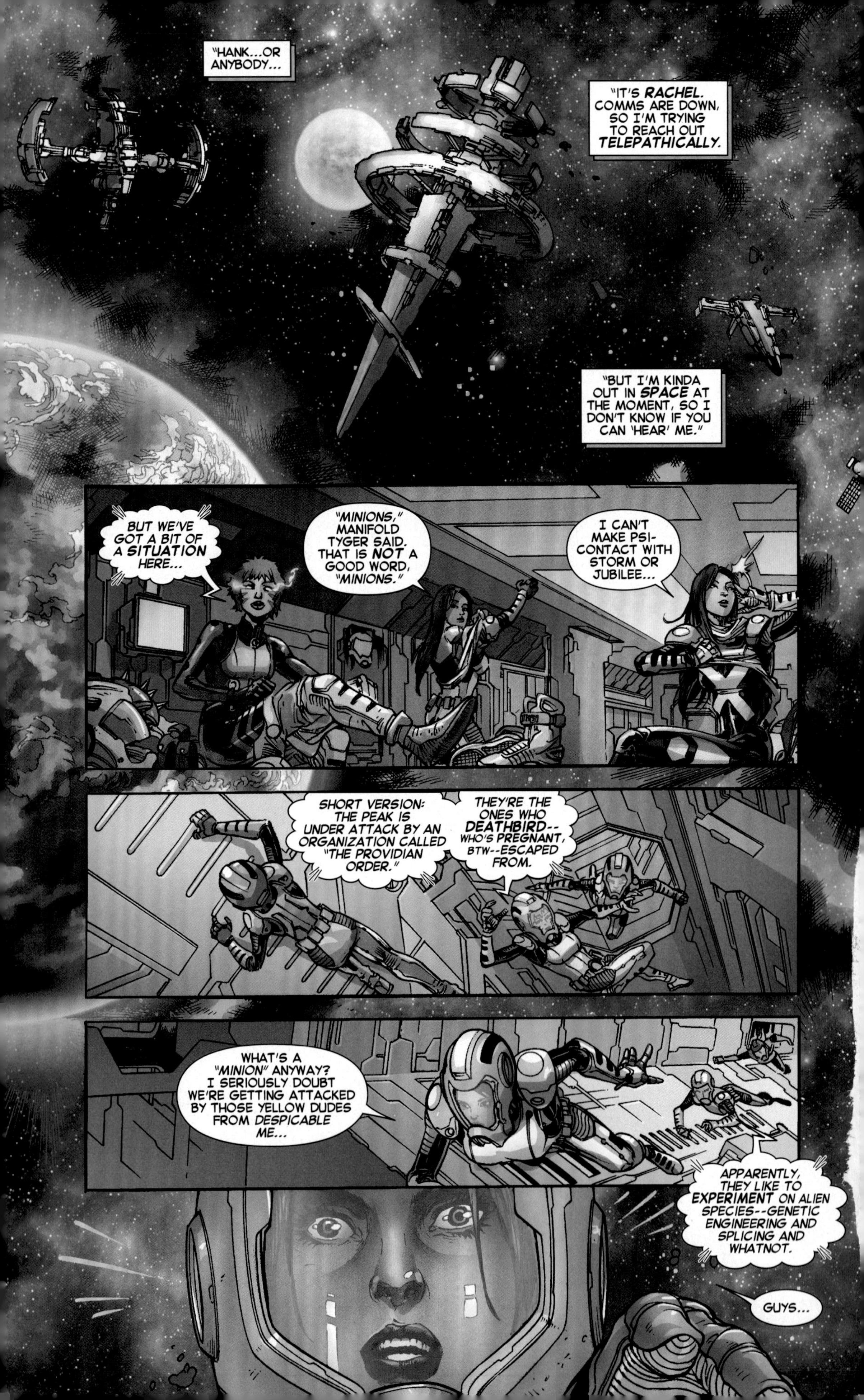
"HANK...OR ANYBODY...
"IT'S RACHEL. COMMS ARE DOWN, SO I'M TRYING TO REACH OUT TELEPATHICALLY.
"BUT I'M KINDA OUT IN SPACE AT THE MOMENT, SO I DON'T KNOW IF YOU CAN 'HEAR' ME."
BUT WE'VE GOT A BIT OF A SITUATION HERE...
"MINIONS," MANIFOLD TYGER SAID. THAT IS NOT A GOOD WORD, "MINIONS."
I CAN'T MAKE PSI-CONTACT WITH STORM OR JUBILEE...
SHORT VERSION: THE PEAK IS UNDER ATTACK BY AN ORGANIZATION CALLED "THE PROVIDIAN ORDER."
THEY'RE THE ONES WHO DEATHBIRD--WHO'S PREGNANT, BTW--ESCAPED FROM.
WHAT'S A "MINION" ANYWAY? I SERIOUSLY DOUBT WE'RE GETTING ATTACKED BY THOSE YELLOW DUDES FROM DESPICABLE ME...
APPARENTLY, THEY LIKE TO EXPERIMENT ON ALIEN SPECIES--GENETIC ENGINEERING AND SPLICING AND WHATNOT.
GUYS...

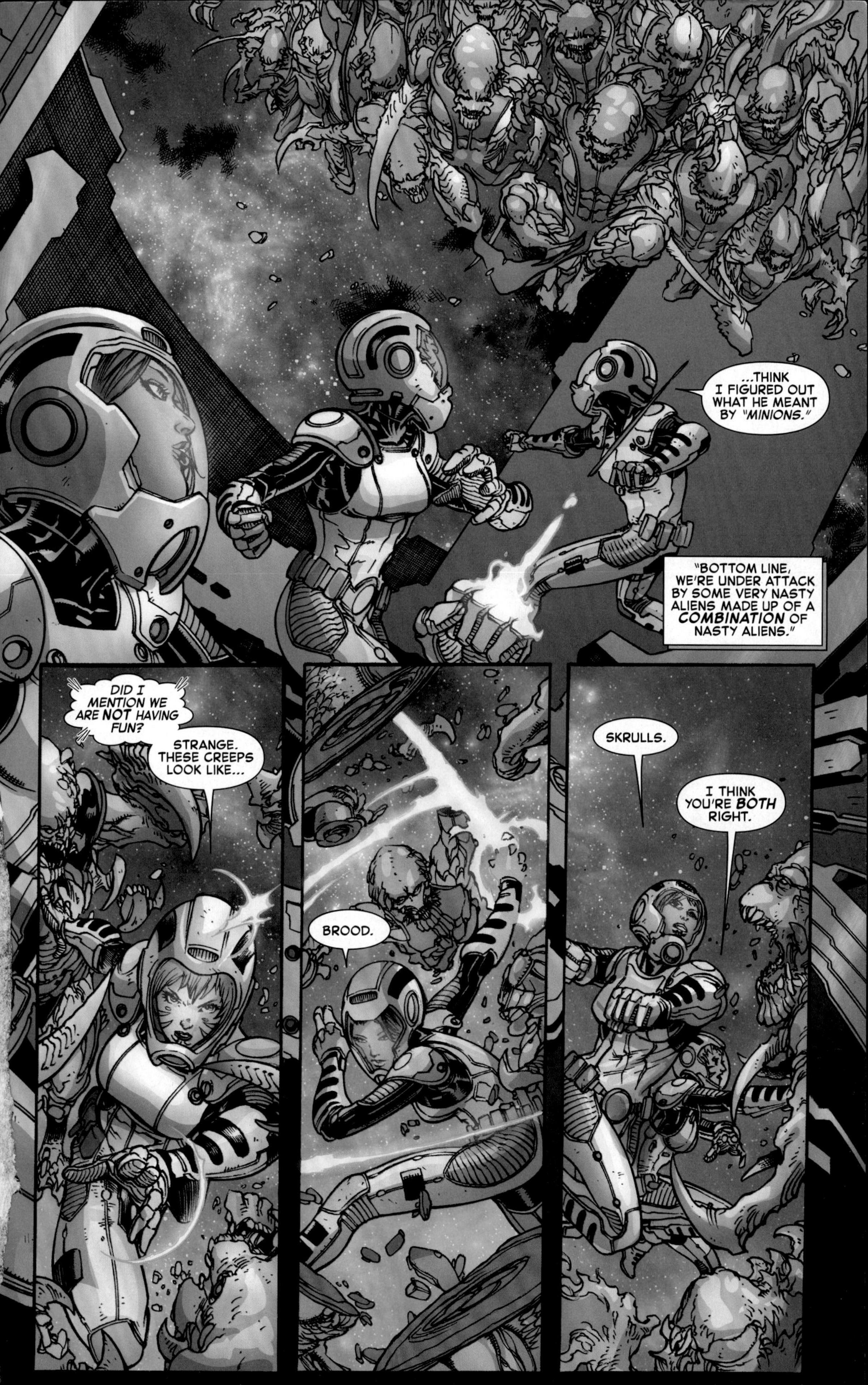
...THINK I FIGURED OUT WHAT HE MEANT BY "MINIONS."
"BOTTOM LINE, WE'RE UNDER ATTACK BY SOME VERY NASTY ALIENS MADE UP OF A COMBINATION OF NASTY ALIENS."
DID I MENTION WE ARE NOT HAVING FUN?
STRANGE. THESE CREEPS LOOK LIKE...
BROOD.
SKRULLS.
I THINK YOU'RE BOTH RIGHT.

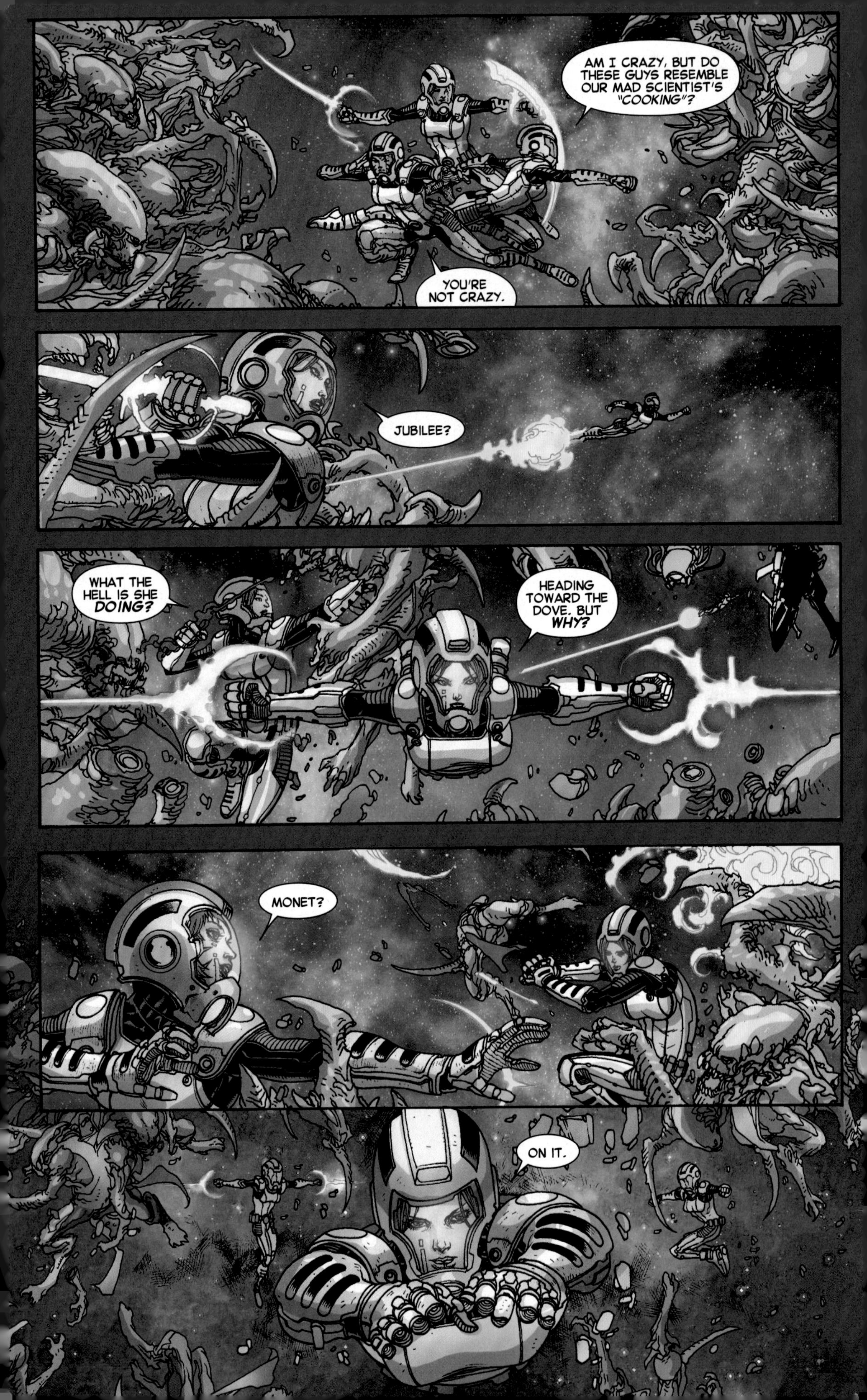
AM I CRAZY, BUT DO THESE GUYS RESEMBLE OUR MAD SCIENTIST'S "COOKING"?
YOU'RE NOT CRAZY.
JUBILEE?
WHAT THE HELL IS SHE DOING?
HEADING TOWARD THE DOVE. BUT WHY?
MONET?
ON IT.

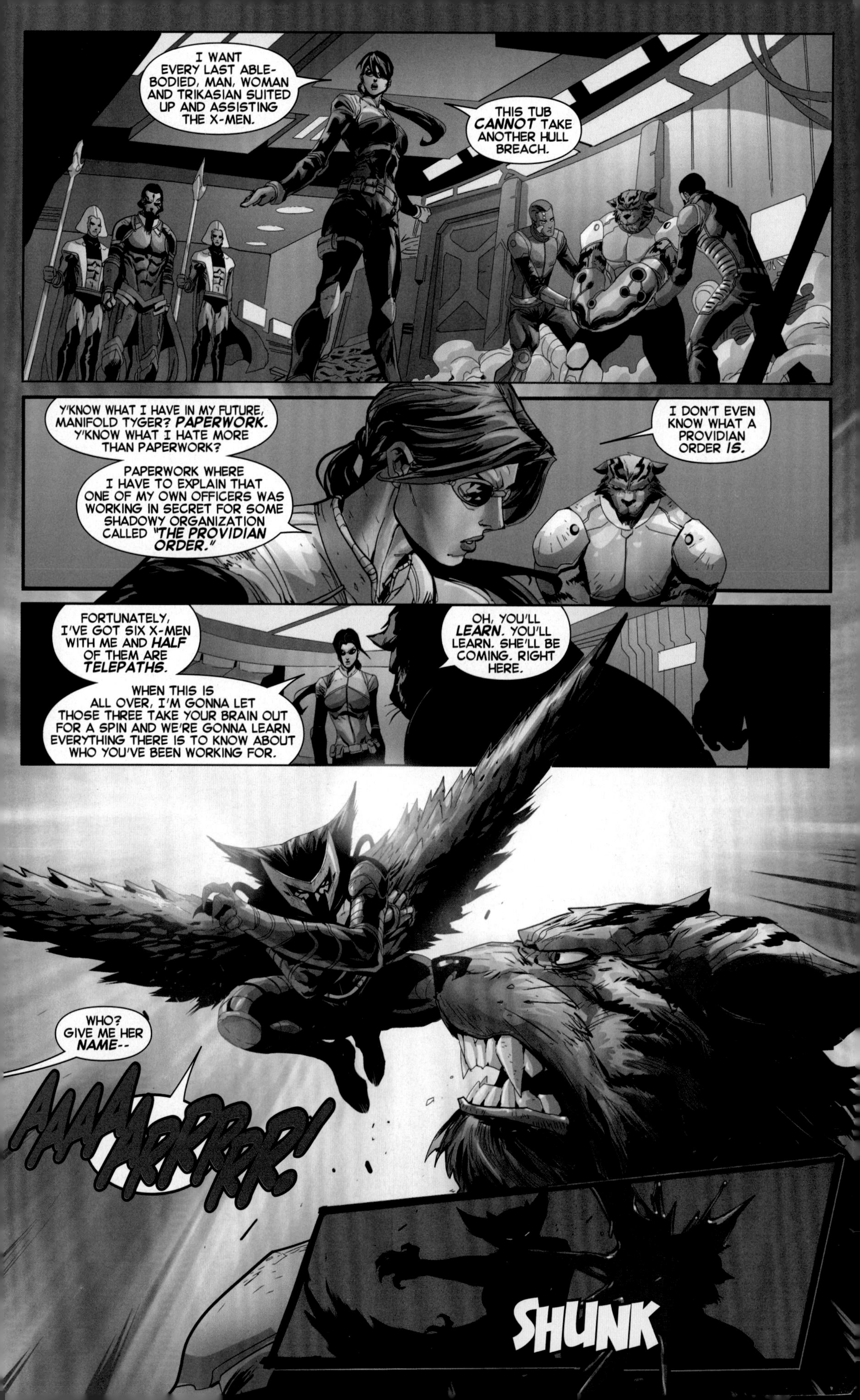

I WANT EVERY LAST ABLE-BODIED, MAN, WOMAN AND TRIKASIAN SUITED UP AND ASSISTING THE X-MEN.
THIS TUB CANNOT TAKE ANOTHER HULL BREACH.
Y'KNOW WHAT I HAVE IN MY FUTURE, MANIFOLD TYGER? PAPERWORK. Y'KNOW WHAT I HATE MORE THAN PAPERWORK?
PAPERWORK WHERE I HAVE TO EXPLAIN THAT ONE OF MY OWN OFFICERS WAS WORKING IN SECRET FOR SOME SHADOWY ORGANIZATION CALLED "THE PROVIDIAN ORDER."
I DON'T EVEN KNOW WHAT A PROVIDIAN ORDER IS.
FORTUNATELY, I'VE GOT SIX X-MEN WITH ME AND HALF OF THEM ARE TELEPATHS.
WHEN THIS IS ALL OVER, I'M GONNA LET THOSE THREE TAKE YOUR BRAIN OUT FOR A SPIN AND WE'RE GONNA LEARN EVERYTHING THERE IS TO KNOW ABOUT WHO YOU'VE BEEN WORKING FOR.
OH, YOU'LL LEARN. YOU'LL LEARN. SHE'LL BE COMING. RIGHT HERE.
WHO? GIVE ME HER NAME--
AAAARRRRR!
SHUNK

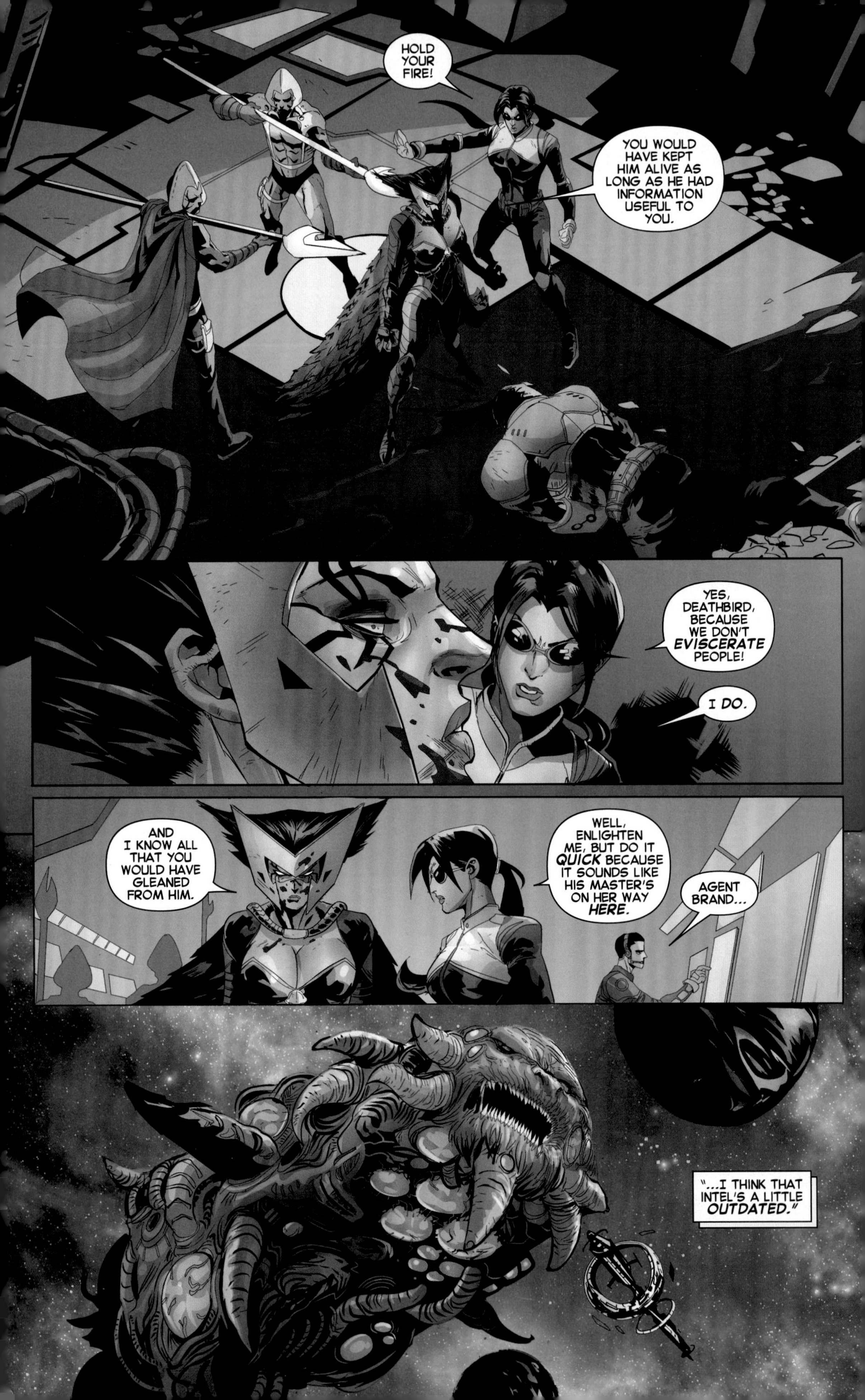
HOLD YOUR FIRE!
YOU WOULD HAVE KEPT HIM ALIVE AS LONG AS HE HAD INFORMATION USEFUL TO YOU.
YES, DEATHBIRD, BECAUSE WE DON'T EVISCERATE PEOPLE!
I DO.
AND I KNOW ALL THAT YOU WOULD HAVE GLEANED FROM HIM.
WELL, ENLIGHTEN ME, BUT DO IT QUICK BECAUSE IT SOUNDS LIKE HIS MASTER'S ON HER WAY HERE.
AGENT BRAND...
"...I THINK THAT INTEL'S A LITTLE OUTDATED."

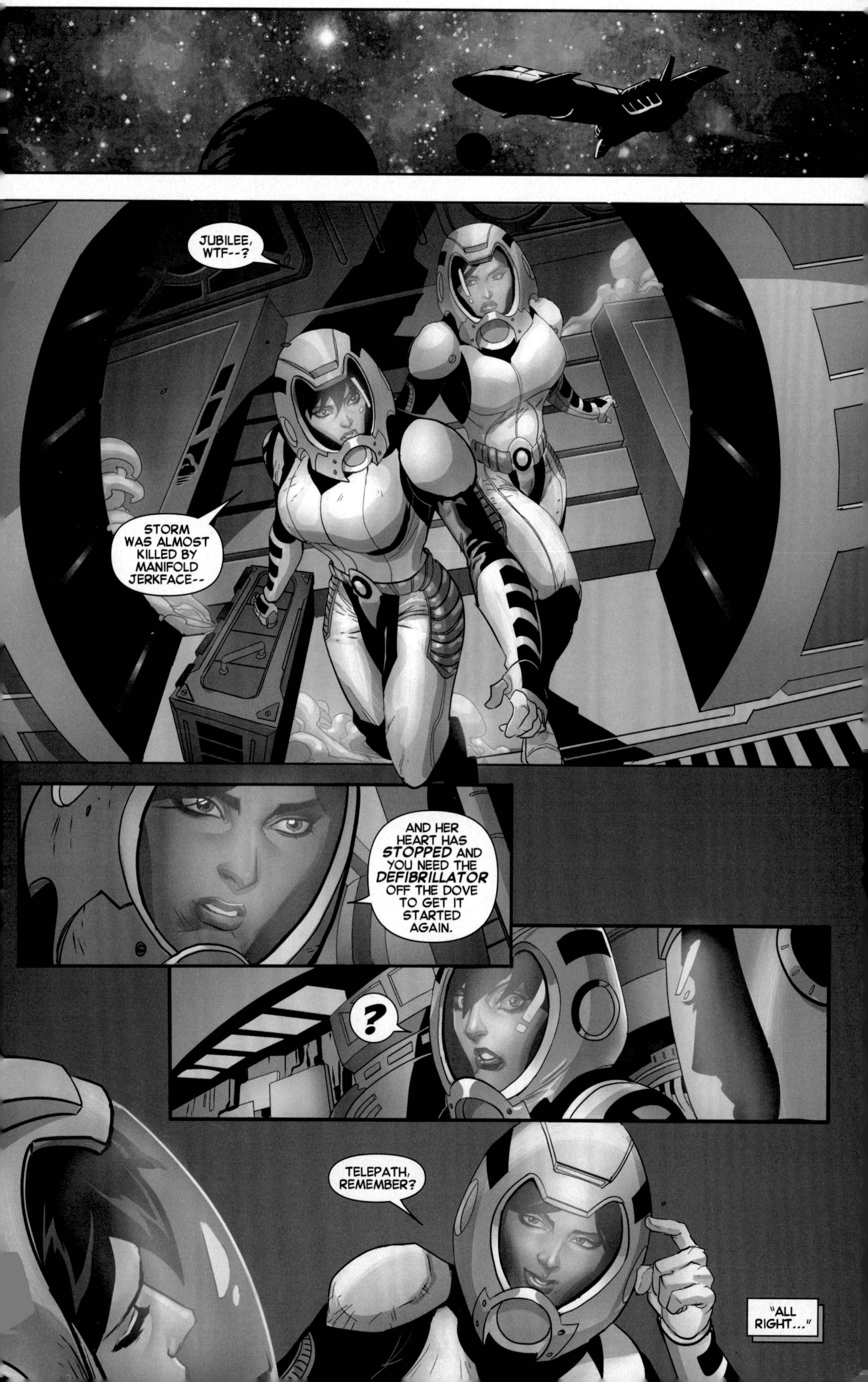
JUBILEE, WTF--?
STORM WAS ALMOST KILLED BY MANIFOLD JERKFACE--
AND HER HEART HAS STOPPED AND YOU NEED THE DEFIBRILLATOR OFF THE DOVE TO GET IT STARTED AGAIN.
?
TELEPATH, REMEMBER?
"ALL RIGHT..."

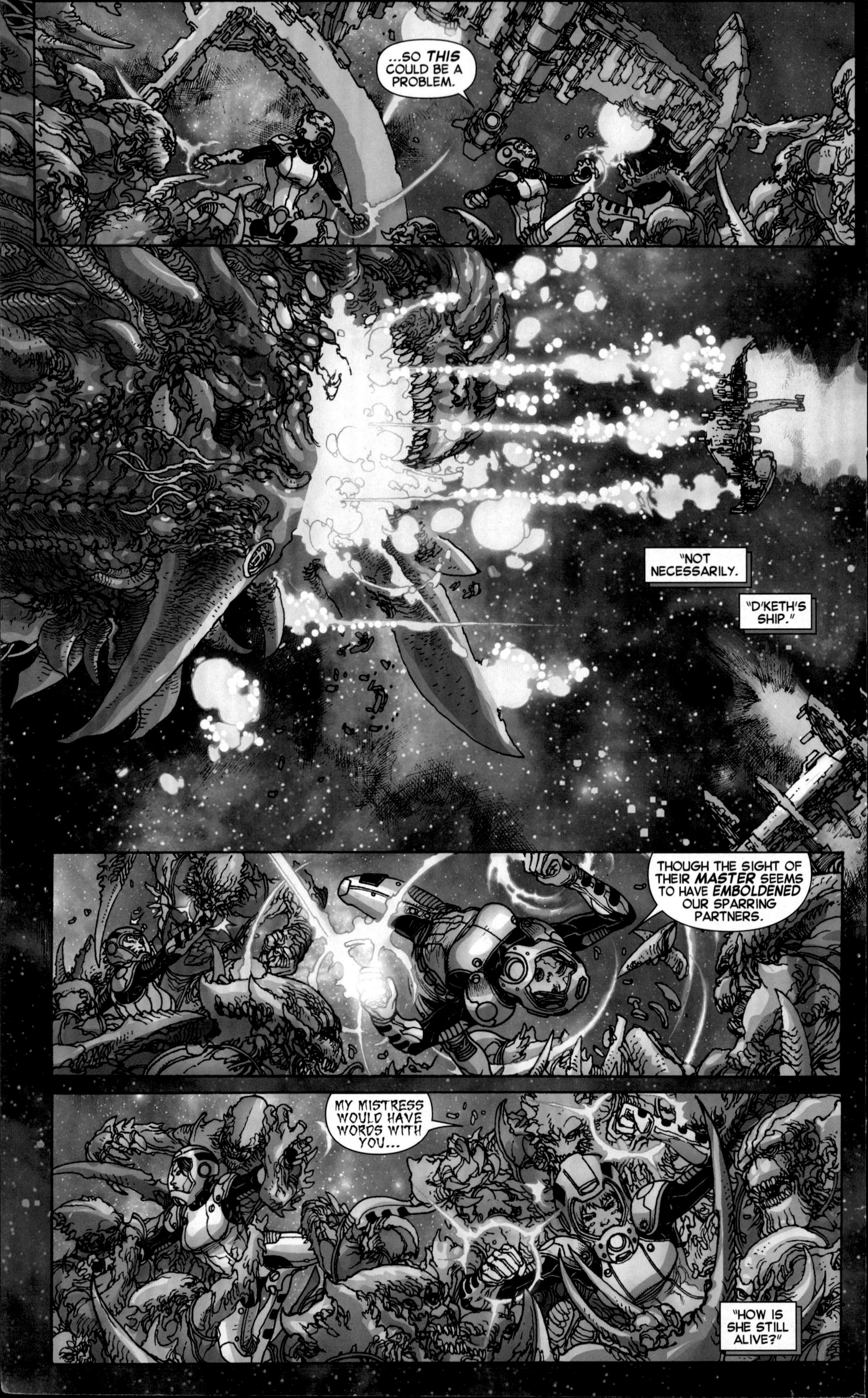
...SO THIS COULD BE A PROBLEM.
"NOT NECESSARILY.
"D'KETH'S SHIP."
THOUGH THE SIGHT OF THEIR MASTER SEEMS TO HAVE EMBOLDENED OUR SPARRING PARTNERS.
MY MISTRESS WOULD HAVE WORDS WITH YOU...
"HOW IS SHE STILL ALIVE?"

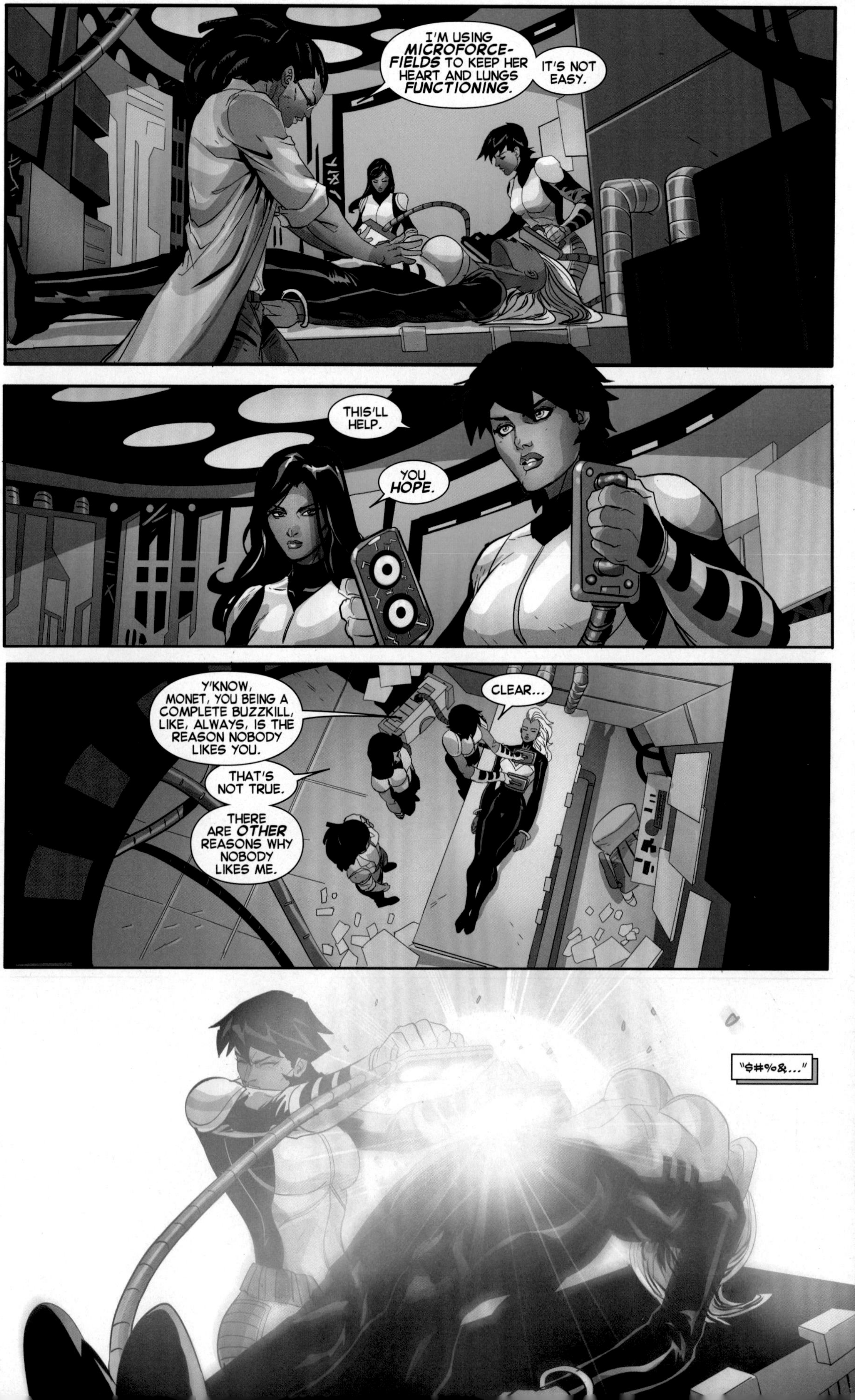
I'M USING MICROFORCE-FIELDS TO KEEP HER HEART AND LUNGS FUNCTIONING.
IT'S NOT EASY.
THIS'LL HELP.
YOU HOPE.
Y'KNOW, MONET, YOU BEING A COMPLETE BUZZKILL, LIKE, ALWAYS, IS THE REASON NOBODY LIKES YOU.
CLEAR...
THAT'S NOT TRUE.
THERE ARE OTHER REASONS WHY NOBODY LIKES ME.
"$#%&..."

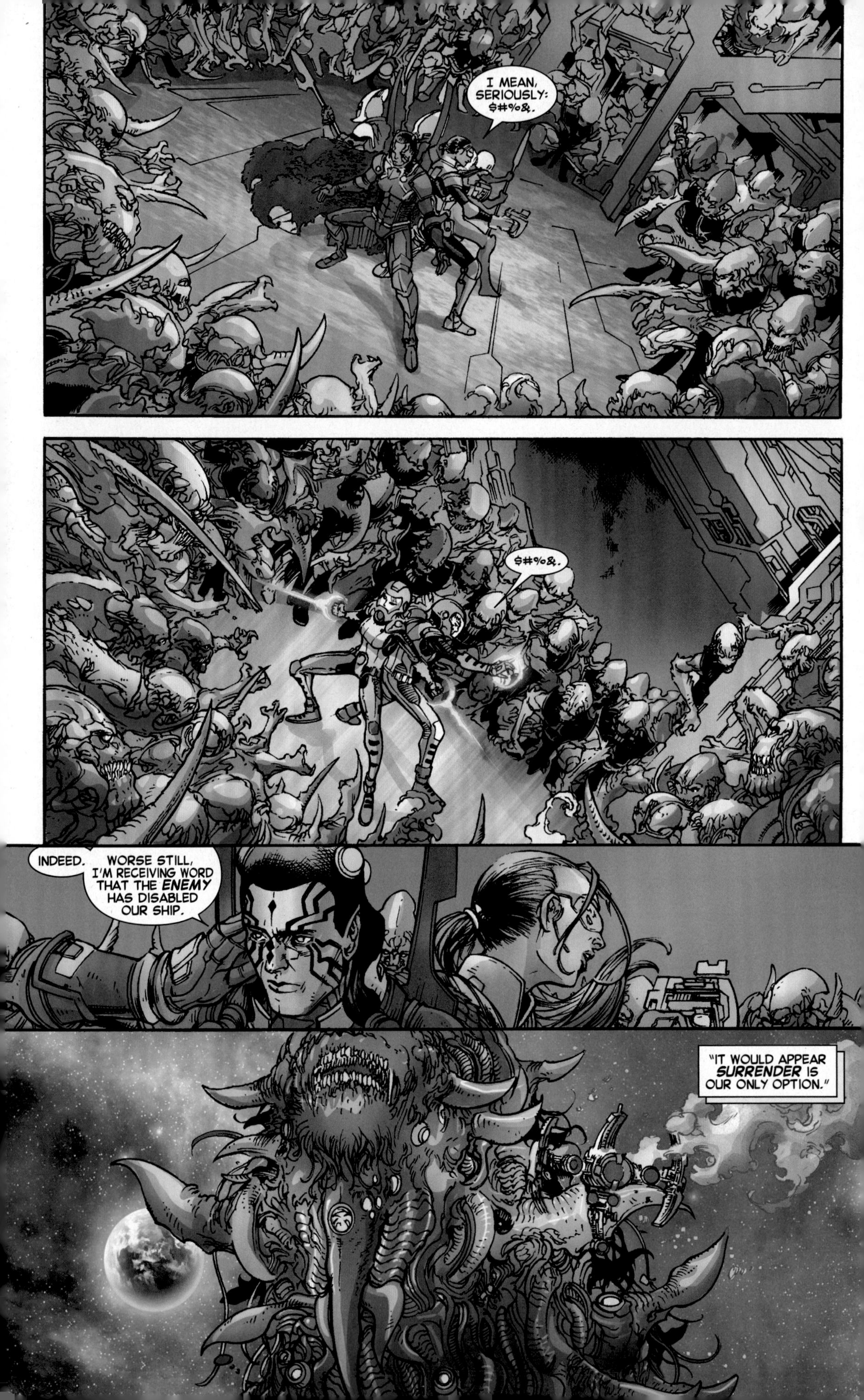
I MEAN, SERIOUSLY: $#%&.
$#%&.
INDEED.
WORSE STILL, I'M RECEIVING WORD THAT THE ENEMY HAS DISABLED OUR SHIP.
"IT WOULD APPEAR SURRENDER IS OUR ONLY OPTION."

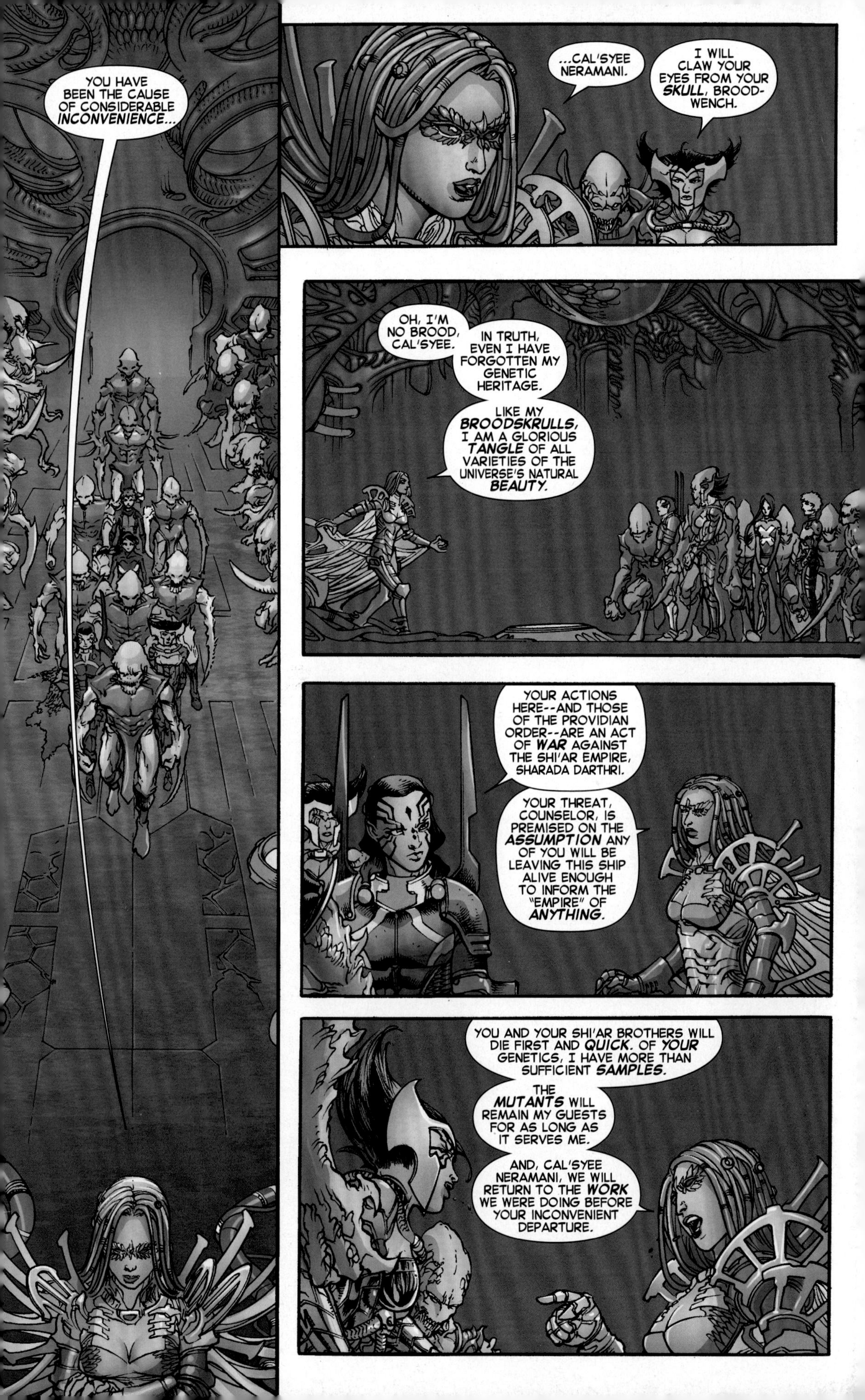
YOU HAVE BEEN THE CAUSE OF CONSIDERABLE INCONVENIENCE...
...CAL'SYEE NERAMANI.
I WILL CLAW YOUR EYES FROM YOUR SKULL, BROOD-WENCH.
OH, I'M NO BROOD, CAL'SYEE.
IN TRUTH, EVEN I HAVE FORGOTTEN MY GENETIC HERITAGE.
LIKE MY BROODSKRULLS, I AM A GLORIOUS TANGLE OF ALL VARIETIES OF THE UNIVERSE'S NATURAL BEAUTY.
YOUR ACTIONS HERE--AND THOSE OF THE PROVIDIAN ORDER--ARE AN ACT OF WAR AGAINST THE SHI'AR EMPIRE, SHARADA DARTHRI.
YOUR THREAT, COUNSELOR, IS PREMISED ON THE ASSUMPTION ANY OF YOU WILL BE LEAVING THIS SHIP ALIVE ENOUGH TO INFORM THE "EMPIRE" OF ANYTHING.
YOU AND YOUR SHI'AR BROTHERS WILL DIE FIRST AND QUICK. OF YOUR GENETICS, I HAVE MORE THAN SUFFICIENT SAMPLES.
THE MUTANTS WILL REMAIN MY GUESTS FOR AS LONG AS IT SERVES ME.
AND, CAL'SYEE NERAMANI, WE WILL RETURN TO THE WORK WE WERE DOING BEFORE YOUR INCONVENIENT DEPARTURE.

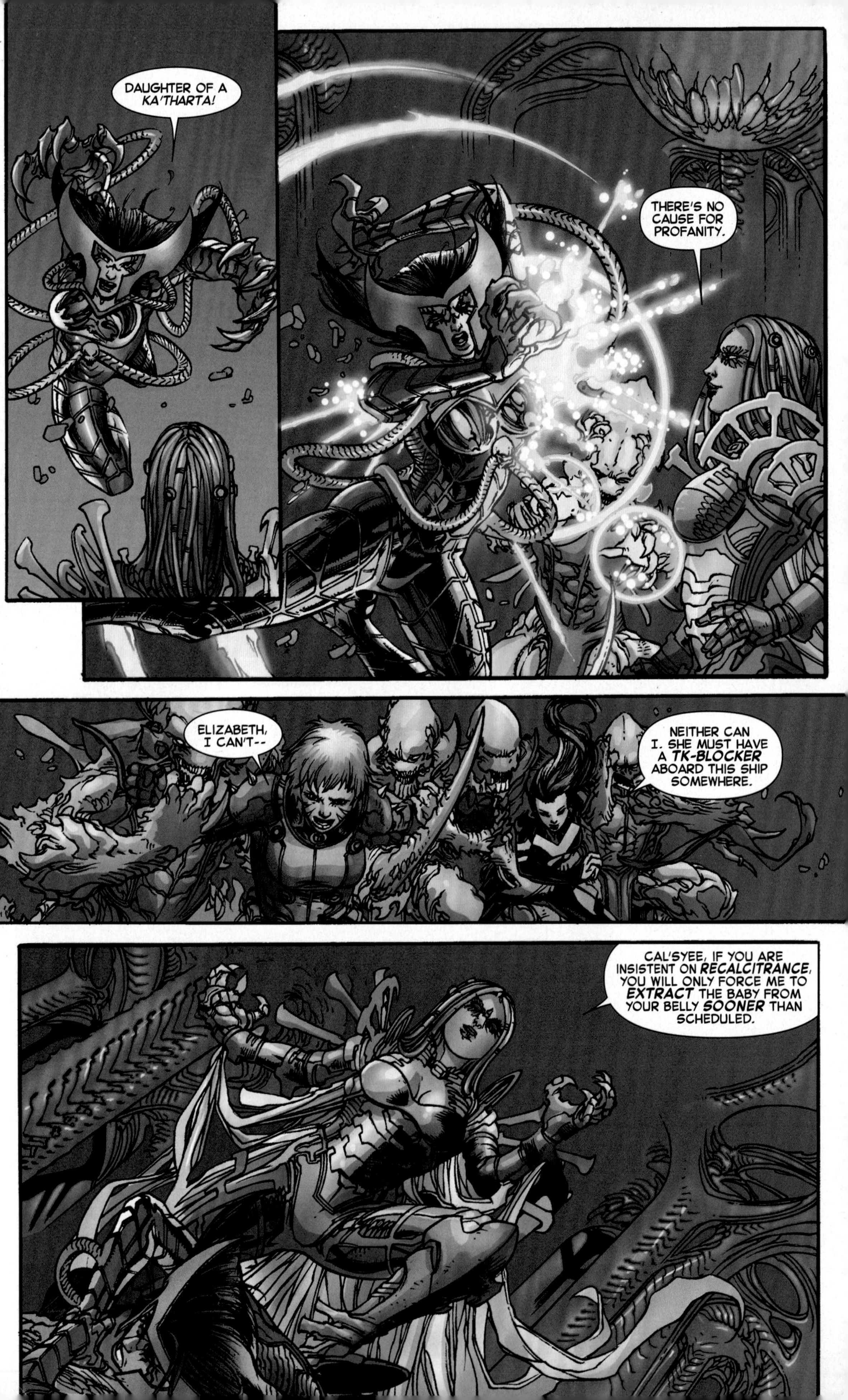
DAUGHTER OF A *KA'THARTA!*
THERE'S NO CAUSE FOR PROFANITY.
ELIZABETH, I CAN'T--
NEITHER CAN I. SHE MUST HAVE A ***TK-BLOCKER*** ABOARD THIS SHIP SOMEWHERE.
CAL'SYEE, IF YOU ARE INSISTENT ON ***RECALCITRANCE***, YOU WILL ONLY FORCE ME TO ***EXTRACT*** THE BABY FROM YOUR BELLY ***SOONER*** THAN SCHEDULED.

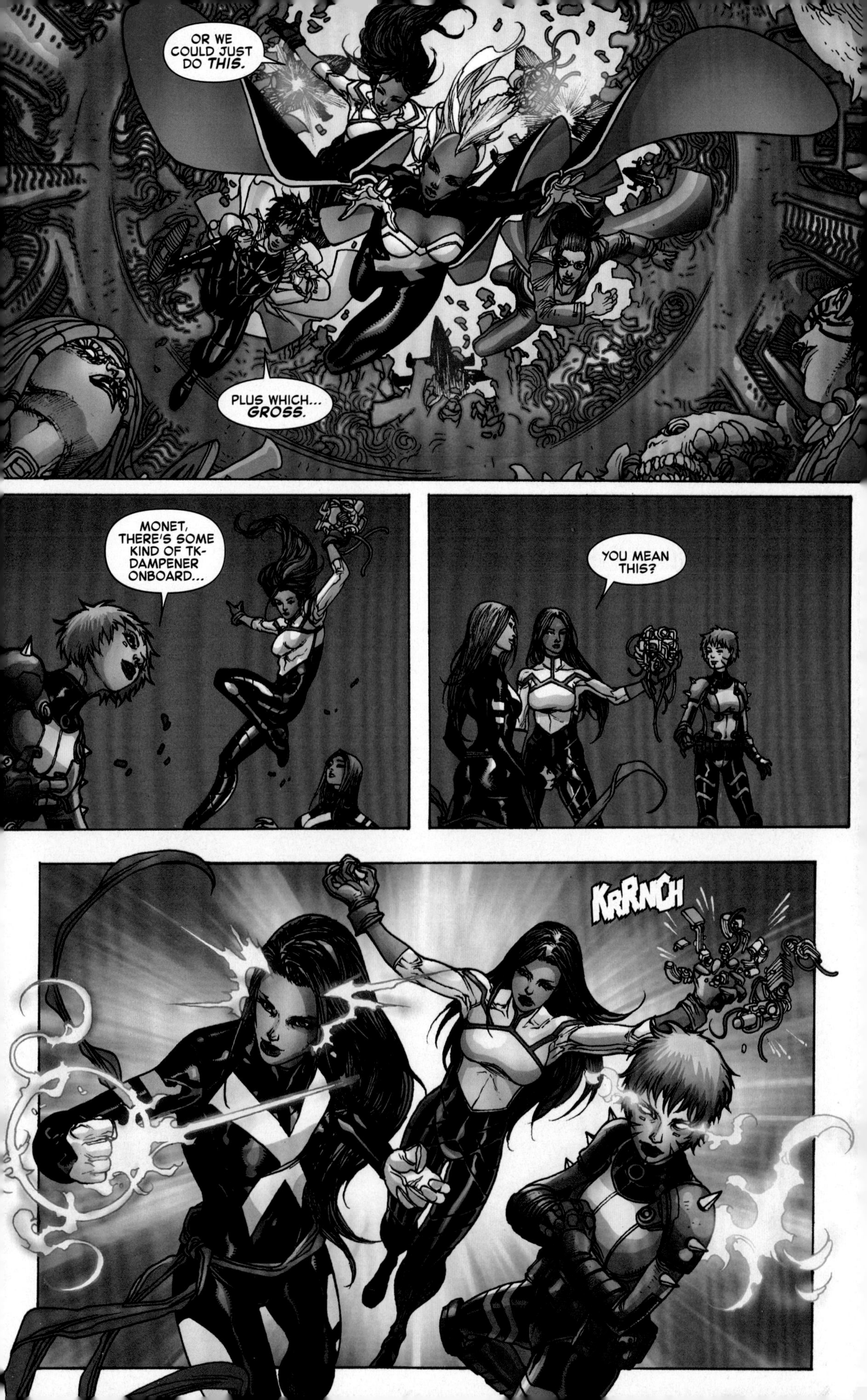
OR WE COULD JUST DO THIS.
PLUS WHICH... GROSS.
MONET, THERE'S SOME KIND OF TK-DAMPENER ONBOARD...
YOU MEAN THIS?
KRRNCH

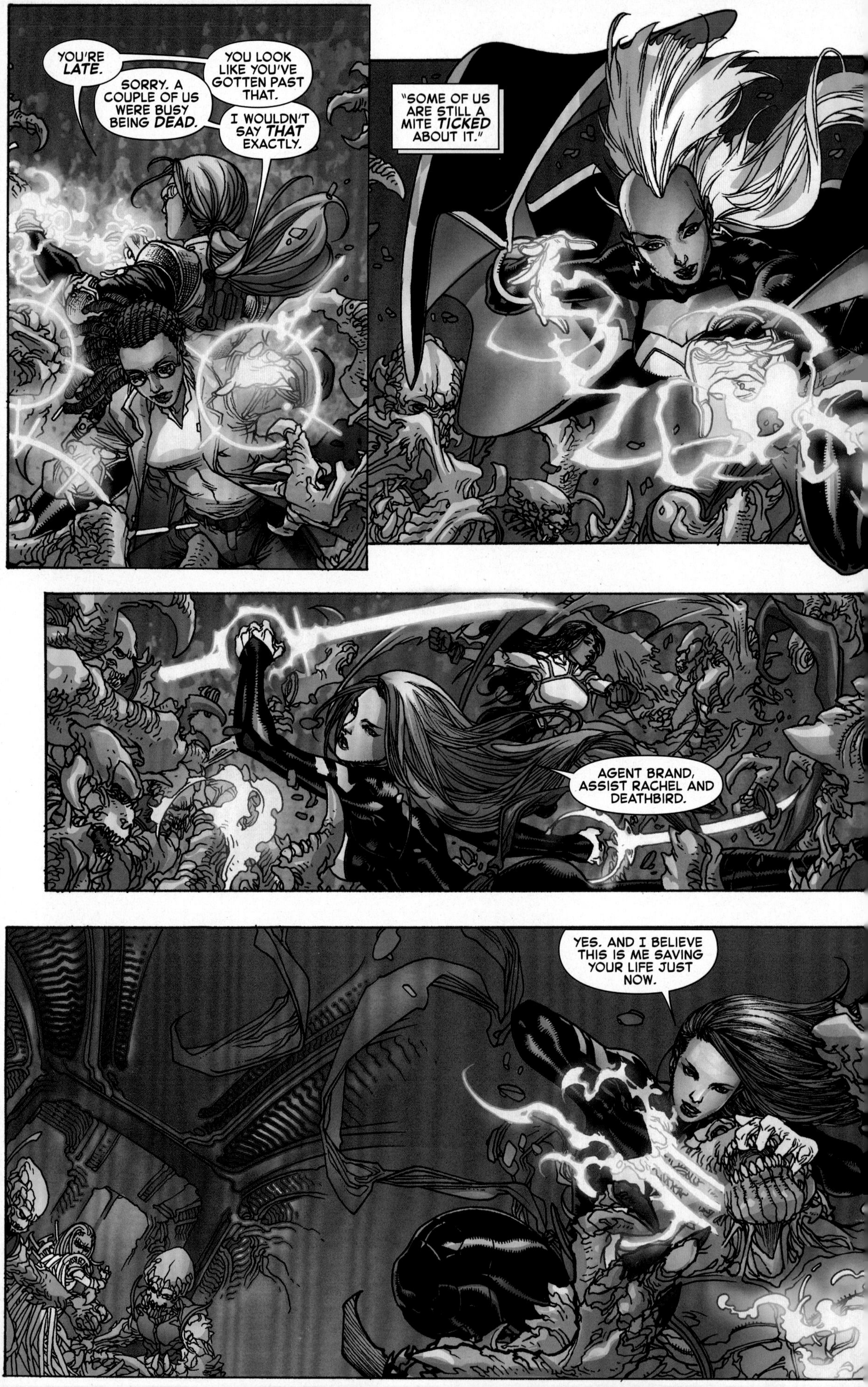
YOU'RE LATE.
SORRY. A COUPLE OF US WERE BUSY BEING DEAD.
YOU LOOK LIKE YOU'VE GOTTEN PAST THAT.
I WOULDN'T SAY THAT EXACTLY.
"SOME OF US ARE STILL A MITE TICKED ABOUT IT."
AGENT BRAND, ASSIST RACHEL AND DEATHBIRD.
YES. AND I BELIEVE THIS IS ME SAVING YOUR LIFE JUST NOW.

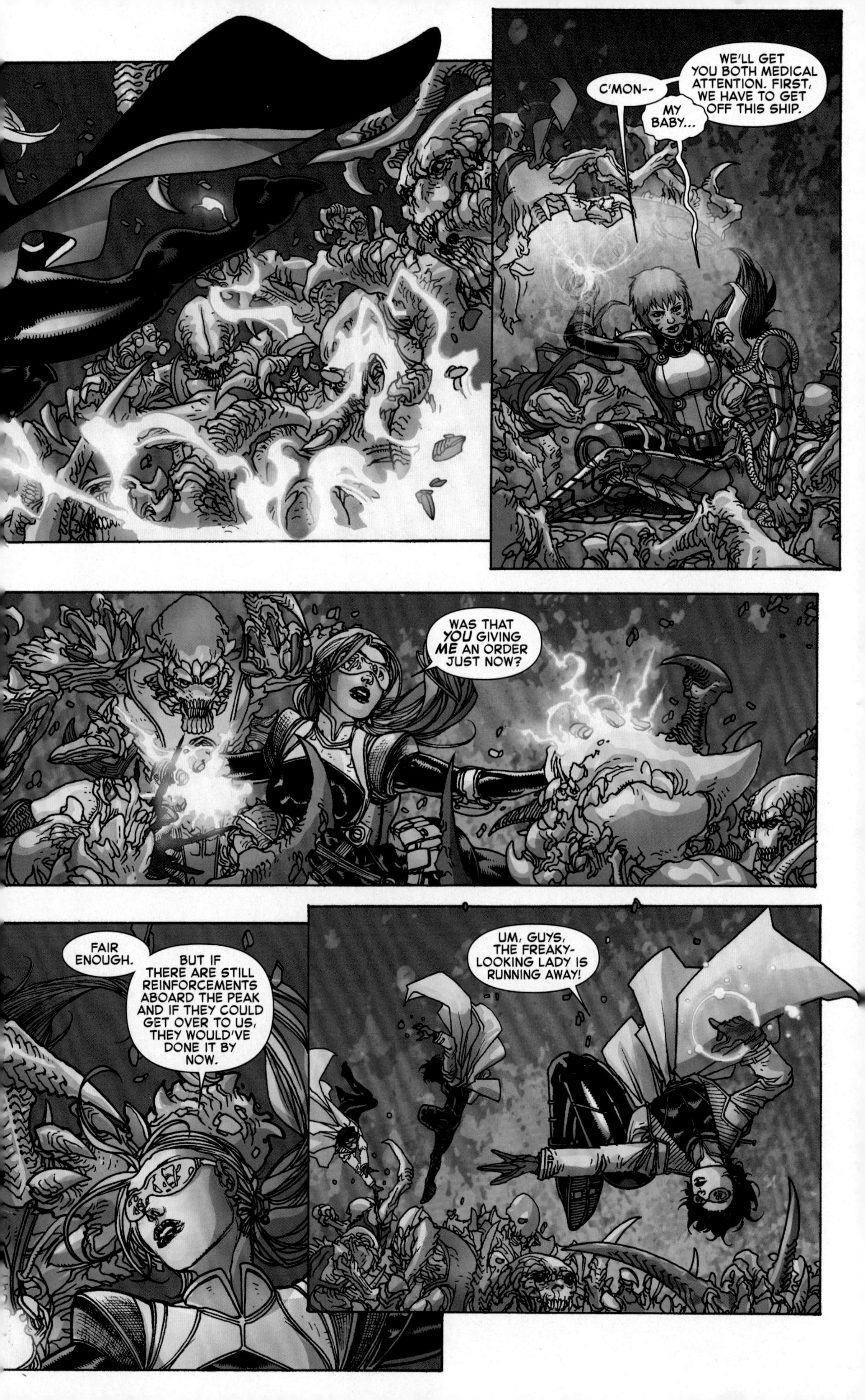
C'MON--
WE'LL GET YOU BOTH MEDICAL ATTENTION. FIRST, WE HAVE TO GET OFF THIS SHIP.
MY BABY...
WAS THAT YOU GIVING ME AN ORDER JUST NOW?
FAIR ENOUGH.
BUT IF THERE ARE STILL REINFORCEMENTS ABOARD THE PEAK AND IF THEY COULD GET OVER TO US, THEY WOULD'VE DONE IT BY NOW.
UM, GUYS, THE FREAKY-LOOKING LADY IS RUNNING AWAY!

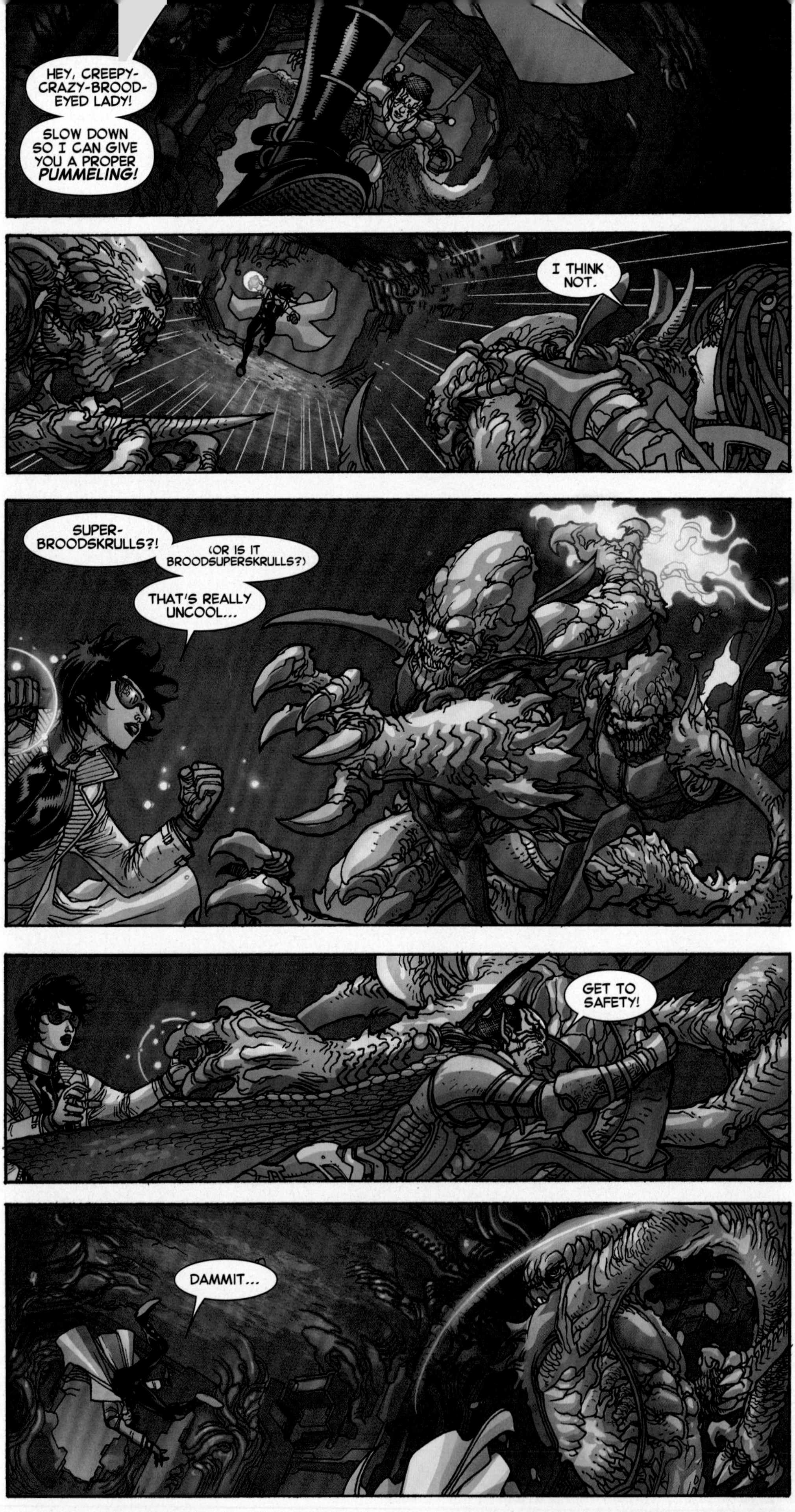
HEY, CREEPY-CRAZY-BROOD-EYED LADY!
SLOW DOWN SO I CAN GIVE YOU A PROPER *PUMMELING!*
I THINK NOT.
SUPER-BROODSKRULLS?!
(OR IS IT BROODSUPERSKRULLS?)
THAT'S REALLY UNCOOL...
GET TO SAFETY!
DAMMIT...

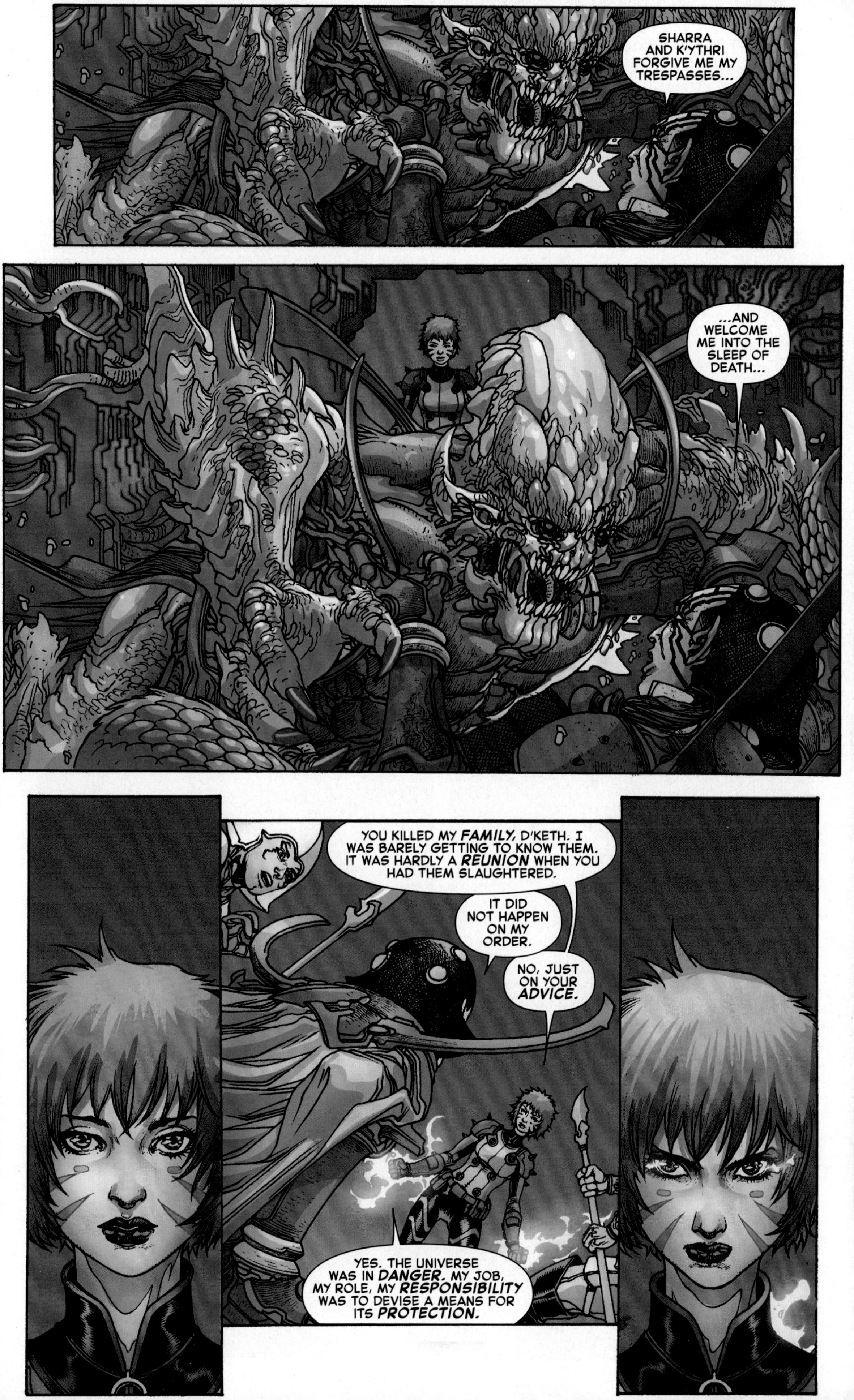
SHARRA AND K'YTHRI FORGIVE ME MY TRESPASSES...
...AND WELCOME ME INTO THE SLEEP OF DEATH...
YOU KILLED MY FAMILY, D'KETH. I WAS BARELY GETTING TO KNOW THEM. IT WAS HARDLY A REUNION WHEN YOU HAD THEM SLAUGHTERED.
IT DID NOT HAPPEN ON MY ORDER.
NO, JUST ON YOUR ADVICE.
YES. THE UNIVERSE WAS IN DANGER. MY JOB, MY ROLE, MY RESPONSIBILITY WAS TO DEVISE A MEANS FOR ITS PROTECTION.

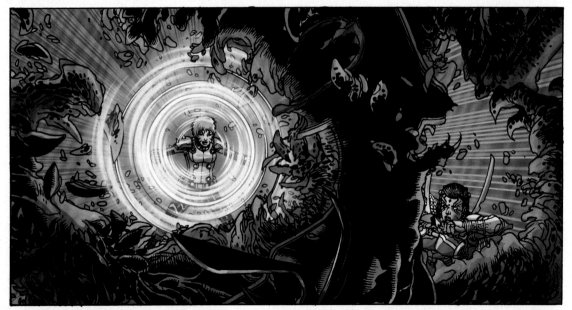

THEY WERE GOING TO KILL ME...

I KNOW.

JUBILEE?

HEAD HURTS LIKE CRAZY.

SPEAKING OF CRAZY...

"...OUR FRIEND'S STILL RUNNING."

GOING SOMEWHERE?

BECAUSE I BELIEVE WE HAVE *MUCH* TO DISCUSS.

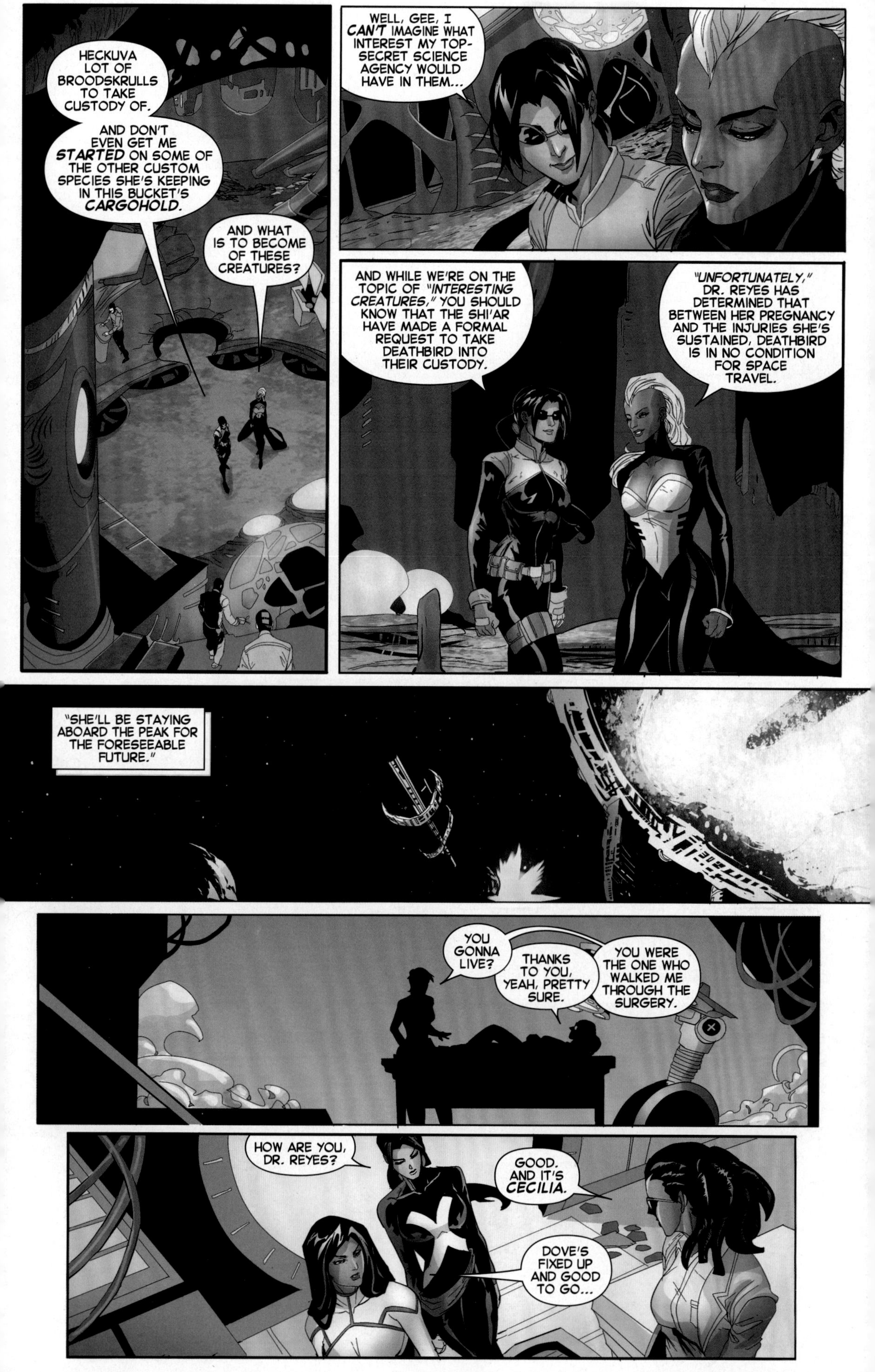
HECKUVA LOT OF BROODSKRULLS TO TAKE CUSTODY OF.
AND DON'T EVEN GET ME STARTED ON SOME OF THE OTHER CUSTOM SPECIES SHE'S KEEPING IN THIS BUCKET'S CARGOHOLD.
AND WHAT IS TO BECOME OF THESE CREATURES?
WELL, GEE, I CAN'T IMAGINE WHAT INTEREST MY TOP-SECRET SCIENCE AGENCY WOULD HAVE IN THEM...
AND WHILE WE'RE ON THE TOPIC OF "INTERESTING CREATURES," YOU SHOULD KNOW THAT THE SHI'AR HAVE MADE A FORMAL REQUEST TO TAKE DEATHBIRD INTO THEIR CUSTODY.
"UNFORTUNATELY," DR. REYES HAS DETERMINED THAT BETWEEN HER PREGNANCY AND THE INJURIES SHE'S SUSTAINED, DEATHBIRD IS IN NO CONDITION FOR SPACE TRAVEL.
"SHE'LL BE STAYING ABOARD THE PEAK FOR THE FORESEEABLE FUTURE."
YOU GONNA LIVE?
THANKS TO YOU, YEAH, PRETTY SURE.
YOU WERE THE ONE WHO WALKED ME THROUGH THE SURGERY.
HOW ARE YOU, DR. REYES?
GOOD. AND IT'S CECILIA.
DOVE'S FIXED UP AND GOOD TO GO...

"WE'RE JUST WAITING ON RACHEL."

THE ORDER OF K'THARI IS RIGHTFULLY YOURS...

IF YOU THINK I WANT *ANYTHING* FROM THE WORLD THAT KILLED MY *FAMILY*, YOU'RE EVEN MORE DELUDED THAN I THOUGHT, D'KETH.

THIS.

PHYLLIS DENNEFER

JEAN GREY

JOSH REY

GAILYN

JULIAN GREY

GREY
JOHN & ELAINE

I JUST TRIED TO BE THE PERSON I THINK YOU *WANTED* ME TO BE.

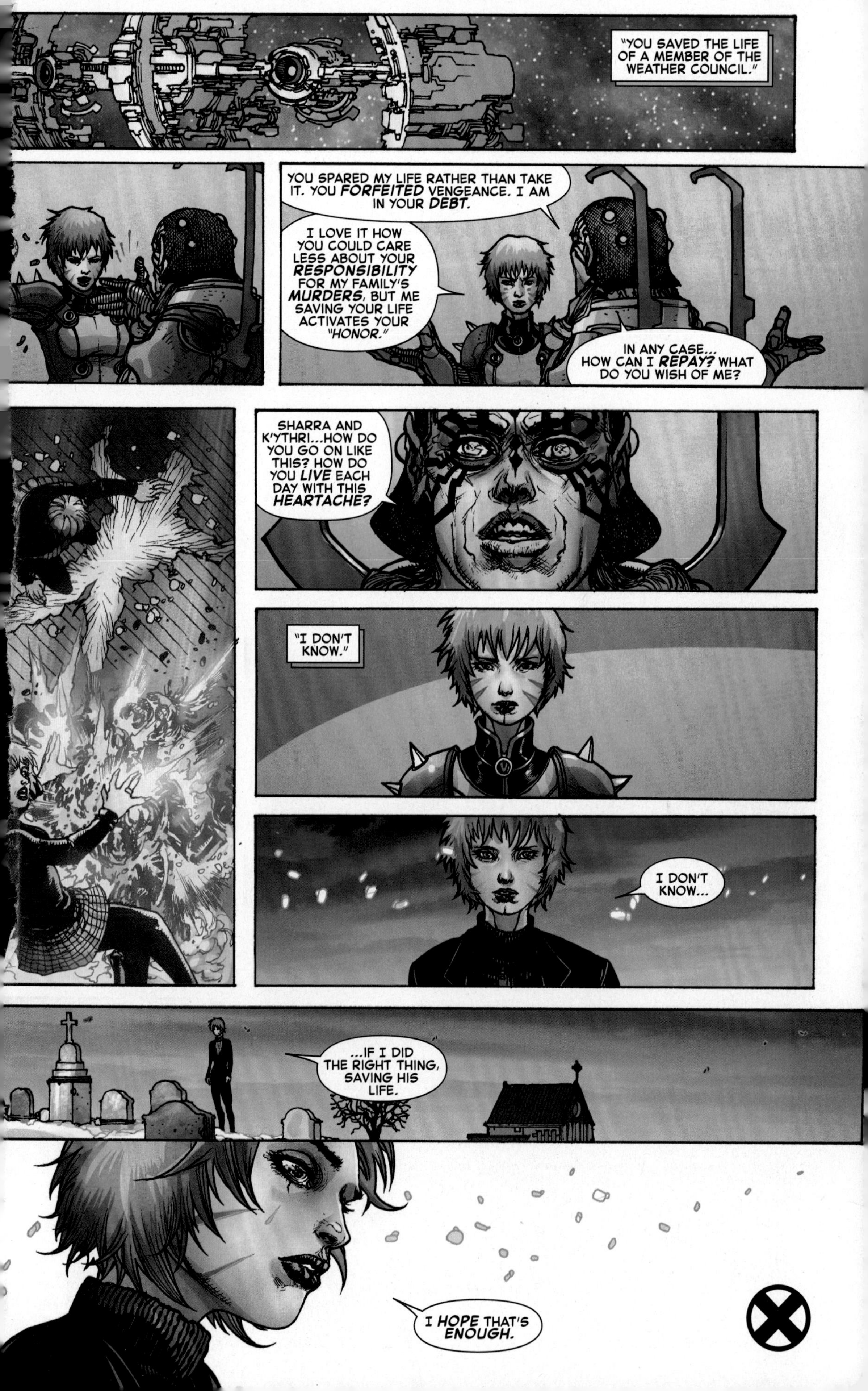
"YOU SAVED THE LIFE OF A MEMBER OF THE WEATHER COUNCIL."
YOU SPARED MY LIFE RATHER THAN TAKE IT. YOU FORFEITED VENGEANCE. I AM IN YOUR DEBT.
I LOVE IT HOW YOU COULD CARE LESS ABOUT YOUR RESPONSIBILITY FOR MY FAMILY'S MURDERS, BUT ME SAVING YOUR LIFE ACTIVATES YOUR "HONOR."
IN ANY CASE... HOW CAN I REPAY? WHAT DO YOU WISH OF ME?
SHARRA AND K'YTHRI...HOW DO YOU GO ON LIKE THIS? HOW DO YOU LIVE EACH DAY WITH THIS HEARTACHE?
"I DON'T KNOW."
I DON'T KNOW...
...IF I DID THE RIGHT THING, SAVING HIS LIFE.
I HOPE THAT'S ENOUGH.

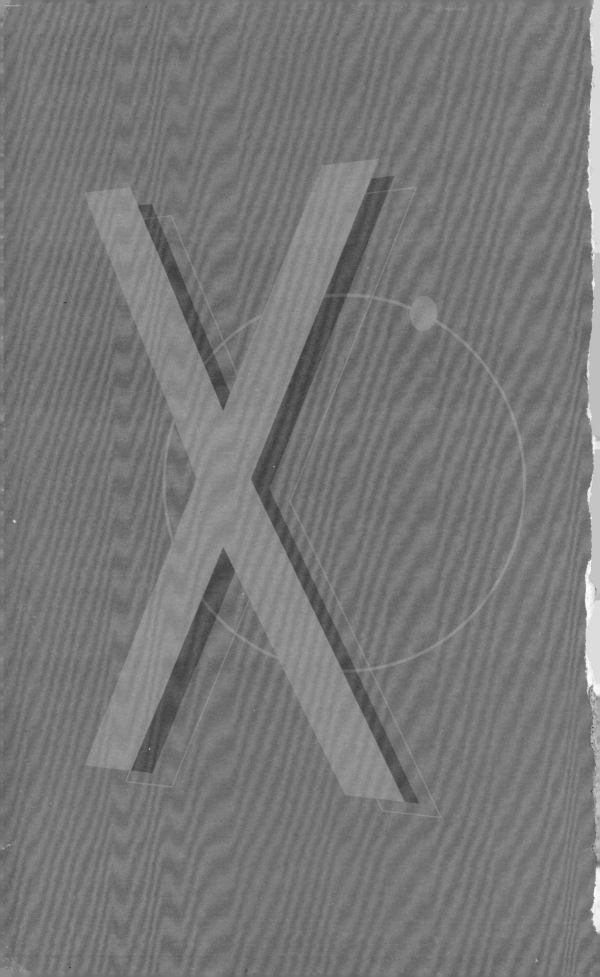